History

a visual encyclopedia

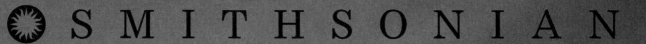
SMITHSONIAN

History

a visual encyclopedia

DK

DK Delhi

Senior Editors Sreshtha Bhattacharya, Virien Chopra
Senior Art Editors Ira Sharma, Shreya Anand
Project Art Editor Sanjay Chauhan
Editorial team Kathakali Banerjee, Upamanyu Das, Rupa Rao, Bipasha Roy, Neha Ruth Samuel
Art Editors Noopur Dalal, Tanisha Mandal
Assistant Art Editor Aparajita Sen
Cartographer Mohammad Hassan
Project Picture Researcher Aditya Katyal
Picture Research Manager Taiyaba Khatoon
Managing Editor Kingshuk Ghoshal
Managing Art Editor Govind Mittal
DTP Designers Pawan Kumar, Vikram Singh
Senior DTP Designer Harish Aggarwal
Pre-production Manager Balwant Singh
Production Manager Pankaj Sharma
Jacket Designer Tanya Mehrotra
DK Delhi Editorial Head Glenda Fernandes
DK Delhi Design Head Malavika Talukder

DK London

Senior Editor Sam Atkinson
Senior Art Editor Jacqui Swan
Project Editor Edward Aves
Editor Mani Ramaswamy
US Senior Editor Megan Douglass
US Executive Editor Lori Cates Hand
Picture Researcher Nic Dean
Managing Editor Rachel Fox
Managing Art Editor Owen Peyton Jones
Production Editor Kavita Varma
Senior Production Controller Meskerem Berhane
Jacket Designer Stephanie Cheng Hui Tan
Jacket Design Development Manager Sophia MTT
Publisher Andrew Macintyre
Associate Publishing Director Liz Wheeler
Art Director Karen Self
Publishing Director Jonathan Metcalf

General Consultant Philip Parker
Contributors Simon Adams, Sufiya Ahmed, Peter Chrisp, Ben Ffrancon Davies, Cora Dessalines, Susan Kennedy, Andrea Mills

First American Edition, 2022
Published in the United States by DK Publishing
1450 Broadway, Suite 801, New York, NY 10018

DK books are available at special discounts when purchased in bulk for sales promotions, premiums, fund-raising, or educational use. For details, contact: DK Publishing Special Markets, 1450 Broadway, Suite 801, New York, NY 10018
SpecialSales@dk.com

Printed and bound in UAE

For the curious
www.dk.com

Contents

BEFORE 500 CE

By around 13,000 BCE, early humans had spread throughout the globe. While in some parts of the world humankind continued to live as nomads, in others people began to farm the land, settling down in villages, towns, and eventually cities. Great civilizations arose as warfare and trade created ancient empires. Some of these civilizations, such as those of ancient Egypt and China, lasted for thousands of years.

Human ancestors

Modern humans (*Homo sapiens*) are a type of ape that evolved from a common ape ancestor in Africa, and our closest living relatives today are chimpanzees. Chimp and human ancestors separated more than six million years ago, when one group of apes, called hominins, began to walk upright. Hominins then went on to evolve bigger brains and develop humanlike behavior.

Some four million years ago, several species of upright walking apes, called Australopithecines, spread across the grasslands of East Africa. By 2.4 million years ago, *Homo habilis* ("handy man") were making stone tools, marking the beginning of the Paleolithic Age (Early Stone Age). *Homo habilis* were 40–50 in (1–1.3 m) tall on average and hominins continued to grow taller until the appearance 1.9 million years ago of *Homo erectus* ("upright man"), who were about as tall as modern humans. *Homo erectus* developed leaf-shaped hand axes, the first tools made to a design, and learned how to control fire. *Homo erectus* are thought to be the first hominins to leave Africa and move into Asia. Evolution continued until around 300,000 years ago when our own species, *Homo sapiens*, appeared in Africa. We later spread to every part of the world, replacing all of the other surviving human species.

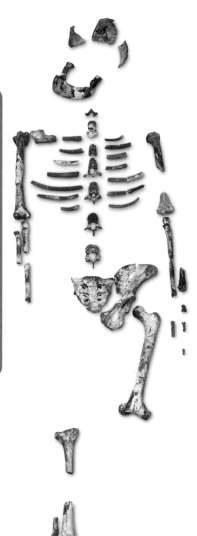

▲ AUSTRALOPITHECUS
Walking upright helped Australopithecus *stay cool and see further, and freed up their hands to carry and throw. Their short legs suggest they would not have been fast runners. This skeleton of a female, nicknamed Lucy, was discovered in Ethiopia in 1974.*

Homo erectus *may have been hairier than humans today.*

▲ EARLY TOOLS
Homo habilis *used broken river pebbles as tools. These stones could crack nuts and smash open animal bones to reach the healthy marrow inside. It is likely that* Homo habilis *were scavengers, feeding on animals killed by other predators, rather than hunting regularly themselves.*

◄ HOMO HEIDELBERGENSIS

Named after Heidelberg in Germany, where their remains were first found, Homo heidelbergensis emerged around 700,000 years ago. They were the first species to build shelters and regularly hunt large animals, using wooden spears. They moved from Africa into Europe, which then had a warm climate, and continued to evolve—becoming Homo neanderthalensis in Europe and Asia and Homo sapiens in Africa.

◄ NEANDERTHALS

Our closest relatives, Homo neanderthalensis, lived in western Asia and Europe from 400,000 years ago. They had brains as big as a modern human's and wore animal-skin clothing. There is evidence that they buried their dead with offerings of flowers.

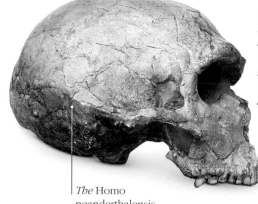

The Homo neanderthalensis *skull is longer and flatter than a modern human's.*

▼ MAKING FIRE

Homo erectus are thought to have been the first species to have used fire for cooking. This made it easier to digest meat, which may have led to the growth of bigger brains and smaller teeth. Fire also offered protection from predators, and allowed groups to stay active in the dark. Sitting around a fire may have encouraged the development of language.

Burning wood from lightning strikes was used to build the first fires.

CHILD IN TIME

Turkana Boy is the nickname of this young *Homo ergaster*—a variety of *Homo erectus*—whose almost complete skeleton was found in Kenya in 1984. He lived 1.6 million years ago. Although he was only between 7 and 11 years old, he was almost fully grown, at 5 ft 3 in (1.6 m) tall.

Out of Africa

Our species—modern humans, or *Homo sapiens*—evolved in Africa around 300,000 years ago. Yet it took more than 100,000 years before we began to leave the continent and spread across other parts of the world. Traveling mostly on foot, and later by boat, modern humans eventually settled almost every part of the planet.

BEFORE 500 CE

The journey out of Africa was made possible due to changes in the climate. Around 194,000 years ago (YA), a warm, wet period turned the previously impassable Sinai Desert (the region linking Africa and Asia) into a green and fertile strip of land, allowing people to move there from Egypt. The descendants of those who took this route gradually died out as the climate became dry again.

Much later, during the Ice Age about 80,000 years ago, low sea levels enabled people to wade across the shallow Red Sea and reach the Arabian Peninsula in western Asia. At first, they spread east, keeping only to the warmer regions. Around 50,000 years ago, people began to settle, and make the earliest forms of art and music. They also invented new technologies, such as needles and the harpoon (a hunting weapon), and tamed the first dogs.

The ability to survive and adapt to colder climates allowed *Homo sapiens* to move further north, and later reach Europe and the Americas. By around 13,000 BCE, humans had spread into every continent except Antarctica.

TAILORED CLOTHING ▶
Modern humans as well as Neanderthals, an earlier human species, used animal skin for clothing. While Neanderthals wore skins loosely tied around them, modern humans invented bone needles (right), with which they could sew tailored clothes, and even decorate them with objects such as beads.

◀ SETTLING AUSTRALIA
Low sea levels allowed modern humans to move down through Southeast Asia into Australia around 65,000 years ago. These first settlers came across many unfamiliar plants and animals, such as kangaroos and giant flightless birds. They hunted them using wooden spears and curved throwing sticks known as boomerangs (left).

MAMMOTH HUT ▶
Wherever modern humans went, they were able to build shelters, even where there was no wood. During the Ice Age, people hunted mammoths on the treeless plains of Europe and Asia, and built shelters using their bones covered with hides (skins).

MODERN HUMANS

194,000–65,000 YA	65,000 YA		45,000 YA
Modern humans leave Africa and move into Asia. The first wave follows a northern route via modern-day Israel and the next one a southern route via Arabia.	People make the first known sea voyage—a 56-mile (90-km) journey to Australia—perhaps using bamboo rafts.		Modern humans begin making the first art. The oldest known animal cave painting so far is that of a pig in Indonesia.

PREHISTORIC CAVE PAINTING

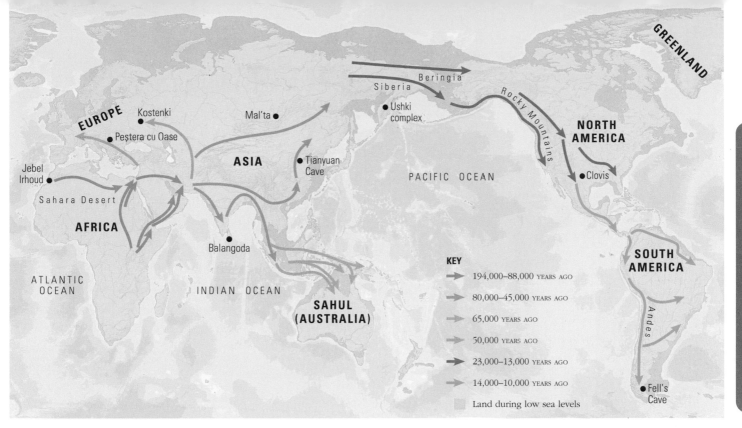

KEY

→	194,000–88,000 YEARS AGO
→	80,000–45,000 YEARS AGO
→	65,000 YEARS AGO
→	50,000 YEARS AGO
→	23,000–13,000 YEARS AGO
→	14,000–10,000 YEARS AGO
▢	Land during low sea levels

HUMAN JOURNEYS ▲

The people who settled the world were hunter-gatherers. They had to keep moving to find fresh sources of food. After leaving Africa, they kept first to the warm south, and then continued eastward, following the coasts, which were rich in resources. They later ventured into the colder climates of northern Asia and the Americas.

HUNTING TOOLS

Inventions that made modern humans successful hunters included bows and arrows and spear-like barbed harpoons for fishing. Spear throwers, which allowed hunters to hurl spears across longer distances, were often decorated with carvings of the animals, such as mammoths.

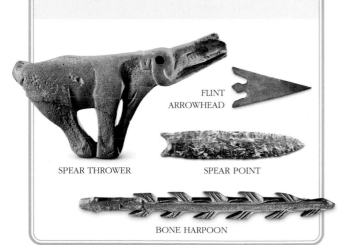

FLINT ARROWHEAD

SPEAR THROWER

SPEAR POINT

BONE HARPOON

▲ END OF THE ICE AGE

The end of the Ice Age, around 12,000 years ago, created a warmer, wetter climate. Cave paintings from the Sahara Desert show people hunting cattle with bows and arrows. The region, which was previously dry and arid (as it is now), had become green and fertile.

30,000–20,000 YA	23,000–13,000 YA	12,000–11,000 YA
The climate enters a phase of severe cold. Many large animals, such as mammoths, become extinct, partly due to hunting by humans.	People move from East Asia into North America, crossing a land bridge created by low sea levels.	Global warming causes ice sheets to melt, creating a warmer climate. People begin to settle down, taking the first steps to farming.

First farmers

For almost all of human prehistory (the time before written records), humans lived as hunter-gatherers, depending on wild foods for survival. But a new way of life began around 10,000 BCE, when people in western Asia started to grow crops—and later, tame wild animals—in a process known as domestication. Humans had become farmers.

Farming changed everything about human life. It was much harder work than gathering food, and it led to a more limited diet. Yet it produced much more food, which could be stored for future use, resulting in population growth. To be near their crops, people settled in villages, which in time grew into towns. Farming required advanced tools to be made—this was the beginning of the Neolithic Age (New Stone Age).

Rather than everyone working in the fields, some people could now specialize in craftwork, such as weaving and pottery.

Farmers needed to know when to plant their crops, so they kept a close track of the seasons using the sun and the stars. This led to new religious beliefs, in which people honored the sun, Earth, and human ancestors, who were thought to watch over the living.

Farming began separately in different parts of the world, each of which developed different crops. While farmers in East Asia grew rice and millet, people in Central America grew maize and beans.

Wild einkorn was domesticated to produce bigger grains.

WILD EINKORN

TEOSINTE

An ear of teosinte has far fewer kernels than modern maize.

◀ **DOMESTICATING PLANTS**
The most important plants domesticated by early farmers were grasslike grain crops, which could be adapted to produce more food and harvested in bulk. Wild einkorn and emmer, two types of wheat, were the first to be domesticated in a region of the Middle East known as the Fertile Crescent. Around 7000 BCE, farmers in modern-day Mexico transformed another grain, the wild teosinte plant, into maize.

Figs were some of the first fruits to be domesticated.

WILD EMMER

FIGS

Woolly coat

Shorter horns

Long curved horns

DOMESTICATED SHEEP

WILD MOUFLON

DOMESTICATING ANIMALS ▶
Early farmers bred animals that were easiest to control. As a result, domesticated animals grew smaller and less aggressive than their wild ancestors. For example, sheep, which were domesticated from the mouflon, lost their long horns and developed woolly coats.

◀ POTTERY
As humans settled in one place, they began to make pottery, which would have been fragile and heavy for hunter-gatherers on the move. Pottery led to changes in the human diet, allowing people to bake bread, make cheese, and boil meat for stews. It was both decorative and useful.

Pots found at Çatalhöyük in modern-day Turkey were used to hold grains and dairy products.

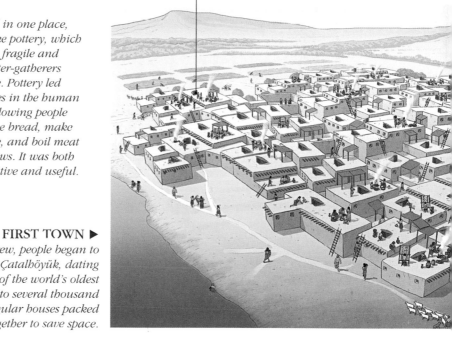

Houses were entered through the roof.

FIRST TOWN ▶
As populations grew, people began to live in dense settlements. Çatalhöyük, dating from 7400–6200 BCE, is one of the world's oldest known towns. It was home to several thousand people who lived in rectangular houses packed together to save space.

EVERYDAY LIFE

When people began to farm, it led to a gradual division between work in the fields and domestic work at home. Women usually took up the responsibilities at home, spending long hours making clothes or grinding grain on a quern (right) to make bread.

ANCESTOR WORSHIP ▶
In the early towns, such as Çatalhöyük and Jericho (in modern-day Palestine), the dead were buried beneath the floors of the houses as a way to remember them. In Jericho, the skulls of ancestors were preserved and given new features, modeled in clay with eyes made of shells.

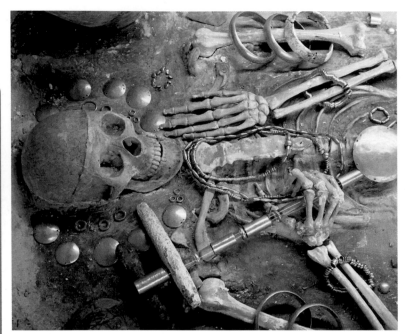

Copper ax
blade tied to a
wooden handle

◄ **PRECIOUS METALS**
*Gold and silver are shiny, rare metals that have
been used to make jewelery since ancient times.
These metals offered people a way to display wealth
and high status. Around 4000 BCE, high-ranking
people at Varna in modern-day Bulgaria were
buried in graves filled with gold ornaments.*

FACT
Ancient Egyptians
found small amounts of
pure iron in meteorites—
rocks from space that hit
Earth. They called this
"metal of heaven."

Working with metals

Early humans made use of stone tools, but somewhere
between 6000 and 2000 BCE, depending on where they
were in the world, people began to use metals widely,
bringing an end to the Stone Age. Unlike stone, metals
could be shaped into any form by molding, beating,
and sharpening. Some metals, such as gold and silver,
were also prized for their beauty.

COPPER TOOLS ►
*The first metal tools were copper
chisels, which were used to build the
Egyptian pyramids. Copper is a soft
metal, so these tools needed constant
resharpening. This well-preserved
ax belonged to Ötzi the Iceman,
whose frozen, 5,300-year-old
body was found in the Alps.*

Metalworking developed in stages,
as people gradually learned how
to work harder metals that proved to
be more useful. Early people used
naturally occurring nuggets of soft
metals, such as lead and copper, to
make jewelry. Later, they learned
to extract these metals from their ores
(metal-bearing rocks) by heating
them in a process called smelting.

The earliest metal tools were
made from copper. In the late
4th millennium BCE, people in western
Asia discovered that adding a small
amount of tin to copper created a

harder material called bronze. As
tin is rare, demand for it gave rise
to long-distance trade, creating great
wealth for the societies that mined
and worked it.

Iron, the most common metal, was
the last to be worked. It is even harder
than bronze and extracting it required
new techniques that were invented
in western Asia around 1500 BCE.
Iron changed everyday life, and
was soon used to make sturdy tools,
weapons, pots, and nails, among
many other useful items.

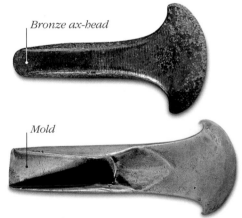

Bronze ax-head

Mold

▲ **BRONZE**
*Bronze was used to make axes by melting
copper and tin together and pouring the
molten mix into molds. It was hard and
long-lasting, which led to the invention
of new weapons, such as the sword.
Bronze could also be hammered into
sheets to make armor.*

◀ IRON WORKING

To extract iron, its ore had to be heated to a high temperature in a charcoal furnace known as a forge. The impurities were beaten out, then the iron was heated to make it malleable (easy to bend), and hammered into shape.

Iron being heated in a furnace, shown in a detail from an ancient Greek vase

Turquoise inlay

BRONZE SCULPTURES

As skills improved, metalworkers made increasingly elaborate artifacts. Bronze, cast in molds, became the most popular metal for sculptures and figurines, which often depicted people, gods, or animals. The Mesopotamian roller below would have been used to make textiles.

The hands of this 8½-ft- (2.6-m-) tall statue once held a curved object.

GREEK LYRE PLAYER

SANXINGDUI STATUE, CHINA

MESOPOTAMIAN ROLLER

◀ AMERICAN METALLURGY

In the Americas, before the arrival of Italian explorer Christopher Columbus, people never learned to use the harder metals. They were, however, skilled at working with gold, silver, and copper, which they used to make religious objects and royal jewelery. In Peru, gold was sacred and known as the "sweat of the sun."

Ceremonial knife from the Sican culture from modern-day Peru

15

Mesopotamian civilizations

More than 5,000 years ago, the world's first known cities appeared in Mesopotamia, a historical region now found largely within the borders of modern-day Iraq. Mesopotamia was also the birthplace of many features of civilization, including rulership by a king or queen, armies, organized religion, and legal systems.

Mesopotamia, which means "the land between the rivers," lay between the Tigris and Euphrates rivers. These waterways flooded every year, which could ruin farmers' crops. The Mesopotamians worked together to control the flood water, building dykes to protect their fields, and canals and reservoirs to store the water for later use. These activities gave rise to a high level of social organization and cooperation. It also created huge harvests, and enough food for growing populations.

It was in southern Mesopotamia, in a land originally called Sumer, that villages grew into the world's first cities. Uruk and Ur had populations of tens of thousands of people. They were ruled over by monarchs who claimed to reign on behalf of the local god.

KEY

Mesopotamia

Sumer

◄ THE TWO RIVERS
The Tigris and Euphrates flow from the mountains of what is now Turkey, through present-day Iraq, and into the Persian Gulf. The Mesopotamian civilization began in Sumer in the southeast and later spread across the whole region.

▼ WARFARE
The world's earliest recorded wars took place in Mesopotamia. Cities fought each other over land, and foreign invaders attacked the region for its great wealth. This mosaic on a box from Ur shows a king and his army celebrating a victory over their enemies.

RISE OF CIVILIZATIONS

c. 4000 BCE	c. 3300–3100 BCE	c. 3000 BCE
The villages in Uruk come together to form the world's first known city. It has walls around its boundaries and contains great monuments. People are divided into classes based on what they do. There were classes for priests, merchants, and craftworkers, among others.	Around a dozen city-states emerge in Sumer, each ruled by a monarch. The Sumerians develop cuneiform, a writing system consisting of marks pressed onto clay tablets.  CUNEIFORM TABLET	The Sumerians learn to make bronze, by mixing tin and copper imported from neighboring lands. The bronze is used to make tools, weapons, and sculptures. The people of Sumer also make four-wheeled chariots for use in warfare.

▲ RELIGION

Each city had a chief god, who was worshipped at a stepped mudbrick temple, called a ziggurat. The god's statue was kept in a shrine at the top. This is the ziggurat of Ur, dedicated to Nanna, the moon god, later renamed Sin. The sides of the structure have been restored with modern-day bricks.

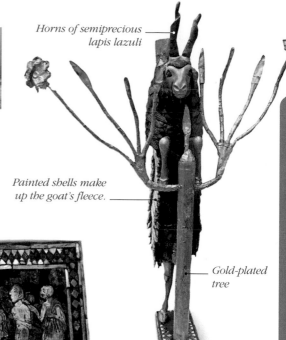

Horns of semiprecious lapis lazuli

Painted shells make up the goat's fleece.

Gold-plated tree

The king is depicted larger than the other figures, which shows his status.

The chariots are pulled by onagers — a type of large, horselike donkey.

Enemy soldiers are trampled under the chariots.

TRADE ▲

Mesopotamia was rich in agricultural products, and exported grain, pottery, and textiles Raw materials, such as metals, timber, and precious stones were imported from neighboring lands. This statuette of a goat, found in a royal tomb in Ur, is made entirely from materials from distant lands.

Shamash, the god of justice

THE CODE OF HAMMURABI ▶

Mesopotamian kings were the first known creators of a system of laws. The most famous of these is the law code of King Hammurabi of Babylon, which was carved on a stele (an upright stone slab) in 1754 BCE. The top of the stele shows the king receiving the laws from Shamash, the Mesopotamian god of justice.

C. 2350 BCE	C. 2100 BCE	C. 1900 BCE
 King Sargon of Akkad, which is a region in the north, conquers Sumer and creates the world's first empire. The Akkadian language later replaces Sumerian in Mesopotamia. SARGON OF AKKAD	The first ziggurat temples are built in Ur, Eridu, Nippur, and Uruk. They tower over the flat landscape of Mesopotamia, displaying the power of the city and its god.	The Amorites, a people from the western deserts, conquer most of Mesopotamia, which they rule from Babylon. They are now known as the Babylonians, and their empire is called Babylonia.

Early Japan

Over a period of about 15,000 years, the people who lived on the Japanese islands in ancient times slowly developed from small and isolated communities of simple hunter-gatherers into complex farming societies with a distinct culture.

Historians and archaeologists aren't sure when humans first reached Japan, although it might have been as early as 35,000 BCE. The age we now call "early Japan" began around 14,000 BCE with the Jomon period. The Jomon people made pottery with a distinctive rope or cord pattern, and formed the earliest communities in Japan. They lived near rivers or the sea, and survived by hunting, fishing, and gathering.

Jomon communities declined around 300 BCE. They were replaced by the Yayoi people, who may have traveled to the Japanese islands from the Korean Peninsula or mainland China. The Yayoi people formed clans, each with a male leader, although women may have also served in this role. Clan heads were also the religious and military leaders of their communities. The various clans often fought each other, and the victors absorbed the defeated clan and its lands into their own.

As some clans began to become larger and more powerful, their culture evolved. The most powerful clan was the Yamato, who conquered all of Japan by the 3rd century CE. This began an era known as the Kofun period, which lasted until the 6th century CE.

FACT
The method of growing rice in flooded fields was introduced to Japan by people who migrated from eastern parts of mainland China.

Reconstructed longhouse

PIT-HOUSES ▶
Many people in early Japan lived in "pit houses"—dwellings that consisted of a sloping roof built over a large hole in the ground, so part of the house was underground. The roofs were covered with grass that helped make them rainproof.

Pitched, thatched roof

Jade beads were used for the necklace.

◀ MAGATAMA JEWELERY
By around 1000 BCE, the people of Japan began making jewelery with curved, comma-shaped beads called magatama. *The beads were made from natural materials such as stone, clay, quartz, or jade. It is thought that the beads were carved to resemble the animal teeth seen on prehistoric jewelery.*

▼ SANNAI-MARUYAMA

Jomon people were living in permanent settlements by around 3500 BCE. The largest of these was the Sannai-Maruyama settlement in northern Japan. Clay figures, tools, and the remains of longhouses, have been found here.

▲ RITUAL BELLS

Metalworking was introduced to Japan during the Yayoi period. Archaeologists have found decorated bronze bells, called dotaku, *at Yayoi sites. Often decorated with images of animals, water, or agricultural objects, the bells may have been used in rituals for good harvests.*

DOGU FIGURINES

Small human- and animal-like figurines, called *dogu*, were made during the Jomon period. Although historians are not exactly sure what their purpose was, they think they might have been used as part of religious rituals, such as to heal the sick or to promote fertility.

DOGU HEAD FROM MIDDLE JOMON PERIOD

DOGU HEAD FROM LATE JOMON PERIOD

DOGU FIGURE FROM FINAL JOMON PERIOD

Wide hips were typical of dogu *figurines.*

◄ BURIAL SITES

The Kofun period gets its name from large burial mounds known as kofun *built for important people such as emperors. Kofun burial mounds came in various shapes but most commonly had an unusual keyhole-shaped design, as seen in the Daisen* Kofun *(left) located near the city of Osaka—the largest* kofun *ever found.*

▲ HANIWA FIGURES

People from the Kofun period built terra-cotta clay figures called haniwa. *Molded into depictions of warriors, birds, boats, weaponry, and the like—*haniwa *were placed around Kofun tombs, possibly to serve and protect the dead in the afterlife, but also to mark where the burial sites were located.*

Ancient Egypt

One of the longest-lasting civilizations in history, ancient Egypt was also one of the most stable. It lasted for more than 3,000 years after its foundation in around 3100 BCE, while empires rose and fell in the Middle East. Throughout this period, Egyptians spoke the same language, and followed the same seasonal routine based on the annual flooding of the Nile River.

▲ GIFT OF THE NILE
The Nile River flowed north through the desert, creating a green, fertile strip where Egyptians built their cities and farmed the land. The deserts that extended on either side protected Egypt from most foreign invaders.

The Egyptians called their country *Kemet*, meaning "black land." The name came from the fertile black silt left behind every year when the Nile River flooded. The flood water went down at exactly the right time of year to plant crops, making the land perfect for farming.

After 3600 BCE, societies in the region developed into two kingdoms—Upper Egypt in the south and Lower Egypt in the north. The two were united around 3100 BCE by a pharaoh (ruler) called Narmer. This unified civilization was at its height during three periods: the Old Kingdom (c. 2682–c. 2182 BCE), the Middle Kingdom (c. 2055–c. 1650 BCE), and the New Kingdom (c. 1550–c. 1069 BCE). While pharaohs of the first two periods built pyramid tombs, later pharaohs were buried in secret tombs in the desert. New Kingdom pharaohs were also warriors and created an empire stretching from the Euphrates River in Asia in the north to Nubia in the south.

Khepresh (blue war crown)

▲ KEEPING RECORDS
The Egyptians invented one of the first writing systems, known as hieroglyphics, around 3300 BCE. It used hundreds of picture signs representing words, sounds, and ideas. Above, scribes are shown taking records of the size of the harvest.

▲ PYRAMIDS

Between c. 2650 BCE and c. 1750 BCE, pharaohs were buried in massive stone tombs called pyramids. The biggest were constructed at Giza in Egypt, shown above. They belong to Khufu (right), his son Khafra (center), and grandson Menkaura (left). The smaller pyramids in front are the tombs of queens.

▼ THE FIRST PHARAOH

Before 3100 BCE, the two kings who ruled Upper and Lower Egypt wore different crowns. Narmer is believed to have united the two kingdoms. The two sides of the Narmer stone palette (below), found in Egypt in the 19th century, show him wearing the crowns of each kingdom.

Narmer wears the red crown of Lower Egypt.

Narmer wears the white crown of the Upper kingdom.

Serpopards (part leopard, part serpent)

Plumed headdress

▲ CHARIOT WARFARE

During the later New Kingdom, pharaohs used fast horse-drawn chariots in times of war. The lightweight chariots allowed the pharaohs, who were armed with bows and arrows, to move swiftly over the battlefield.

CHILD IN TIME

Tutankhamen was only eight or nine when he became pharaoh c. 1333 BCE. After his death c. 1323 BCE, he was buried in a secret tomb, which was discovered in 1922. Filled with treasures, the tomb made the boy pharaoh world famous.

FACT
The Great Pyramid at Giza, Egypt, is the oldest of the Seven Wonders of the Ancient World, and the only one that still stands today.

CUSTOMS AND BELIEFS

The ancient Egyptians believed that they lived in a well-ordered world, overseen by gods. There were many different gods, who were represented in both human and animal form. For example, the mother goddess Hathor was represented either as a cow or as a woman wearing a horned headdress.

Egyptian temples were believed to be the homes of the gods, who were represented by statues. Here, the gods were treated like living beings and given daily meals and clean clothes. During religious festivals, priests took the gods' statues out of their temples on parades featuring musicians and dancers.

The people of Egypt considered their pharaoh to be a link between humans and the gods. In the Old Kingdom, a pharaoh was seen as a living god. From the Middle Kingdom, they were considered to be the representatives of the gods on Earth. As pharaohs took the throne, they were transformed into the earthly form of Horus, the hawk-headed sky god. It was believed that after death, they would be united with Horus's father Osiris, the king of the underworld. Egyptians believed that, after death, they could also live again in the kingdom of Osiris, which was a land just like ancient Egypt.

> **FACT**
> When making a mummy, the Egyptians carefully preserved every organ except the brain, which they threw away. They thought brains served no purpose!

PROTECTOR GODS

Every part of ancient Egyptian life was protected by a god. While Horus watched over the pharaoh, Hathor cared for mothers. Bes guarded the home against snakes and scorpions, and Anubis looked after the mummification process.

ANUBIS

BES

HORUS

HATHOR

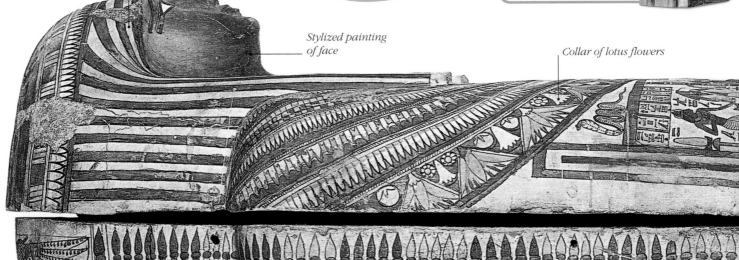

Striped wig worn by gods

Stylized painting of face

Collar of lotus flowers

▲ MAGIC SPELLS

The ancient Egyptians were often buried with a collection of spells to help them travel through the underworld. The spells acted as a passport to the kingdom of Osiris. Here, a person is tested by having their heart weighed against the Feather of Truth.

Obelisk made of pink granite

▲ LUXOR TEMPLE

Unlike most temples, which were dedicated to particular gods, the great temple of Luxor was dedicated to the Royal Ka, the divine soul of the pharaoh. Every year a great festival called Opet was held here, during which the living pharaoh was reborn as a god.

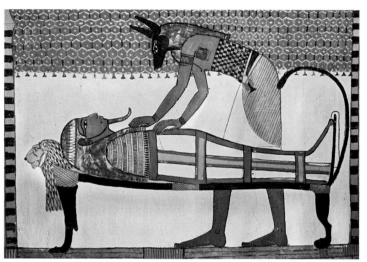

◄ MUMMIFICATION

Egyptians believed that though they could live again after death, their soul would still need a physical body and so they developed a ritual to preserve the dead, known as mummification. Priests wearing the mask of the god Anubis, who oversaw the process, removed the inner organs, dried the flesh, stuffed the body, and wrapped it in linen bandages.

MUMMY CASE ▼

For added protection, a mummy was placed in a case, which was shaped like a body and covered in magic spells. The case was another substitute body for the dead person. The mummy case below belonged to a man called Pensenhor, and was made around the 8th century BCE.

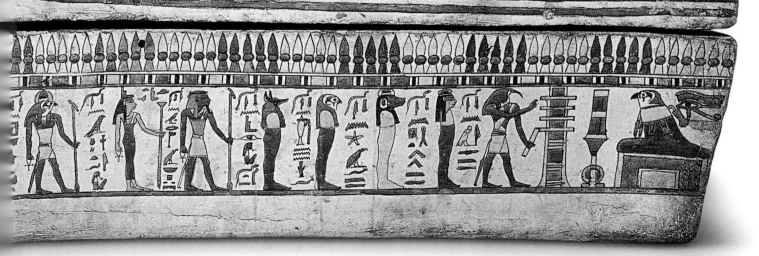

Early African civilizations

Africa was home to some of the wealthiest civilizations of the ancient world. The earliest rose around 5,000 years ago in northeast Africa where the people of ancient Egypt (see pp.20–23) and the Nubia region established civilizations that thrived for several thousand years. Later, advanced cultures emerged in West Africa and in the east, where the Kingdom of Aksum developed into a major world power.

ANCIENT KINGDOMS OF AFRICA

c. 1070 BCE–350 CE
The Kingdom of Kush, in modern-day Sudan, is the most powerful of a series of civilizations that rules in ancient Nubia, south of Egypt along the Nile valley. It is known as the "Land of the Bow," owing to its skilled archers, and grows rich on trading resources and goods such as gold, ivory, and animal pelts.

500 BCE–200 CE
The Nok culture flourishes in modern-day Nigeria. Nok people create impressive terra-cotta artifacts and are also skilled metalworkers, using sophisticated technology to make iron tools and weapons.

NOK TERRA-COTTA FIGURE

202–46 BCE
The Kingdom of Numidia rules a large part of northwest Africa. The Numidian cavalry is famous for its military tactics, which it uses to fight against the Carthaginians in 151–150 BCE.

80 BCE–825 CE
In eastern Africa, the Kingdom of Aksum rises to become a powerful trading empire. It develops a writing system that is still used by modern-day Ethiopian and Eritrean languages. Around 328 CE, the kingdom converts to Christianity.

KUSHITE ART ▶

Like the ancient Egyptians, the people of Kush built many large pyramids over the burial chambers of their kings and queens. These were decorated with detailed paintings and carvings. This carving, on a stone slab found in the royal capital of Meroë, shows a Kushite prince slaying his enemy.

24

Ancient Greece

Often called the "cradle of Western civilization," ancient Greece was one of the first well-developed civilizations in Europe. At its peak, around 2,500 years ago, it stretched across vast areas of the ancient world. The ancient Greeks made important contributions to philosophy, politics, mathematics, science, and the arts. Their influence shaped the Western world.

In ancient times, Greece was not a single unified country, but a collection of more than 1,000 city-states, such as Athens, Sparta, Thebes, and Syracuse. Each city-state was known as a *polis*, and governed itself independently.

These city-states were often at war with each other, with each struggling to be the strongest power in the region. But in the 4th century BCE they were all conquered and brought under the rule of Philip II of Macedonia.

After Philip's death, his son Alexander set about extending Greek territory and influence, building an empire that stretched into North Africa and Central Asia.

Greek power over the ancient world continued until the mighty Roman Empire (see pp.46–47) came to dominance in 146 BCE, although that did not end the influence of Greek culture around the Mediterranean and the Western world.

▲ **CITY-STATES**
Each Greek city-state had its own laws, customs, and currency. Up to the 5th century, Athens was the most powerful city-state. Its most powerful fortress was the Acropolis, built on a hill above the city. At its center was the Parthenon temple, which still stands today.

▲ **ATHENIAN DEMOCRACY**
Athens developed one of the earliest democracies, giving citizens the right to vote, though women and enslaved people were excluded. A device called a kleroterion *(above) was used to choose citizens at random to fill government roles.*

Persian archer wearing clothes with decorated sleeves

▲ GREEK–PERSIAN WARS

From 492 to 449 BCE, various Greek city-states were at war with the Persian Empire (see pp.40–41). To fight this common enemy, many of them joined forces to form the Delian League. The League was founded after the Persians sacked Athens in 478 BCE, and prevented them from permanently taking over parts of Greece.

FACT
The modern-day marathon race has its origin in an ancient Greek story, in which a messenger is said to have run a distance of 26 miles (42 km) from Marathon to Athens without stopping.

ALEXANDER THE GREAT

Alexander the Great (356–323 BCE), was born in Macedonia. As a child he studied under the philosopher Aristotle, and became king of Macedonia in 336 BCE at the age of 20. Alexander's military campaigns helped the spread of Greek culture in the places he conquered.

MAJOR PERIODS

c. 3500–1100 BCE	The Minoan civilization develops on the island of Crete in the Mediterranean Sea. The Minoans build complex cities and large palaces. Their culture spreads to the Greek mainland.
c. 1600–1050 BCE	Influenced by the Minoans, the Mycenaean civilization establishes itself in mainland Greece. The Mycenaeans develop a flourishing culture and are the first people to speak a form of Ancient Greek.
c. 1100–750 BCE	The Minoan and Mycenaean civilizations collapse. In the 8th century BCE, the first city-states emerge and the Greeks start to set up colonies around the Mediterranean and Black seas.
431–404 BCE	The two most powerful city-states, Athens and Sparta, battle for supremacy during the Peloponnesian War. Sparta emerges victorious.
336–323 BCE	Greek territory expands during the reign of Alexander the Great. After his death, the empire splits up into smaller states.
146 BCE	The Roman Republic defeats an alliance of Greek city-states at the Battle of Corinth, beginning the Roman domination of Greece.

◄ ALEXANDER'S CONQUESTS

Alexander the Great inherited a kingdom that included Macedonia and most of the Greek city-states. An incredibly skilled military leader, he went on to conquer parts of western Asia, northern Africa, and northern India, creating one of the largest empires ever to have existed.

KEY ■ Kingdom of Macedonia ■ Alexander's empire

Macedonia · Black Sea · Caspian Sea · Thebes · Athens · Sparta · Anatolia · Crete · Cyprus · Tigris · Mesopotamia · Euphrates · Babylon · Iranian Plateau · Persepolis · Sahara Desert · Nile · EGYPT · Bukhara · Maracanda (Samarkand) · Hindu Kush · Taxila · Indus · Hydraotes · Zaradros · Himalayas · Quetta

ANCIENT GREEK CULTURE

Ancient Greece produced a thriving and influential culture. Some of the scientific ideas to come out of the region were very advanced for the time. For example, Greek astronomer Aristarchus put forward the theory that the sun, not Earth, was the center of the universe. This fact was not widely accepted until more than a thousand years later. Additionally, the mathematician Eratosthenes was the first to accurately estimate the circumference of Earth.

In literature, works by the poets Homer and Sappho continue to be regarded as some of the greatest ever written. The writings of Greek philosophers have had a major impact on Western thinking and culture. Even after the Roman conquest, Greek culture continued its influence. Pre-Christian Roman beliefs, for example, were based on Greek mythology, but with Greek names replaced by Roman ones.

▼ SCIENCE AND MATHEMATICS

The ancient Greeks knew of seven planets in the solar system and had names for 48 constellations, 47 of which are still recognized. Pythagoras's theorem, which explains the relationship between the lengths of a right-angled triangle's sides, was also developed in ancient Greece.

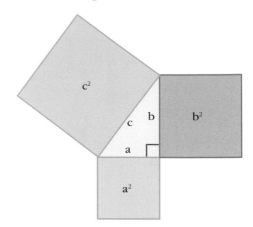

◄ PHILOSOPHY

Philosophers such as Thales of Miletus, Plato (left), Socrates, and Aristotle wrote about what it meant to be human, and about how humans should behave. Their works were so influential that they still form the basis of modern Western philosophy.

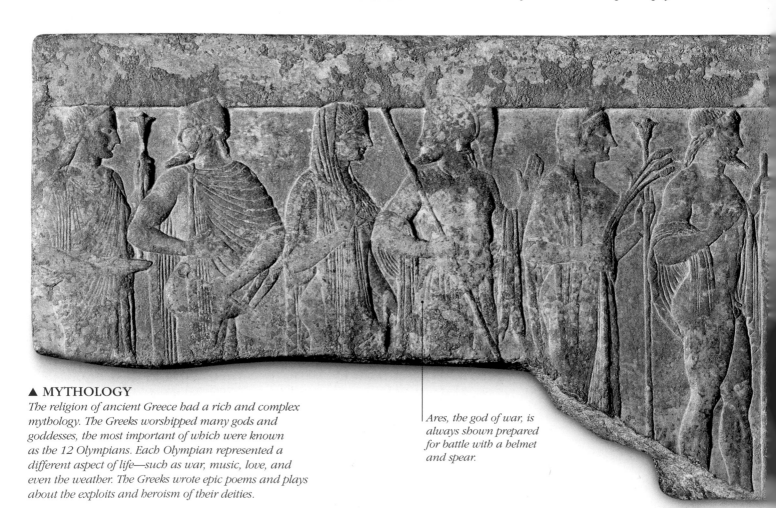

▲ MYTHOLOGY

The religion of ancient Greece had a rich and complex mythology. The Greeks worshipped many gods and goddesses, the most important of which were known as the 12 Olympians. Each Olympian represented a different aspect of life—such as war, music, love, and even the weather. The Greeks wrote epic poems and plays about the exploits and heroism of their deities.

Ares, the god of war, is always shown prepared for battle with a helmet and spear.

HIPPOCRATES

Hippocrates (c.460–370 BCE), is often called the "father of modern medicine." He changed the course of medicine by arguing that illnesses had natural causes and were not punishments sent by the gods.

THEATER ▶
Drama originated in ancient Greece, where people watched plays in open-air venues known as amphitheaters. There were three types of drama—tragedies, comedies, and satyr plays, which were somewhere between the two. Actors often played more than one role, and wore masks to represent the different characters.

WOMEN IN ANCIENT GREECE ▶
Greek women were mostly restricted to the home, unable to vote or own land, although Spartan women enjoyed more freedom and rights than those in other city-states. Girls were sometimes educated, but usually only to prepare them to run a household.

▲ THE OLYMPIC GAMES
In 776 BCE, the first Olympic Games were held in Olympia. These games, which included sports such as boxing, wrestling, running, long jump, javelin, and discus throw, were the inspiration for the modern Olympic Games, which began in 1896.

Artemis, goddess of the hunt, always holds a bow and a quiver of arrows.

The god of music, Apollo, is shown with a lyre.

Ancient monuments

Structures made from rock or stone are often all that remain of past civilizations, and can give us insight into the skills, customs, and beliefs of the people who built them. Hundreds of laborers would have been needed to construct each of these massive monuments.

Megalithic tomb
Munhung-ri Dolmen

Where Pyongyang, North Korea
When c. 3300–1200 BCE

This structure made up of large prehistoric stones, or megaliths, is called a dolmen. Erected in the Bronze Age, it was probably the tomb of an important person. The Korean Peninsula contains more than 40,000 such dolmens—40 percent of the total number in the world.

Limestone marvel
Great Sphinx

Where Giza, Egypt
When c. 2500 BCE

The ancient Egyptians built statues of sphinxes—mythical creatures, usually with a human head and lion's body—to guard tombs and temples. Carved from a single block of limestone, the Great Sphinx of Giza is one of the world's largest stone structures.

The head of the Great Sphinx may represent Pharaoh Khafre.

Buddhist shrine
Great Stupa

Where Sanchi, India
When c. 250 BCE

Stupas are mound-like stone structures built to contain sacred objects known as relics. This stupa was built by the Mauryan emperor Ashoka (see p.44) to hold relics of the Buddha. The carved gateways were added later, and show scenes from the Buddha's life.

Roman amphitheater
The Colosseum

Where Rome, Italy
When 80 CE

In Roman times, bloodthirsty shows such as gladiator fights and wild animal hunts were put on in this vast open-air arena. Its four tiers of stone seating could accommodate up to 50,000 spectators.

Two vertical stones support a flat capstone.

Ancient stone circle
Stonehenge

Where Wiltshire, England
When c. 3000–2200 BCE

The purpose of this huge stone circle is a mystery, but archaeologists have discovered that some of the giant boulders at Stonehenge were dragged into place, probably on sleighs, from nearly 155 miles (250km) away. It is believed that Stonehenge was an important religious or ceremonial site.

Rock-cut tomb
Al-Khazneh

Where Petra, Jordan
When Early 1st century CE

Known as Al-Khazneh ("The Treasury"), this elaborate stone monument was actually the entrance to a royal tomb. It was carved out of a sheer cliff-face by the Nabataeans—Arab traders who built their capital city of Petra in a narrow gorge in the mountains of present-day Jordan.

Raised circular balcony for pilgrims to walk around the stupa

One of the four gateways to the stupa

The columns were carved in a style similar to those found in Greek or Roman temples.

Mesoamerican step pyramid
Pyramid of the Sun

Where Teotihuacán, Mexico
When 2nd to 3rd century CE

Rising 216ft (66m) high, the Pyramid of the Sun was built to mimic the shape of the mountain behind it. It is the largest structure in Teotihuacán—a city in central Mexico built by a civilization that existed centuries before the Aztec Empire.

Carved obelisk
Obelisk of Aksum

Where Aksum, Ethiopia
When 4th century CE

Weighing 220 tons (200 metric tons), this tall monument is made of a single piece of granite, and stands 69ft (21m) high. It was built to mark the burial site of King Ezana of the ancient kingdom of Aksum (see p.45).

31

Ancient India

The earliest civilization on the Indian subcontinent first spread along the Indus River around 2500 BCE. For the next 5,000 years, a series of empires rose and fell in the region, and two of today's major world religions, Hinduism and Buddhism, first appeared on the subcontinent.

▲ **INDUS VALLEY CIVILIZATION**
At its peak, the Indus Valley Civilization stretched from northeast Afghanistan, through Pakistan, and into northwest India. The Indus people developed extensive trade networks across the region. They recorded their transactions on engraved seals, like the one pictured above.

MAJOR EMPIRES

322–185 BCE	Founded by Chandragupta Maurya, the Mauryan Empire grows to become India's largest kingdom, covering nearly all of the Indian subcontinent.
c. 135 BCE–c. 225 CE	The Kushans of Central Asia conquer modern-day Afghanistan and northwest India. Their empire reaches its greatest extent under Kanishka I in the 2nd century CE.
c. 275–c. 897 CE	The Pallava Empire, known for its art and architecture, controls much of south India from its capital at Kanchipuram, Tamil Nadu.
320–c. 550 CE	The reign of the Gupta Empire is a golden age for India. The empire is at peace and grows wealthy from trade. The arts and culture flourish.

GUPTA
PERIOD COIN

The Indus Valley Civilization suddenly declined after 1800 BCE, and nomadic tribes swept in from Central Asia to conquer much of northern India. For the next 1,500 years, the region was divided. During this period the Vedas—sacred texts of Hinduism—were composed. In 326 BCE, the armies of Alexander the Great (see p.27) invaded northern India. This inspired Chandragupta, ruler of the powerful Magadha kingdom, to rise up. He drove out Alexander's successors and in 322 BCE established the Mauryan Empire. The Mauryans expanded to the south, uniting India for the first time.

ASHOKA'S PILLARS ▲
Emperor Ashoka had stone pillars built across his empire, which were carved with inscriptions instructing people how to live a Buddhist life. A pillar at Sarnath, Uttar Pradesh, was topped with a sculpture of four back-to-back lions (above), which in 1950 became India's official emblem.

Chandragupta's grandson, Emperor Ashoka, was one of India's greatest rulers. Following a violent and bloody war, he converted to Buddhism and its influence quickly spread. The Maurya Empire declined after Ashoka's death in c. 231 BCE, and a number of smaller kingdoms came to power. From 320 CE, most of north and central India came under the rule of the Gupta Empire, which promoted Hinduism but was tolerant of other religions.

*A cupola
(small dome)
tops the pyramid.*

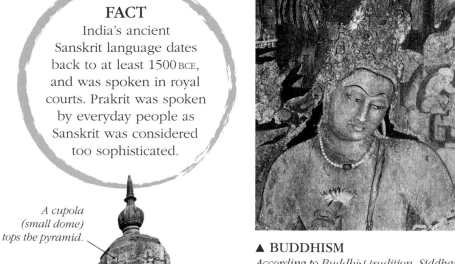

▲ BUDDHISM

*According to Buddhist tradition, Siddhartha
Gautama, known as the Buddha, was
born a prince around 560 BCE in modern-
day Nepal. He left the palace and was
shocked by the poverty he saw. He vowed to
live a simpler life and spent the rest of his
days teaching others how to overcome
suffering. The religion of Buddhism, based
on his teachings, now has more than
500 million followers around the world.*

◄ STONE ARCHITECTURE

*The Pallavas were a dynasty of kings that ruled south
India from the late 3rd century CE. They constructed
many monuments—at first these were cut into the
sides of mountains, but later the Pallavas developed
methods of creating free-standing temples from
stone. The Shore Temple at Mamallapuram, Tamil
Nadu, is their greatest architectural achievement.*

*The structure was
built using blocks
of granite from a
nearby quarry.*

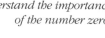

GOLDEN AGE ▲

*The reign of the Guptas was a time
of great progress in math, science,
philosophy, and the arts. In the
6th century CE, the mathematician
Aryabhata (above) was
one of the first people to
understand the importance
of the number zero.*

China's early dynasties

According to Chinese tradition, the first Chinese rulers were the Xia Dynasty, though archaeologists disagree on whether this dynasty existed or not. The Xia are believed to have governed a kingdom on the banks of the Yellow River in the late 3rd to early 2nd millennium BCE. The Xia were later followed by the Shang, the Zhou, and eventually the Qin.

RISE AND FALL OF DYNASTIES

c. 1600–1046 BCE

The Shang kings rule a small northern state, which soon expands to control a large part of China. They use animal bones, covered with ancient Chinese script, that are believed to tell the future. Shang metalworkers master the crafting of bronze items.

SHANG TORTOISE SHELL WITH WRITING

1046–776 BCE

In 1046 BCE, the Shang are overthrown by King Wu of Zhou, who founds his own dynasty. The Zhou kings claim they have been given the right to rule by heaven. This concept of the "Mandate of Heaven" is used by all later Chinese emperors.

ZHOU GOOSE-SHAPED RITUAL VESSEL

776–221 BCE

From 776 BCE onward, the Zhou kings struggle to control the different parts of the kingdom, which disintegrates into many separate states constantly at war with one another. From 476 to 221 BCE, only seven states remain, and the most western state, Qin, conquers the others one by one.

221–210 BCE

The king of Qin, who names himself Shi Huangdi (First Emperor), uses force to unify China, making everyone adopt the same writing script, coinage, and measuring units. But the power of the Qin weakens dramatically after his death in 210 BCE, and the dynasty is overthrown just four years later.

◀ **TERRA-COTTA ARMY**
The First Emperor was buried in a vast tomb built by 700,000 workers. To the east of the tomb, pits held an army of at least 8,000 life-size terra-cotta warriors, created to protect the emperor in the next world.

The Phoenicians

From their homeland on the coast of what is now Lebanon and parts of Syria and Israel, the Phoenicians became the leading seafaring merchants of the ancient world. From the 10th century BCE, they sailed the Mediterranean, searching for new markets, founding colonies, and spreading their culture, including their language and alphabet.

The Phoenicians lived in around a dozen coastal cities, including Byblos, Tyre, and Sidon, each of which was ruled by a king. The hills of their homeland were covered with tall cedar trees, which the Phoenicians used to build their ships. They also sold the cedar wood to Egypt, Greece, and Mesopotamia.

The Phoenicians founded trading stations across the Mediterranean, such as Carthage in North Africa. They also explored the Atlantic coast of Europe, the Indian Ocean and—according to one ancient historian—in c. 500 BCE, sailed around Africa, in search of new markets.

Phoenician cities were centers of fine craftwork, producing glassware, metalwork, textiles, and furniture decorated with ivory. Phoenician traders exchanged these for products not available in their cities, such as tin and silver from Spain, copper from Cyprus, incense from Arabia, and ivory from Egypt.

▲ PHOENICIAN BIREME
The Phoenicians used their cedar to build warships. Their standard warship was a bireme—a ship powered by two decks of oars. The Persian Empire's navy was made up of Phoenician ships.

▲ TYRIAN PURPLE
The Phoenician city of Tyre was famous for a purple dye made from the shells of a Murex sea snail. It took tens of thousands of snails to make a small amount of this dye, which came to be known as Tyrian purple. Cloth dyed with Tyrian purple was highly valued, and was worn mostly by kings and emperors.

▼ PHOENICIAN CRAFTS
Phoenician crafts were influenced by the different cultures they encountered. This Phoenician carved ivory panel, found in present-day Iraq, combines an Egyptian sphinx and a Mesopotamian lamassu (a human-headed winged lion).

The sphinx wears a striped headcloth as worn by Egyptian pharaohs.

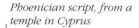

Phoenician script, from a temple in Cyprus

▲ PHOENICIAN ALPHABET
Unlike Mesopotamian or Egyptian scripts that had hundreds of signs, the Phoenician alphabet had just 22, all standing for consonants. Easy to learn, it was adapted by the Greeks, who added vowel signs, and then later by the Romans.

◀ MOUNTED BOWMAN
In warfare and hunting, nomads used a short, powerful bow made from wood, horn, and sinew, fired from horseback. This felt hanging, from a Siberian kurgan, shows a horseman with a short bow case at his side.

Two Scythians fight a mounted Greek soldier.

▲ SCYTHIAN GOLD
The richest kurgans *belonged to the tribe of the Scythians, who lived in what is now southern Siberia from around the 7th century* BCE. *This Greek gold comb was found in the tomb of a king, whose body was completely covered in gold items.*

Steppe nomads

The steppes of Eurasia are a vast, dry, treeless plain, stretching from Europe to the borders of China. Although not suitable for farming, the land is good for grazing animals. For 5,500 years, the steppes have been the home of horse-riding nomads, people who are constantly on the move, searching for fresh pastures.

Early steppe nomads spent their lives on horseback, accompanying sheep, goats, camels, and cattle on great journeys. They used carts to carry their belongings, including the tents in which they slept each night. At the edges of the steppe, they would trade horses and animal products with settled peoples, who in turn provided them with metals and other goods. Steppe nomads buried their dead beneath mounds, each called a *kurgan*, often full of treasures acquired through trading and raiding.

In the first millennium BCE, nomadic tribes began to gather in huge mobile hordes, threatening settled civilizations. From the 5th century BCE, the Xiongnu of Mongolia regularly raided China. To meet the threat, in 215 BCE, China's first emperor, Qin Shi Huangdi, built a great wall across his northern frontier. Later, in the 1st century CE, the Kushans from Central Asia conquered Afghanistan and northwest India. They were followed, in the 4th and 5th centuries, by the Huns, whose empire stretched from western Asia into Europe.

ATTILA THE HUN

Attila ruled the Huns from 434–453 CE. During his reign, the Huns conquered lands from the Rhine in western Europe to the Caspian Sea in Central Asia. Western European empires came to fear Attila's plundering armies.

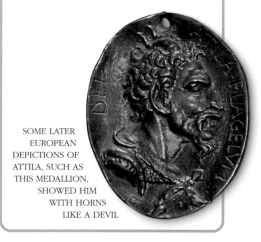

SOME LATER EUROPEAN DEPICTIONS OF ATTILA, SUCH AS THIS MEDALLION, SHOWED HIM WITH HORNS LIKE A DEVIL

Ancient Maya

In around 2000 BCE, the eastern part of Central America and modern-day Mexico saw the rise of the Maya civilization, which grew to become one of the most advanced of its time. The ancient Maya constructed large cities in which they built tall pyramid temples. They also made beautiful works of art, and created a sophisticated writing system.

The Maya homeland contained a central rainforest, with dry regions to the north, and highlands to the south. They cleared areas of rainforest for farmland to grow crops, which could support grand cities with tens of thousands of people.

The Maya were greatly influenced by other civilizations of the region, such as the Olmecs and the Zapotecs. From them they inherited a calendar system. Ancient Maya people were able to predict eclipses and the movements of the moon as well as the planet Venus, and used their understanding of the skies to create an accurate calendar.

After 800 CE many Maya cities had begun to decline or collapse. Some historians believe that this was due to constant warfare and decreasing natural resources.

▲ ROYAL RITUALS
Maya kings and queens believed they were descended from gods, and offered their blood in rituals to contact and honor them. They often drew a thorn-studded rope across their tongue to draw blood. This stone carving shows a queen of Yaxchilan performing a bloodletting ceremony.

▼ PYRAMID TEMPLE
The center of every Maya city was a ceremonial area, with tall pyramids that were topped with temples. These pyramids were sometimes tombs for kings who were worshipped in the temple. Below is the temple of King Pakal the Great of the city of Palenque.

▲ WRITING
The Maya created a complete writing system using symbols called glyphs to represent both words and syllables, and produced books with pages made of tree bark. The glyphs run along the top of the page shown above.

Priests performed rituals at the temple on top of the pyramid.

The nine terraces of the pyramid represent the nine levels of the Maya underworld.

MAJOR PERIODS

1800 BCE–250 CE	The first Maya villages appear around 1800 BCE. By around 500 BCE, these have begun to grow into large cities with ceremonial centers. The Maya also develop a system of writing.
250–950 CE	Maya civilization reaches its height. Cities are ruled by powerful kings who build monuments that record the date of their kingdoms.
950–1520 CE	Following a long period of drought, cities in the central rainforest are abandoned. However, Maya cities in the north and south of the region continue to grow.
1520–1697	Spanish colonists invade the region, but face fierce resistance from the Maya. It takes the colonists almost 200 years to complete their invasion.

▲ WARFARE

Maya leaders displayed their fitness to rule through their success in warfare. The aim was not to kill enemies, but to capture them for later sacrifice to the gods. Maya warriors often wore jaguar headdresses and skins into battle to symbolize victory, as shown in this painting from a Maya site in Mexico.

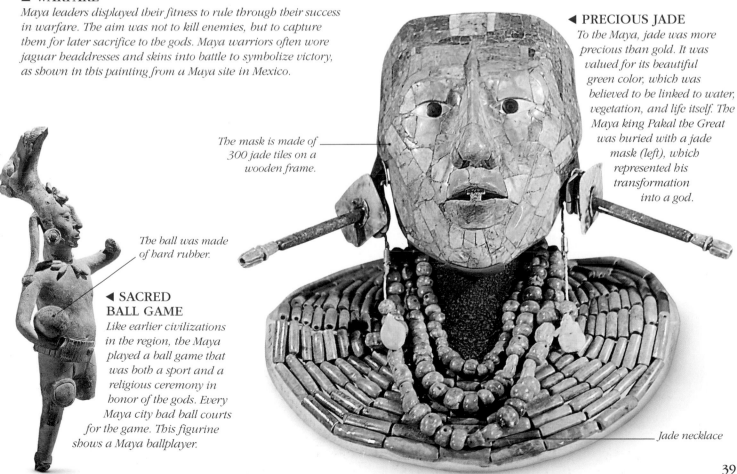

◄ PRECIOUS JADE

To the Maya, jade was more precious than gold. It was valued for its beautiful green color, which was believed to be linked to water, vegetation, and life itself. The Maya king Pakal the Great was buried with a jade mask (left), which represented his transformation into a god.

The mask is made of 300 jade tiles on a wooden frame.

The ball was made of hard rubber.

◄ SACRED BALL GAME

Like earlier civilizations in the region, the Maya played a ball game that was both a sport and a religious ceremony in honor of the gods. Every Maya city had ball courts for the game. This figurine shows a Maya ballplayer.

Jade necklace

The Persian Empire

In the 6th century BCE, Cyrus II, king of the small city-state of Persis (in modern-day Iran), began a series of conquests that led to the creation of the world's first superpower. At its peak, the Persian Empire he founded controlled territories in Africa, Asia, and Europe.

▲ PERSEPOLIS
In 518 BCE, Darius I founded a new capital, Persepolis, where he built a vast palace. During Nowruz, the annual spring festival, people from all over the empire brought gifts to Persepolis. The city was burned down by Alexander the Great in 330 BCE.

DARIUS I

The third of the Persian Empire's great kings, Darius I (reigned 522–486 BCE) was a gifted leader. He improved his empire's organization and completed many building projects. Though he expanded the empire to its greatest extent, he failed to conquer the Greek city-states.

A brilliant military commander, Cyrus the Great—as he came to be called—conquered three neighboring empires over a period of just 11 years. Though ferocious in battle, he was generous toward those he defeated, and allowed people in the captured territories to retain their religions, beliefs, and customs. After his death, his son Cambyses II expanded the empire by conquering Egypt. The empire reached its peak under Darius I who extended its territory into Europe. The empire received tributes (gifts, such as gold) from the conquered territories, and punished any rebellion swiftly.

There was a long rivalry between the Persians and their western neighbors, the Greeks, and in 330 BCE the Persian Empire eventually fell to the massive army of Alexander the Great (see p.27). Following Alexander's conquest, there were two later Persian empires, the Parthian and Sasanian, the latter of which was defeated by Arab invaders in 642 CE.

CONNECTING THE EMPIRE ▶
The Persian Empire was better run and better connected than any previous empire. Each province was run by a powerful satrap (governor), who was allowed to make decisions independent of the king. Darius I developed a new postal system, and built new roads to connect the empire—the most important was the Royal Road, which connected his capital, Susa, with the Mediterranean coast. People rode in chariots, much like this model of a satrap's vehicle.

EXTENT OF THE EMPIRE ▲

Cyrus the Great conquered the Median Empire, of which Persis was a part, in 550 BCE, then the empire of Lydia in 546 BCE, and Babylon in 539 BCE. Under later kings the empire continued to grow and at its height under Darius I stretched from southeastern Europe to northwest India— the largest empire the world had ever seen.

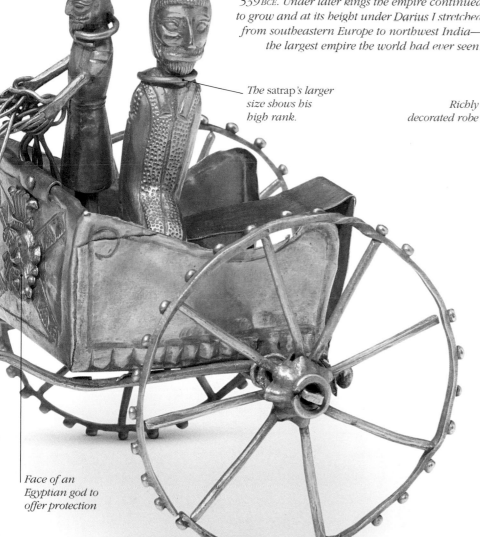

The satrap's larger size shows his high rank.

Face of an Egyptian god to offer protection

Richly decorated robe

▲ ROYAL ARMY

The Persian army included an elite force of 10,000 troops that served as the king's personal bodyguards. They were called "Immortals" because as soon as one died, they were replaced to keep the number at 10,000. The mosaic above shows one of Darius I's loyal soldiers, at his palace in Susa.

▲ LATER PERSIA

After being defeated by Greece, Persian power was revived first under the Parthian Empire (247 BCE–224 CE), followed by the Sasanian Empire (224–651 CE). Both came into conflict with the Roman and Byzantine empires. This coin shows Ardashir I (reigned 224–242 CE), the founder of the Sasanian Empire.

The movable wings actually flapped during battle.

Celtic Europe

From the 6th century BCE, the Iron Age civilization of the Celts stretched across much of Europe. The Celts, who originated from north of the Alps, lived in many large tribes and never saw themselves as a single people. They were fierce warriors and skilled metalworkers.

The Celts spoke a group of related languages, connected to modern Irish and Welsh, and shared customs, religious beliefs, and styles of art. The name "Celt" comes from *Keltoi*— the Greek name for a particular tribe living in France. The Romans called them "Galli" (Gauls), which led to the lands they settled being called Gaul (France), Galicia (in Spain), and Galatia (in Turkey).

Much of what we know of the Celts comes from the writings of the Romans, who eventually conquered most of their lands. The Romans were startled by the independence of Celtic women, who could rule as queens and go into battle. They were also shocked by some of the Celtic religious practices, which included human sacrifice. In Britain and Gaul, this was carried out by priests called druids.

SPREAD OF THE CELTS

800–500 BCE

The first recorded Celtic culture emerges in modern-day Austria. People of the Hallstatt culture bury their dead with bronze ornaments decorated with geometric patterns.

BRONZE BROOCH
FROM HALLSTATT

◀ METALWORK
Celts were expert metalworkers, decorating bronze artifacts, such as shields and the backs of mirrors, with elaborate patterns. Many bronze items have been found in rivers and lakes, where they were thrown as offerings to gods. This shield was found in the Thames River, near Battersea, London, UK.

Red glass studs inlaid on the bronze Battersea Shield

BOUDICCA

Following the Roman conquest of southern Britain, Queen Boudicca of the Iceni, a Celtic tribe in eastern England, led a great uprising against the invaders. In 61 BCE, her army sacked three Roman towns before being defeated.

▲ HILLFORTS
In Britain, Celtic tribes built great hillforts, which were defended by deep ditches and tall earth banks topped by timber walls. Maiden Castle (above) in southern England is one such example. It was home to hundreds of people who lived in thatched wooden roundhouses.

▼ RELIGION
The Celts worshipped hundreds of gods and offered them precious objects and sacrifices. Each clan had its own deities, but some gods were followed over a wider area under different names. One of them was the nature god, who the Gauls called Cernunnos.

The nature god is surrounded by wild animals.

◀ COINS
After coming into contact with the Romans and the Greeks through trade, the Celts initially copied their coins. This Celtic gold coin, featuring a horse, was inspired by one issued by King Philip of Macedonia. Later, the Celts developed their own style, designing coins featuring images of deities and local chiefs.

450 BCE	400–390 BCE	279–278 BCE	58–51 BCE
A second Celtic culture, called La Tène, spreads from present-day Switzerland across much of Europe, stretching from Spain to Romania. Its metalwork has swirling patterns.	The Celtic Senones tribe invades what is now Italy, sacking Rome in 390 BCE. The Romans pay them a huge sum in gold to leave.	A massive Celtic army invades Greece but is eventually turned back. Part of the army moves into Anatolia, in modern-day Turkey, settling the area of Galatia.	The Celts' dominance across northern Europe comes to an end when Roman general Julius Caesar conquers Gaul and part of Britain.

Egyptian pharaohs wore a false beard as part of their regalia.

Leaders of the ancient world

Across the ancient world, many extraordinary kings and queens left their mark on history. Some were remarkable military strategists who outwitted their enemies, while others ruled by brute force. Still others were great administrators, and successfully governed large and complex empires.

Egyptian pharaoh
Hatshepsut

Where Egyptian Empire, North Africa
When c. 1507–1458 BCE

One of the few female rulers of Egypt to rule in her own right, Hatshepsut acted as regent to her stepson Thutmose III before becoming pharaoh herself. She reigned for about 20 years. Many statues of the time portrayed her in the traditional clothes worn by male pharaohs, complete with false beard.

Mauryan emperor
Ashoka

Where Indian subcontinent, South Asia
When c. 304–c. 232 BCE

Ashoka the Great, ruler of the Mauryan Empire of South Asia, fought many violent battles on his path to power before embracing Buddhism, a religion that teaches nonviolence. Following the conquest of Kalinga, in modern-day India, he gave up war to spread the message of Buddhism throughout his empire and beyond.

Qin emperor
Qin Shi Huangdi

Where China, Asia
When 259–210 BCE

Zheng, king of Qin, took the name Qin Shi Huangdi (meaning "First Qin Emperor") after conquering six other Chinese states and uniting them under the same laws, written language, and currency. After his death, Zheng was buried with the Terra-Cotta Army—a magnificent collection of sculpted clay warriors meant to protect him in the afterlife (see pp. 34–35).

Roman ruler
Caesar Augustus

Where Roman Empire, Europe
When 63 BCE–14 CE

After decades of civil war, Caesar Augustus restored peace to the Roman world, and was proclaimed the first Roman emperor in 27 BCE. During his 40-year reign, he reformed the army and government, laying the foundations for a stable empire.

Palmyrene queen
Septimia Zenobia

Where Palmyrene Empire, Western Asia
When c. 240–c. 274 CE

Zenobia ruled the wealthy city of Palmyra (modern-day Syria), then part of the Roman Empire. At a time of turmoil in Rome, Zenobia seized the chance to set up an independent kingdom and conquered a large part of the Roman Empire. She declared herself empress but was later defeated. In this 19th-century portrait, she is shown in chains.

Headdress decorated with turquoise stones

Aksumite king
Ezana

Where Kingdom of Aksum, Eastern Africa
When c. 303–350 CE

Ezana was the ruler of the ancient city of Aksum in what is now Eritrea and northern Ethiopia. At about the same time that the Roman Empire adopted Christianity, he was converted to the Christian faith by a missionary from Syria. As a result, Aksum became the first Christian kingdom in Africa.

Ezana wears a crown and is flanked by two stalks of wheat.

Visigoth leader
Alaric I

Where Parts of Roman Empire, Europe
When 370–410 CE

The Visigoths were a Germanic people living on the eastern border of the Roman Empire. In 410 CE, their king Alaric I led an army to attack and plunder the city of Rome. This act contributed to the fall of the Western Roman Empire.

Maya ruler
K'inich Janaab' Pakal

Where Palenque, North America
When 603–683 CE

In 615 CE, at the age of 12, K'inich Janaab' Pakal became the *ajaw* (ruler) of the Maya city-state of Palenque, in modern-day Mexico. His reign of 68 years is one of the longest in history. Pakal's palace at Palenque still stands today.

45

Ancient Rome

From a small farming settlement in the 10th century BCE, ancient Rome grew to become one of the largest empires in history. At its peak, the Roman Empire was home to as many as 70 million people, covered much of Europe and North Africa, and extended well into Asia.

Early Rome was originally ruled by kings, but in 509 BCE the Romans overthrew the seventh king, Tarquin the Proud, and set up a republic. Rome was now run by a system of elected officials, led by two consuls who ruled alongside a council called the Senate. This council was initially made up only of patricians (wealthy landowners), but over time the plebeians (poorer citizens) managed to win more political power.

Rome prospered and grew. It expanded south into Sicily and North Africa, and by the 2nd century BCE the Romans were in control of most of the Mediterranean. After around 100 BCE, civil war began to tear the Roman Republic apart. After a long power battle, Julius Caesar became dictator for life in 44 BCE, but was soon killed. His heir, Augustus, then defeated his rivals to become the first emperor of Rome in 27 BCE. The Roman Republic had become the Roman Empire, and once again power rested almost entirely with one person. It would remain this way, passing from emperor to emperor, for the next 500 years.

Helmet crests were made of feathers or horse hair.

ROMULUS AND REMUS ▲
According to legend, Rome was founded by twin brothers Romulus and Remus, who were sons of the war god Mars. They were raised by a female wolf. Romulus killed his brother and became the first king, giving the city his name.

◄ ROMAN SENATE
Only men could join the Senate. Originally, its role was only to offer advice to the king, but during the Roman Republic it became much more powerful, making key decisions. The Senate's role diminished when Rome became an empire.

THE ROMAN EMPIRE

27 BCE	69–79 CE
Julius Caesar's heir Augustus defeats his rivals to become the first emperor of Rome.	After a year of civil wars, Vespasian emerges victorious and restores some stability. He builds the huge Colosseum amphitheater in Rome, which still stands today.

◀ THE ROMAN ARMY

Well organized and highly trained, the Roman army conquered vast areas along the Mediterranean and beyond. It was made up of Roman citizens as well as people from conquered territories in Africa, the Middle East, and elsewhere. One of the elite units of the army was the Praetorian Guard (left), which served as bodyguards for the emperors.

The curved shield protects the soldier's body.

JULIUS CAESAR

Julius Caesar (100–44 BCE) was one of the most powerful politicians and military leaders of ancient Rome. He conquered Gaul (modern-day France) and seized power in 47 BCE after defeating his rival, Pompey, in a civil war.

◀ AQUEDUCTS

The Romans built aqueducts (bridges that carry water over rivers and valleys) to supply public baths, fountains, farms, and more. Many of these ancient structures are still standing today, such as the Pont du Gard (left) in Nîmes, France.

ROMAN EMPIRE AT ITS HEIGHT ▶

The empire reached its greatest expanse around 117 CE. Extending all the way around the Mediterranean and up as far as Britain, it stretched 2,800 miles (4,500 km) from east to west and 2,300 miles (3,700 km) from north to south.

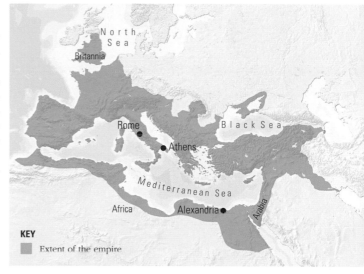

North Sea

Britannia

Rome

Athens

Black Sea

Mediterranean Sea

Africa

Alexandria

Arabia

KEY

Extent of the empire

117–139 CE	284–305 CE	312–330 CE	476 CE
To protect his massive empire, Emperor Hadrian builds defenses along frontiers.	The empire is now too big to manage, so Emperor Diocletian splits it in two: east and west.	Emperor Constantine reunites the empire, but establishes his capital in modern-day Turkey rather than in Rome.	Germanic chief Odoacer overthrows the last Western Roman emperor. The Eastern Empire will survive for another 1,000 years.

EMPEROR HADRIAN ON A ROMAN COIN

LIFE IN THE ROMAN EMPIRE

The Roman Empire was a multicultural society, made up of people not just from Europe but also from Africa and the Middle East.

The Romans were innovators, and their technological advances allowed them to improve their quality of life. They built strong roads to connect the empire, and invented concrete, which made their structures last. Many of their buildings even had underfloor heating, which worked by feeding warm air through underground channels.

Culture and literature flourished, too. Ancient Roman writers such as Virgil, Cicero, and Ovid created some of the most famous texts in history, and are still studied today. Many written records from ancient Rome help us piece together a vivid image of what life was like back then.

FACT
In 79 CE, the volcano Mount Vesuvius erupted, spewing out volcanic lava and ash that destroyed and preserved the Roman towns of Pompeii and Herculaneum. They were rediscovered only in modern times.

▲ FLOURISHING TRADE
Trade was essential to the survival of the empire, particularly the large cities, which needed to import food to feed ever-growing populations. Rome traded via both land and sea. Everyday items such as wine and grain were traded within the empire but many luxury items came from beyond its borders, such as silk from China.

SOCIAL CLASSES ▶

Roman society was split into two main classes—the wealthy patricians and the poorer plebeians. Enslaved people belonged to neither class and were considered to be the property of their owners. It was, however, possible to gain freedom from slavery and live as a freedman or freedwoman.

An enslaved person serves a drink to his enslaver.

◀ WOMEN IN ROMAN SOCIETY

Women had very few rights in the Roman Empire and were generally not able to take part in political life. They were expected to raise families and run households, though those from poor backgrounds also had to work to earn an income.

◀ PUBLIC BATHS

Every Roman town had a public bathhouse, which was not just a place to wash and relax but also to meet up with friends. Hot pools and steam rooms were usually heated by an underfloor heating system from a furnace but the Roman Baths in the city of Bath, England, were built above natural hot springs.

◀ GLADIATORS

Bloodthirsty battles between trained fighters called gladiators were popular in ancient Rome. Spectators would crowd amphitheaters to watch the fights, which were often to the death. Gladiators were usually enslaved people or prisoners who had been condemned to death, though some became major celebrities.

The grill on the bronze gladiator helmet protects the face.

ROMAN GODS

Before Christianity became the main religion of the empire in the 4th century CE, the Romans worshipped many gods and goddesses. Each god watched over a different aspect of life. The Romans built temples to the main gods, such as Jupiter (the god of the sky), where animal sacrifices were sometimes performed.

Mithras, a sun god

JUPITER

Lares, guardian spirits

ALTAR TO LARES AUGUSTI

MITHRAS SLAYING THE BULL

▲ **EMPEROR GAOZU**

Liu Bang began life as a peasant and then became a bandit and rebel chieftain. Out of the chaos that followed the collapse of the ruling Qin empire, he emerged as the most powerful leader. In 202 BCE, he declared himself founder of the new Han Dynasty, and took the title Emperor Gaozu.

EMPEROR WU

Emperor Wu (reigned 141–87 BCE) was the seventh ruler of the Han Dynasty. Under his long rule, China became a powerful empire. Wu was inspired by the teachings of the philosopher Confucius, which emphasize respecting others and honoring tradition. He made Confucianism the official school of thought for his kingdom.

▼ **TOMBS AND TREASURES**

The Han believed in the afterlife, and were buried with belongings they felt their souls would need after death. The very wealthy, such as members of the royal family, were laid to rest in suits made out of expensive jade.

Han China

After the death of the first emperor, Qin Shi Huangdi, in 210 BCE, civil war broke out across China. In 202 BCE, the Han Dynasty took power and reunified the kingdom. Han emperors organized the empire well. Under their rule, China went through an age of economic prosperity, and many new inventions improved daily life.

Han rule over China falls into two distinct periods—the Western Han period up to c. 9 CE, when the capital was at Chang'an, and the Eastern Han period from c. 25 CE until 220 CE, when Luoyang became the capital. The years in between saw the brief rule of the Xin Dynasty.

The Han set up an efficient civil service to manage their vast empire, and established a permanent army paid for by taxes, and not by the training of peasants. However, Eastern Han rule was not very stable, and the transfer of power from one leader to the next was seldom trouble-free. There were often power struggles between members of the imperial family, officials, and warlords, while peasant uprisings weakened the government's grip on power. As the ruling elite became increasingly cut off from ordinary people, those excluded from power began to arm themselves. After a major rebellion in 184 CE, the Han Empire finally collapsed in 220 CE, bringing in an era of rival warlords.

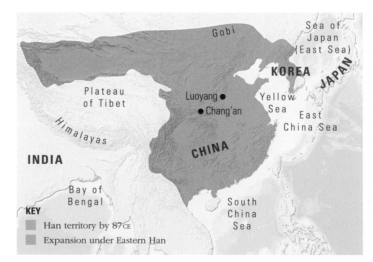

KEY
- Han territory by 87 CE
- Expansion under Eastern Han

◄ **EXPANDING THE EMPIRE**

By 87 CE, the Han Empire covered much of eastern modern China, along with northern Vietnam and Korea. During the Eastern Han period, the emperors made alliances with tribes in the north and the west, extending the empire as far as Central Asia.

Jade was believed to protect the body from decay.

HAN INVENTIONS

Many advances were made during the Han era. Inventions included the first magnetic compass, the wheelbarrow, and an early seismoscope (a device to detect earthquakes). Most important of all was the invention of paper by Cai Lun in 105 CE. The paper was made from tree bark, hemp, and linen.

MAGNETIC COMPASS

Shock waves trigger a ball to drop into the mouth of one of the frogs.

PAPER

SEISMOSCOPE   WHEELBARROW

▲ THE SILK ROAD

The trade route known later as the Silk Road first opened up during the Han era, connecting China to Europe across Central Asia. Chinese merchants grew rich selling goods such as silk and ceramics, while gold and ivory were imported from the west. Ideas and technologies, such as that of papermaking, also spread along the route.

▲ BUDDHISM IN CHINA

Buddhism was introduced to China from India along the Silk Road, reaching the royal court in Luoyang by 65 CE. The first Buddhist temple, the White Horse Temple (above), was built in the city in 68 CE.

51

A Vandal horseman hunts a stag.

A Barbary stag, a type of red deer found in North Africa

The most powerful Germanic king was Theodoric the Great (reigned 493–526 CE). From 511 CE, he ruled both the Ostrogoths and the Visigoths, governing a kingdom that stretched from modern-day Spain to Italy.

COIN DEPICTING THEODORIC

▲ VANDALS IN AFRICA

In 429 CE, the Vandals crossed into Africa and founded a kingdom that included Sicily, Malta, Sardinia, and Corsica. In 455 CE, they sacked Rome, which is why "vandalism" now means deliberate destruction. Despite this, wealthy Vandals in Africa lived like Romans, in villas decorated with mosaics (above).

Germanic peoples

The first Germanic peoples came from modern-day Scandinavia and were probably driven south by climate change. By the 3rd century BCE, many tribes had settled in the area east of the Rhine River and north of the Danube River. The Romans called this region Germania, and tried several times to conquer it but failed. For several centuries the two cultures lived alongside each other in relative peace.

In the 370s CE, the nomadic Huns (see p.37) swept west from Central Asia into Germania, forcing several tribes to flee further west into the Western Roman Empire in search of new lands to settle. A series of wars followed and in 476 CE the Western Roman Empire fell.

The Germanic peoples formed new kingdoms across the former empire—the Visigoths in Gaul and modern-day Spain, the Ostrogoths in Italy, the Vandals in North Africa, the Angles and Saxons in Britain, and the Franks in Gaul.

These Germanic peoples wanted to exploit the wealth of the former Roman Empire rather than plunder it. Influenced by Roman culture, kings modeled themselves on Roman emperors. They became Christians, though many continued to worship Germanic gods. Most adopted new languages based on Latin, though in remote Britain the Anglo-Saxon kingdoms kept their language, which developed into English. Over the next 300 years, some of these Germanic kingdoms would grow into the major powers of medieval Europe.

◄ OSTROGOTHS IN ITALY

The Ostrogoths, or eastern Goths, built up an empire that stretched north of the Black Sea in eastern Europe. In 493 CE, led by Theodoric the Great, they conquered modern-day Italy and established the Ostrogothic Kingdom. The empire reached its peak under the rule of Theodoric the Great who was buried in a grand mausoleum (left) at Ravenna, Italy. After his death, the Ostrogoths suffered repeated invasions by the Byzantine Empire, resulting in their decline.

◀ VISIGOTHS IN SPAIN

The Visigoths (western Goths) were among a group of early Germanic people to cross into the Roman Empire in 376 CE. They founded a kingdom in southern Gaul, which later included much of modern-day Spain. Visigothic jewelers made eagle brooches decorated with colored glass and gemstones called garnets. The eagle was a popular design, adopted from Roman imperial insignia.

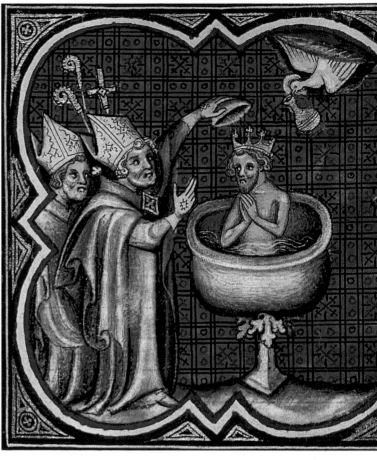

▲ FRANKS IN GAUL

In the late 5th century, the Franks, who had settled in the region of western Europe called Gaul, were united into a single nation by their king, Clovis I (reigned 481–511 CE). In 496 CE, he converted to Christianity (above). Gaul came to be known as Francia (modern-day France)—the land of the Franks.

— *Red garnets embedded in a metal frame*

SUTTON HOO TREASURES

In the 620s, an Anglo-Saxon king was buried at Sutton Hoo (in modern-day Suffolk, UK) in a ship filled with royal treasure. An excavation in 1939 uncovered several artifacts, including a helmet based on a Roman design, a richly decorated belt buckle, a lid for a purse, and other valuable items.

— *Mask attached to helmet to protect the warrior's face*

HELMET

PURSE LID

BELT BUCKLE

500–1450

Civilizations throughout the world flourished during this period. Empires in China, India, and parts of Africa underwent golden ages of culture, and the Aztec and Inca civilizations in the Americas reached their peak. Christianity spread from the Middle East, eventually dominating Europe, but then a new religion arose—Islam. This quickly spread from the Middle East, bringing a new faith and culture to many parts of Asia and Africa.

Medieval India

500–1450

With the fall of the Gupta Empire in the 6th century, India entered a period in which the Hindu religion was revived, and Buddhism went into a rapid decline. From the 13th century, the first Muslim rulers established their empires in the region. Islamic kingdoms were founded in the north, while Hindu empires flourished in the south. The period ended with the beginning of the Mughal Empire in 1526.

After the breakup of the Gupta Empire (see pp.32–33), which had dominated much of India, new kingdoms came to power. In the late 10th century, the Cholas conquered rival kingdoms in the south. The Chola Empire grew rich through trade with Southeast Asia, and oversaw a golden age of art and architecture. Later, in the 14th century, the powerful new Vijayanagar Empire emerged in India's southwest and remained in control of the south for three centuries. Both the Chola and the Vijayanagar built magnificent temples decorated with scenes from Hindu mythology.

In the north, the invasion of Muslim armies from Central Asia in the late 12th century led to the establishment of the Delhi Sultanate—the first Islamic empire in India—in 1206. It ruled large parts of India for 320 years, until its defeat by the Mughals (see pp.120–121).

Flames surround Lord Shiva.

Shiva is shown mid-dance.

◀ **CHOLA ART**
The early Chola kings focused on extending their rule, building an empire that spanned south India and northern Sri Lanka, but later Chola rulers oversaw a period of high culture. The Chola built grand temples and are famous for their bronze sculptures. This one shows the Hindu god Shiva—in his form of Nataraja, Lord of the Dance.

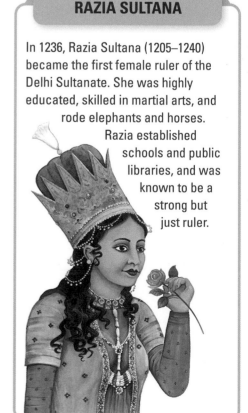

RAZIA SULTANA

In 1236, Razia Sultana (1205–1240) became the first female ruler of the Delhi Sultanate. She was highly educated, skilled in martial arts, and rode elephants and horses. Razia established schools and public libraries, and was known to be a strong but just ruler.

VIJAYANAGAR ART
Art and architecture flourished during the reign of Vijayanagar kings. Spectacular temples were built out of stone and decorated with elaborate murals and carvings. This mural covers the walls and ceilings of the entrance hall at the Veerabhadra Temple in Lepakshi (modern-day Andhra Pradesh).

◀ QUTB MINAR
The formerly enslaved soldier Qutb al-Din Aibak rose through the ranks of the military of the Ghorid Dynasty to become the first ruler of the Delhi Sultanate in 1206. To commemorate his victories, he ordered the building of the sandstone Qutb Minar minaret (left), which still towers over South Delhi.

HAMPI ▶
The Vijayanagar Empire was founded by two Hindu brothers, who set up a new capital called Vijayanagara (modern-day Hampi). It was filled with exquisite monuments, such as this stone chariot, and by 1500 it had become the world's second-largest city after Beijing.

THE DELHI SULTANATE

1206–1290 CE	1290–1320 CE	1320–1451 CE	1451–1526 CE
The former general Qutb al-Din Aibak establishes the Mamluk Dynasty, the first dynasty to rule over the Delhi Sultanate.	The Khaliji Dynasty comes to power after a revolution, and extends the territory under the Delhi Sultanate's control to cover much of western India.	The Delhi Sultanate reaches the peak of its power under the Tughlaq Dynasty (1320–1413), which is succeeded by the Sayyid Dynasty (1414–1451).	The Lodi Dynasty briefly revives the Delhi Sultanate's power, but after a series of rebellions it falls to Mughal forces in 1526.

The Byzantine Empire

The halo represents the religious authority of the emperor over the Church.

In 395 CE, the Roman Empire was split into the Western and Eastern empires for the final time. While the Western Roman Empire fell to the Germanic tribes by 476 CE, the Eastern Empire, which came to be known as the Byzantine Empire, thrived and outlasted its western counterpart by almost a thousand years.

The Byzantine Empire was ruled from Constantinople (modern-day Istanbul), which had become the capital of the Eastern Roman Empire c. 324 CE. The city soon became one of the largest and richest in all of Europe, a position it held until the early 13th century.

During its thousand-year existence, the Byzantine Empire developed sophisticated legal systems. It also created its own version of Christianity called Eastern Orthodoxy, which had a strong influence on Byzantine art and architecture. Almost all forms of art produced during this time expressed religious ideas and themes.

The empire began to decline from the 11th century onward, although it held on for another 400 years, before falling to the Ottoman Turks (see pp.100–101) who captured Constantinople in 1453.

Tyrian purple robes were a symbol of royalty.

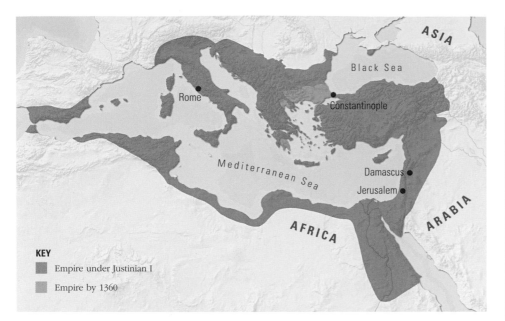

KEY

■ Empire under Justinian I

■ Empire by 1360

▲ RISE AND FALL OF THE EMPIRE

In the 6th century, the empire stretched around most of the Mediterranean Sea, but it lost important territory, such as the lands of Egypt and Syria, to Muslim armies soon after. By 1360, it had shrunk considerably, and it continued to lose territory until it collapsed entirely in 1453.

EASTERN ORTHODOX CHURCH ▶

The Roman Catholic and Eastern Orthodox Churches disagreed on how they understood Christianity and worshipped God. The Orthodox Church did not recognize the authority of the Pope. These differences grew over the centuries, leading the two Churches to formally part ways in 1054.

The third slanted crossbeam makes this instantly recognizable as an Orthodox cross.

▼ HAGIA SOPHIA

Built as a Christian church, the Hagia Sophia (meaning "Divine Wisdom") was completed in 537ce. After Constantinople fell to the Ottomans in 1453, it was turned into a mosque. The building's architecture reflects a mix of both Christian and Islamic influences.

The dome represents heaven and the afterlife. It was the largest dome in the world until the 15th century.

Islamic minarets were added in the 15th and 16th centuries.

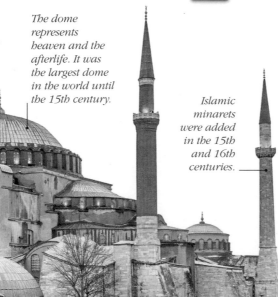

MAJOR EVENTS

306–337
Constantine I becomes the first emperor of the Eastern Roman Empire. He establishes a new eastern capital, Constantinople, named after himself.

527–565
Justinian I comes to power and reconquers some of the land lost after the fall of the Western Roman Empire. This includes parts of Africa, Italy, and Spain.

600–900
The first coins to depict Jesus Christ are minted during the reign of Justinian II. The design of Christ with long hair and a beard became standard for all future coins.

GOLD COIN SHOWING CHRIST

976–1025
The reign of Basil II begins a golden age for the empire. Under his rule, the empire becomes wealthier and extends its territory into the Balkans and beyond.

1071
Conflicts between the Byzantine and the Seljuk empires lead to the Battle of Manzikert. The Seljuks win, weakening Byzantine power in Anatolia (part of modern-day Turkey).

1095–1204
Roman Catholic armies attempt to recapture Jerusalem during the Crusades. During the Fllourth Crusade (1202–1204), they attack and ransack Constantinople.

1204–1453
Weakened from constant invasions, Constantinople is reduced to a city-state, and falls to the Ottomans in 1453.

The spread of Christianity

From its beginnings in the 1st century CE, Christianity spread from the Middle East to Europe. The mighty Roman Empire made Christianity its official religion in the 4th century, and even after the fall of Rome in the 5th century, the conversion of Germanic kings and their people from paganism to Christianity extended its influence further across Europe. The Church dominated all aspects of everyday life for medieval Christians, from monarchs to peasants. As its influence grew, the Church became wealthy, and a powerful political force in Europe. It owned vast areas of land, had some control over the decisions of Europe's rulers, and could even raise its own armies.

◄ SAINT AUGUSTINE

Saint Augustine of Canterbury was sent from Rome to England by Pope Gregory to convert the Anglo-Saxons from paganism to Christianity. He arrived in 597 and successfully converted King Aethelberht I of Kent and many of his subjects. He became the first Archbishop of Canterbury; a position that still exists today.

SAINT BONIFACE ►

Born in Anglo-Saxon England, Saint Boniface led missions to the Frankish Empire during the 8th century to convert the Germanic peoples there and establish Christian churches. Following his success, he was known as the "Apostle to the Germans." Boniface was killed in 754 and became recognized as a saint soon after.

61

The early Islamic world

In the early 7th century, the new religion of Islam, founded by the Prophet Muhammad, began to spread through the Arabian Peninsula. By the end of the century, Islam had spread to the north coast of Africa and parts of Central Asia through military conquest and trade. This Islamic Empire continued to grow over the following centuries.

The Islamic Caliphate (empire) was ruled by a series of caliphs (leaders). Muhammad's successors established the Rashidun Caliphate, which ruled until 661. The empire expanded rapidly as powerful Muslim armies conquered land across the Middle East, including in Persia, Syria, and Egypt.

The Umayyad Dynasty then came to power, and advanced further into North Africa and as far as Spain.

The empire reached its peak under the Abbasid Dynasty in the 8th century, when it was one of the largest the world had ever seen, stretching from southern Europe across North Africa and much of Asia. The early Abbasids oversaw a golden age of learning and scientific progress. Yet gradually they lost territory and were finally overthrown by an invading Mongol army in the mid-13th century.

Caliph Harun al-Rashid ruled the Abbasid Dynasty from 786 to 809, at the start of the Islamic golden age.

◀ **ABBASID CALIPHATE**
The Abbasid Dynasty seized power in 750 and established Baghdad (in modern-day Iraq) as their capital. Scientists, philosophers, scholars, and artists gathered in the city during what became known as the Islamic golden age. The caliphate ended when the Mongol army invaded in 1258 (see p.88).

▼ **UMAYYAD CALIPHATE**
After the death of the last Rashidun caliph in 661, Syrian governor Mu'awiya took power. He became the first caliph of the Umayyad Dynasty, and moved the capital to Damascus. The Dome of the Rock shrine—one of Islam's holiest sites—was built in the city of Jerusalem by the Umayyads in the late 7th century.

KEY
- Muslim Lands by 632
- Muslim Lands by 656
- Muslim Lands by 756

ASIA
Samarkand
Kabul
Iranian Plateau
EUROPE
Black Sea
PERSIA
Constantinople
ANATOLIA
Isfahan
Rome
Baghdad
SYRIA
Jerusalem
Cordova
Mediterranean Sea
Cairo
Medina
Atlas Mountains
Mecca
EGYPT
Red Sea
Arabian Sea
AFRICA

▲ **MAP OF THE EARLY ISLAMIC EMPIRE**
During the early years of Islamic rule, Muslim armies conquered large areas of the Middle East, North Africa, and Central Asia. As the empire grew, goods were traded across continents and Islamic culture and beliefs spread farther eastwards. It also led to great advances in maths, science, and the arts.

FATIMID
GOLD COIN

▲ FATIMID CALIPHATE

In the 10th century, the Fatimids, who claimed to be descendants of the Prophet Muhammad's daughter, rose to power. A rival dynasty to the Abbasids, they ruled across North Africa, Egypt, and most of Syria from 909 to 1171. The Fatimids grew rich through trade in the Mediterranean and Red seas.

◄ SELJUK EMPIRE

The Seljuk Empire was founded in the 11th century CE and lasted until the 14th century CE. The Seljuks established a vast empire that at its peak stretched from modern-day Turkey to Pakistan. In 1073, they captured the city of Jerusalem. This led to Christian armies mounting the First Crusade in 1096 in order to wrestle the city back from Muslim control.

Seljuk warriors were skilled riders and fought on horseback.

SALAH AL-DIN

Salah al-din (reigned 1174–1193) overthrew the Fatimids and founded the Ayyubid Dynasty. He became the first sultan of Egypt and Syria, and then conquered neighboring Muslim states. He is best known for his role in the Third Crusade when he recaptured Jerusalem from Christian armies in 1187.

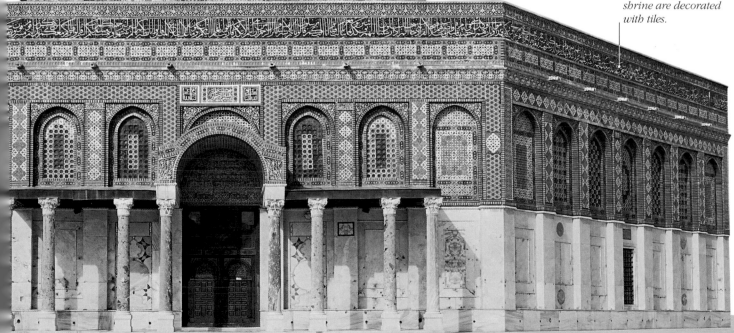

The walls of the shrine are decorated with tiles.

ISLAMIC ART AND SCIENCE

The rule of the Abbasid Dynasty (750–1258) is considered a golden age of Islam. Science, culture, and art flourished as great thinkers from across the empire flocked to the new capital Baghdad, which also became a center for trade. Classical Greek texts were translated into Arabic, leading to important advances in the fields of math, astronomy, the arts, philosophy, and medicine. The thirst for knowledge in Baghdad was helped by the new practice of book binding. The Abbasids also learned how to make paper from the Chinese and could now produce it on a large scale, making books more widely available. The famous collection of Arabic folk tales, *One Thousand and One Nights*, was compiled during the golden age of Islam.

▲ HOUSE OF WISDOM

Baghdad was a center of learning and its libraries were stocked with books on medicine, mathematics, astronomy, philosophy, and poetry. Abbasid Caliph Haroun al-Rashid founded the House of Wisdom, also known as the Grand Library of Baghdad, which flourished under his son, al-Ma'mun, in the early 9th century.

▼ DECORATIVE ART

In Islamic architecture, geometric patterns rather than human or animal figures were commonly used as decoration. These patterns included repeated circles, squares, stars, and multi-sided polygons. The Jameh mosque in the city of Yazd in Iran, built in the 14th century, is decorated with exquisite geometric designs.

FACT
The Fatimid Caliphate, rulers of Egypt, built the Al-Azhar mosque for their new capital city of Cairo in 972. This place of learning became the world's second oldest university.

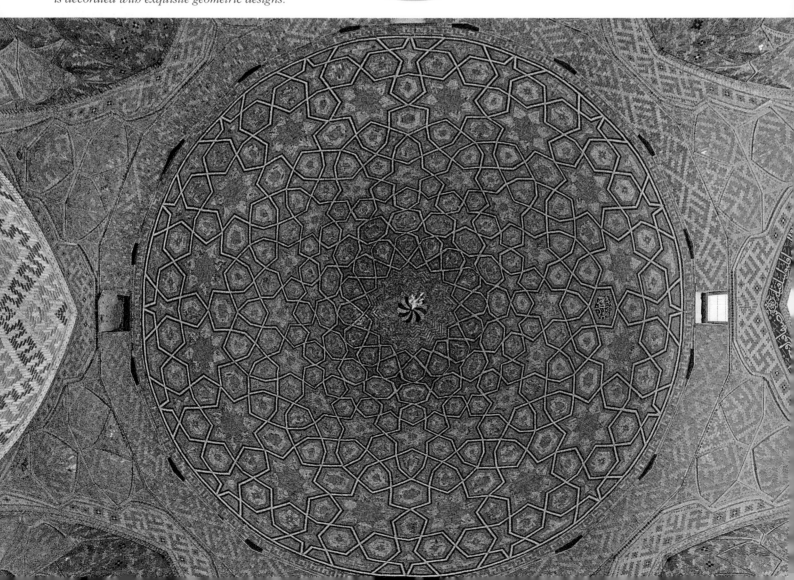

▲ CANON OF MEDICINE
In the 11th century, Persian physician Ibn Sina, also known as Avicenna, wrote an encyclopedia of medicine—the Canon of Medicine—*which was used as a medical textbook for more than 700 years. It included information on how our bodies work and the causes of health and illness.*

The turban represents Islamic culture.

▲ UNIVERSITY OF QARAWIYYIN
The Islamic Empire established some of the world's earliest universities. In 859, Fatima Al-Fihri founded the Al-Qarawiyyin mosque in Fez, Morocco, which became a top center of Islamic learning. The complex included a prayer space, courtyard, library, and school rooms. It is considered to be the oldest university in the world.

The dragons represent Chinese culture.

Astrolabes were made of iron or brass.

OMAR KHAYYAM

Omar Khayyam (1048–1131), was born during the reign of the Seljuks. The Persian mathematician, astronomer, philosopher, and poet is known for his contribution to math and for his "Rubáiyát"—a collection of quatrains (four-line poems) about the different stages of life, including love, loss, and death.

▲ THE ELEPHANT CLOCK
Engineer Ismail al-Jazari (1136–1206) invented the "Elephant Clock" which used the flow of water between bowls to measure time. A tank was hidden in the belly of the elephant where water poured from one basin to another. The design represents the diversity of cultures in Islam.

▲ ASTRONOMY
Scientists in the Islamic world were very interested in astronomy. They developed astrolabes to calculate the position of the sun and stars. These devices were used to tell the time and they could also indicate the direction of Mecca, which Muslims must face toward for prayer.

▲ CHANG'AN

In the 7th century, the Tang capital Chang'an (present-day Xi'an) was the world's most populous city, with around one million people living within its city walls and another million in the suburbs beyond. Dating from this time, the Giant Wild Goose Pagoda (above) still stands today. It was built to store Buddhist sacred texts.

Tang and Song China

After the fall of the Han Dynasty in the 3rd century CE, China experienced centuries of unrest. But in 618, the rebel leader Li Yuan set up the Tang Dynasty, which lasted until 907. Another period of turmoil followed before the general Zhao Kuangyin established the Song Dynasty (960–1279). Historians see both of these periods as high points of Chinese civilization.

In the Tang era, the development of woodblock printing in the 7th century allowed the publication of many new texts, helping to improve literacy. China began expanding its control to the west and south, and soon became a powerful influence over neighboring Japan and Korea.

Thanks in part to improved methods of growing rice, the population of China grew rapidly during the Song period, reaching 200 million people by the end of the dynasty in 1279. This population growth allowed Song China to prosper economically and a new merchant class emerged. Technology also flourished under the Song, with many new inventions and discoveries.

Under both dynasties, emperors ruled with the help of an efficient civil service—government employees who administered the laws of the country.

TANG DYNASTY

618 Military leader Li Yuan seizes power and declares himself the founder of the new Tang Dynasty. He rules as Emperor Gaozu.

630 Emperor Taizong defeats the Eastern Turks, making China the dominant power in East and Central Asia.

690–705 Empress Wu Zetian comes to power and rules over the short-lived Wu Zhou Dynasty.

751 The Abbasid Caliphate armies defeat the Chinese at the Battle of Talas in Central Asia. This stops China's westward expansion.

907 Weakened by uprisings, the Tang Dynasty is overthrown by a military governor called Zhu Wen, who is later replaced by the Song Dynasty.

▲ THE CIVIL SERVICE
Men wishing to work for the Song Dynasty's government had to take a written literary exam that required knowledge of the writings of Confucius. This meant that entry to the civil service was on merit rather than through family connections.

Early gunpowder was made of saltpeter, sulfur, and charcoal.

▲ INVENTIONS
There were many technological advances during the Song Dynasty. Important inventions included paper money, movable type—which made it possible to mass produce books—and gunpowder. A formula for gunpowder was first recorded in a military book in 1044.

WU ZETIAN

First as the powerful wife of Emperor Gaozong and eventually as sole ruler from 690 to 705, Wu Zetian was the only woman to rule China in her own right. She was an effective leader, introducing reforms to the economy and education system.

SONG CITIES
Cities flourished under the Song, crowded with markets and shops selling goods of every kind. People gathered in entertainment quarters to enjoy themselves during festivals. The people of Kaifeng (the Northern Song capital) are shown celebrating the Qingming festival in this copy of a Song Dynasty painting.

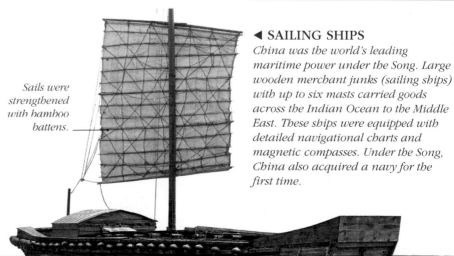

Sails were strengthened with bamboo battens.

◄ SAILING SHIPS
China was the world's leading maritime power under the Song. Large wooden merchant junks (sailing ships) with up to six masts carried goods across the Indian Ocean to the Middle East. These ships were equipped with detailed navigational charts and magnetic compasses. Under the Song, China also acquired a navy for the first time.

ARTS AND CUSTOMS

Cultural life in China blossomed under the Tang and Song dynasties. The empire was usually at peace, and its increasing wealth and prosperity allowed art and culture to flourish. The Tang period is known for its poetry and painting, beautiful porcelain, and glazed earthenware—particularly the ornate clay figures that were placed in graves to accompany the dead.

Under the Song, Chinese painting reached its peak, while porcelain and ceramics were produced to a very high standard. Poetry flourished, and theater and drama became more complex. The largest theaters in Kaifeng, capital of the Northern Song, could entertain audiences of several thousand. The development of gunpowder enabled the use of fireworks in public festivities, where large displays were often accompanied by dancers moving through clouds of colored smoke.

A saddle with a curved seat provided stability for the rider.

▶ HORSES

When the Tang came to power, the government owned only around 5,000 horses, but within 50 years that number had increased to more than 700,000. For the Tang, horses symbolized status and military power. Only the nobility, including women, were permitted to ride. Tomb figures from the period include many horses along with other animals.

POLO PLAYER

EVERYDAY LIFE

During the Tang period, Chinese citizens—especially the upper classes—had a lot of free time to devote to leisure activities. They enjoyed archery, hunting, cuju (a game similar to soccer), tug-of-war, and many more sports. Polo was introduced from Persia in around 700 and became popular among both men and women.

FACT
The first known written document on tea—*Ch'a Ching* (*The Classic of Tea*) by Chinese writer Lu Yu—was composed during the Tang period.

PORCELAIN ▶

The technique for making porcelain was perfected around 700. It was manufactured using clay for the body, ash for the glaze, and minerals to make the pigments. Tang Dynasty porcelain was exported as far as Africa.

Dragon-shaped porcelain detail

Women rode for both hunting and pleasure.

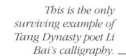

This is the only surviving example of Tang Dynasty poet Li Bai's calligraphy.

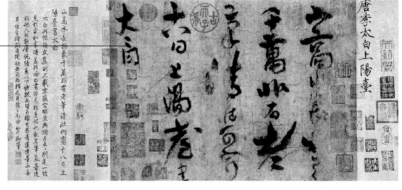

POETRY ▲

The Tang period was a golden age of poetry in China. More than 3,000 poets are recorded from this time, along with about 48,900 of their poems. Writing poetry was a skill required for those wishing to pass civil exams. One of the famed poets of this time was Li Bai.

▼ SILK

Song women wove silk threads to make into clothes and to be decorated and hung as wall tapestries, while professional weavers created prized fabrics such as brocades and damasks. Song Brocade—China's most luxurious silk today—was woven during this period.

▲ LANDSCAPE PAINTING

Under the Song, the subjects typically depicted in paintings shifted from people and events at court to dramatic landscape scenes. Brush strokes were more important than color, which was used sparingly. Landscape painting reached new heights in this period.

Kingdoms of Southeast Asia

Southeast Asia lies at one of the world's great crossroads, in the middle of a sea-based trade route linking India and China. From the 7th century onward, wealthy kingdoms rose across the region. The culture and politics of these kingdoms were influenced by their powerful neighbors, and, later, by contact with the Islamic world.

The kingdoms that thrived in present-day Cambodia, Myanmar (Burma), and Thailand were land-based and drew their wealth from rice farming. Other kingdoms, such as Champa in modern-day Vietnam and the Srivijaya Empire of Sumatra (in modern-day Indonesia) grew rich on sea trade. These kingdoms adopted Hinduism and Buddhism from India. Both religions spread rapidly and influenced all parts of life. The rulers of the powerful Khmer Empire in present-day Cambodia, for example, believed they were god-kings related to Hindu deities. They built grand cities influenced by the cultures and kingdoms of India. Other kingdoms such as Dai Viet (in modern-day Vietnam) were dominated by China.

In around 1400, the Malacca Sultanate—the first Islamic sultanate in Southeast Asia—was founded in Malaysia. However, its wealth as a trading hub soon attracted the interest of European powers. Malacca was conquered by the Portuguese in 1511, beginning a new era of European colonization of Southeast Asia.

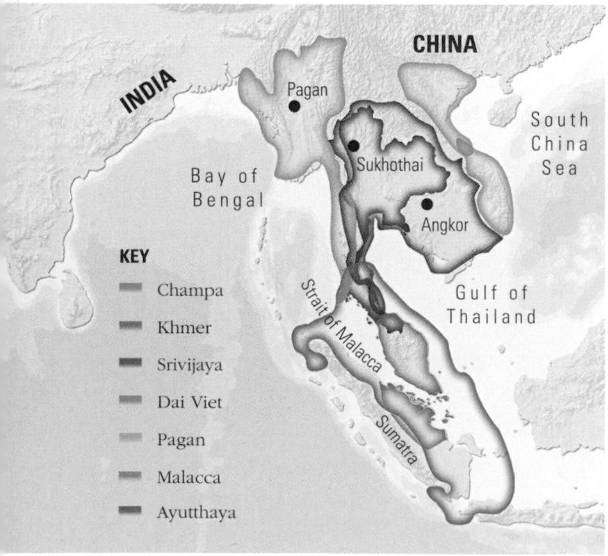

Red-brick temple of Shiva at the My Son complex in Vietnam

▲ MAJOR KINGDOMS

The kingdoms of Southeast Asia rose and fell over time. This map shows the furthest extent of each empire at its peak.

KEY
- Champa
- Khmer
- Srivijaya
- Dai Viet
- Pagan
- Malacca
- Ayutthaya

(Map labels: INDIA, CHINA, Pagan, Bay of Bengal, Sukhothai, Angkor, South China Sea, Gulf of Thailand, Strait of Malacca, Sumatra)

CHAMPA ▶

On the southern coast of Vietnam, the Champa Kingdom lasted from the 2nd century CE to the 17th century but was at its height in the 9th and 10th centuries. The Cham people built temples to the Hindu deity Shiva with distinctive red brick towers. They were often at war with their Khmer and Dai Viet neighbors.

Dating to 684 CE, this inscription praises the establishment of a park by the Srivijaya king Sri Jayanasa.

◀ SRIVIJAYA EMPIRE

The Buddhist Srivijaya Kingdom rose around 650 CE in present-day Sumatra and extended its rule to include the Malay Peninsula and parts of Java and Borneo. After its fall in the 13th century, it was largely forgotten until modern times when historians began piecing together its history with the help of inscriptions such as this one.

PAGAN KINGDOM

From the 1050s to the 1280s, Pagan, in what is now Myanmar, was the capital of the first Burmese kingdom. It was one of the greatest Buddhist centers in Southeast Asia. Pagan kings built 10,000 Buddhist monuments, of which more than 2,000 still survive today.

KHMER EMPIRE ▶

From around the 9th to the 13th centuries, the most powerful kingdom in Southeast Asia was the Khmer Empire. Khmer kings established their capital at Angkor (in present-day Cambodia), where they built Angkor Wat—the largest temple complex in the world. It is decorated with people and scenes from Hindu mythology.

THAI KINGDOMS ▼

After freeing themselves from Khmer rule in the 13th century, the Thai established two kingdoms—Sukhothai in the north and Ayutthaya in the south. Ayutthaya went on to unite present-day Thailand, and became one of the leading regional powers from the 14th to 18th centuries.

Statue of Buddha at Wat Mahathat in Sukhothai Historical Park, Thailand

◀ DAI VIET

China heavily influenced the culture of northern Vietnam. After nearly a thousand years under Chinese rule, it was unified in 968 CE into an empire called Dai Viet by the military leader Dinh Bo Linh, who became its first emperor. He is shown here wearing regal clothes in the Chinese style.

▲ MESA VERDE

The Ancestral Puebloans inhabited southwest North America between c. 100 CE and c. 1600. They moved from a hunter-gatherer lifestyle to farming when they began to create permanent settlements. In the mountainous terrain of the region they constructed great villages in the shelter of overhanging cliffs. The biggest example is the Cliff Palace at Mesa Verde in Colorado, built between 1150 and 1300 using materials such as sandstone and mortar.

Cultures of North America

The first human inhabitants of North America were present at least 23,000 to 21,000 years ago according to archeological evidence. For thousands of years, a rich mix of civilizations and cultures used the varied landscape of North America for hunting, fishing, and farming.

EVERYDAY LIFE

Maize was first grown in the dry land of the southwest around 4,000 years ago, before spreading into the north. Maize grew quickly and was easy to harvest, making it a vital food for early civilizations on the North American continent.

There are conflicting theories about the first humans in North America, and where they came from. Indigenous people have their own beliefs about how they arrived on the continent. The earliest tribes to arrive were hunters and gatherers, some of them nomadic, who kept on moving to follow migrating herds of animals.

Over time, advanced cultures began to develop, whose people grew a variety of crops, built homes, and handcrafted tools and other artifacts. From around 500 BCE, the Adena people of the Eastern Woodlands, an area that stretched from the Atlantic Ocean to the Great Plains, farmed the land and built large earth mounds that served as ceremonial sites. A few centuries later, the Hopewell people set up villages and made pottery in the same region. By 800 CE, the Ancestral Puebloans had built large homes from earth and stone in the southwest. Gradually, these civilizations expanded and spread across the continent. By the late 1400s, North America was home to almost 60 million Indigenous people.

▲ DISTRIBUTION OF COMMUNITIES

Prehistoric farming and mound-building communities were spread out across North America. The Ancestral Puebloans and other farming communities such as the Hohokam and Mogollon people lived in the southwest, while the Mississippians built their communities around large earthen mounds in the eastern and northern regions.

ARCTIC PEOPLE ▼

The Thule people lived in the Arctic regions of North America from about 1000 CE. They survived the freezing conditions by wearing clothes made from animal fur and building homes with animal bones and skins. They were skilled hunters, targeting walruses, whales, and seals using handcrafted harpoons and slate knives.

Sledge made of seal bones and skin

IROQUOIS ▶

The Great Lakes of North America were settled by Iroquois nations in the mid-15th century. Their village homes, called longhouses, were built next to the water for canoeing and fishing. Longhouses were made of wood covered in elm bark. There was a door at both ends and a hole in the roof to let out smoke from fires lit for warmth and cooking.

MISSISSIPPIAN CRAFTS

Early pottery from Mississippian communities was plain and practical, with pots and jars that proved useful for storing crops and carrying water. As potters and sculptors became more skilled, they created elaborate designs. Decorative pieces included shells, pipes, crockery, and clay heads made as offerings to the dead.

CARVED SHELL

FROG-SHAPED PIPE

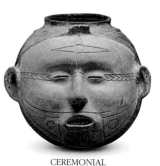

CEREMONIAL VESSEL

▲ MISSISSIPPIAN CULTURE

The people of the Mississippian culture were farmers who grew crops such as maize and beans. They built houses and other buildings on large earth mounds in the Mississippi Valley. The mound city of Cahokia (above) near the modern-day city of St. Louis, Missouri, was once home to thousands of people.

The shoguns of Japan

Up until the late 12th century, power in Japan rested squarely with the emperor, who controlled political life. From 1192 until 1868, however, Japan was in effect ruled by a series of shoguns (military dictators), who dominated the government of Japan and reduced the power of the emperor.

Shoguns had existed for centuries as military commanders in the emperor's service, but they slowly gained more and more political power.

Following a civil war, Minamoto Yoritomo set up a military government in Kamakura, independent of the imperial court in Kyoto. He seized power over his rival lords and founded the Kamakura Shogunate in 1192. Minamoto established a feudal system. The emperor, shogun, and *daimyo* (landowning nobles) formed the higher levels of this

system, followed by the samurai. Peasants, craftworkers, merchants, and servants were at the bottom.

Clan wars were common during the Kamakura and later shogunates until the Battle of Sekigahara in 1600, when Tokugawa Ieyasu united the country. He founded the Tokugawa Shogunate in 1603, which ruled Japan until 1867 when the 15th Tokugawa shogun—Yoshinobu—was exiled, and power returned to the emperor.

MAJOR SHOGUNATES

1185–1333
Minamoto Yoritomo becomes the first all-powerful shogun and establishes the Kamakura Shogunate. It lasts until 1333 when Emperor Go-Daigo restores imperial rule after victory in the Genkō War.

1338–1573
A former Kamakura general called Ashikaga Takauji—who helped Emperor Go-Daigo win the Genkō War—establishes the Ashikaga Shogunate. It collapses in 1467, after which Japan enters a long period of civil war.

1603–1868
Thirty years after the final fall of the Ashikaga Shogunate, Tokugawa Ieyasu establishes the Tokugawa Shogunate, which presides over a peaceful era that lasts for more than 250 years.

TOKUGAWA IEYASU

MINAMOTO YORITOMO

In 1180, an ambitious young noble named Minamoto Yoritomo (1147–1199), started a war against the rival Taira clan, which dominated the imperial court. After defeating his rival, Yoritomo became the first shogun to have complete political control, meaning that he effectively controlled Japan until his death.

▲ **FEUDAL JAPAN**
Under the feudal system, the emperor granted land to the daimyo. *Samurai were responsible for protecting the* daimyo, *the lands, and the people who worked in the region. The samurai grew in influence and became an elite class in themselves.*

▲ BATTLE OF DAN-NO-URA
Fought at sea, the Battle of Dan-no-ura was a decisive battle of the Genpei War (1180–1185). The Taira clan's defeat ended their control of Japan and led directly to the establishment of the first shogunate under Minamoto Yoritomo.

◄ SAMURAI CODE
The samurai were strictly bound to the bushido *code of conduct, which emphasized the importance of honor and discipline. Samurai who failed to live up to these ideals sometimes took their own lives in a ritual suicide known as* seppuku.

ARMS AND ARMOR

The weaponry and armor of the samurai was not just key to their military success, but also a symbol of their elite social status. Their main weapons were the deadly *katana* and the shorter *wakizashi* swords, the *tanto* knife used for stabbing, and a long pole weapon called a *naginata*. Since they fought without shields, their armor covered them from head to toe.

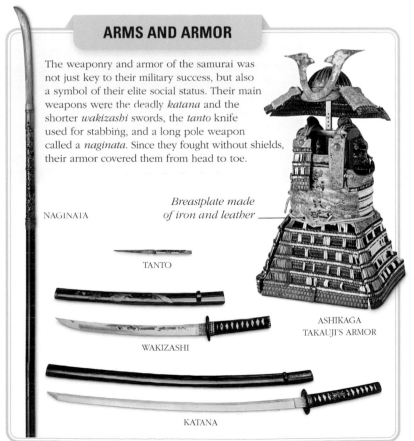

NAGINATA

Breastplate made of iron and leather

TANTO

WAKIZASHI

ASHIKAGA TAKAUJI'S ARMOR

KATANA

SHINOBI ►
The Shinobi— *or ninjas—were another type of soldier in feudal Japan, and were considered socially inferior to the samurai. These masters of stealth acted as spies and assassins, operating in secret to surprise their targets.*

Medieval western Europe

The period between the 5th and 15th centuries was an era of great change for western Europe. New kingdoms emerged and grew rich, yet this was also a time of constant warfare and widespread poverty. Power and wealth belonged to the monarchs, the nobles, and the Church, while the vast majority of people remained poor.

After the fall of the Western Roman Empire in 476 CE, new cultures influenced by Roman, Germanic, and Celtic traditions took hold across the continent. Around the same period, Christianity rapidly spread and new nations were born led by Christian monarchs.

By the 10th century, much of Europe was organized into a feudal system, in which kings gave land to the nobility, who, in return, provided them with armies during wartime. At the bottom of this system were the peasants, who worked the land.

At this time, culture and art across Europe began to flourish. The first university in Europe was founded in the 11th century, and advances in art and architecture gave rise to brilliant artworks and buildings that survive to this day.

Toward the end of the 15th century, the medieval period gave way to the Renaissance (see pp.104–105), when an explosion of new ideas transformed western Europe yet again.

▲ THE CRUSADES
From the 11th to the 13th centuries, Christian armies from Europe fought a series of religious wars known as the Crusades against Muslim forces in the eastern Mediterranean. The Crusaders, which included warriors such as Richard the Lionheart (above), wanted to regain Jerusalem—a sacred place for Christianity and Islam—from Muslim control, but their campaign ultimately failed.

▲ POWER OF THE CHURCH
The Catholic Church's power grew rapidly during this period, eventually holding a huge influence over everyday medieval life. Elaborate churches and cathedrals, such as Beauvais Cathedral in France (above), were built as spectacular monuments to God.

◄ KNIGHTS
Knights were an elite class of horseback warriors who fought in times of war for the king or queen. In peacetime, they demonstrated their fighting skills at jousting tournaments—in which two knights would charge each other with long lances—a popular form of entertainment.

ISLAMIC KINGDOMS ►
In the 8th century, Muslims from North Africa conquered Spain. They brought new foods, such as oranges and almonds, and new technologies, and introduced a unique style of Islamic architecture. One of the most beautiful examples is the Alhambra palace in Granada, which was built by the Nasrid Dynasty—the last of the Islamic kingdoms to fall to Christian rulers in 1492.

◄ THE BLACK DEATH

An explosive outbreak of bubonic plague, a highly contagious disease known as the Black Death, ravaged Europe from 1347 until 1351, killing around a third of the continent's population. It took until the start of the 16th century for Europe's population to recover to its pre-plague level. The horrors of the plague were often represented in the form of dancing skeletons.

Leader of the Frankish kingdom (in modern-day France and Germany), Charlemagne (c.748–814) went on to unite large parts of western and central Europe. He was crowned emperor of the Romans in 800 CE.

COIN DEPICTING CHARLEMAGNE

▼ THE HUNDRED YEARS' WAR

Beginning in 1337, the Hundred Years' War was a series of battles fought between England and France over English claims to the French throne. The first major battle took place at Crécy (below), where an English army of 12,000 defeated an army of more than 30,000 French soldiers. Ultimately, though, the French won the right to rule unchallenged, and by 1453 had pushed the English out of almost all of France.

The Vikings

A seafaring people, the Vikings originated in modern-day Sweden, Norway, and Denmark. They were known and feared across Europe for their violent raids (attacks), but they also traded peacefully with other lands. Between the 9th and 11th centuries, Vikings established trading outposts in the British Isles, mainland Europe, and even as far away as North America.

▲ VIKING RAIDERS

Vikings launched surprise attacks on coastal communities that had little or no way of defending themselves. They raided England and Francia (modern-day France) so often that these kingdoms started collecting a tax (later often called the danegeld) to pay off the Vikings and prevent them from stealing and destroying property.

One of the earliest significant Viking raids was on Lindisfarne in England in 793. The Vikings went on to settle permanently in parts of England and Ireland, as well as Iceland and Greenland. They also penetrated deep into eastern Europe and set up a kingdom called the Kievan Rus', which gives Russia its modern name. As they settled, the Vikings began to trade, exchanging timber, iron, and furs for spices, salt, silk, and more. Around the end of the 10th century, they started minting their own coins.

Before Christianity became their main religion in the 11th century, the Vikings had their own religion with many deities. Their mythology is still influential in the modern day—several film characters of the Marvel Universe, such as Thor and Loki, are based on old Scandinavian religious figures.

During the height of their power, the Vikings successfully raided or conquered wherever they went. However, a series of defeats in battle in the 11th century, including the loss of a Norwegian force to the English army at the Battle of Stamford Bridge in 1066, brought the Viking Age to an end.

LEIF ERIKSON

Around 1002, Viking explorer Leif Erikson (c.970–1020) reached what is now Newfoundland, Canada, and set up a settlement called Vinland there. He was probably the first European person to reach the Americas, arriving almost 500 years before Christopher Columbus.

The mast would have a square sail attached to it.

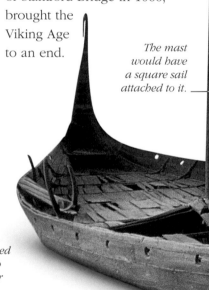

A spindle was used to twist wool into yarn (thread) for making clothes.

◄ VIKING WOMEN

Although Viking women did not enjoy the same status as men, they did have certain freedoms that were unusual for the time. They were allowed to own property and could also divorce their husbands in certain situations. While the men were away raiding, the women were in charge of making clothes and running the home and farms. Some women achieved significant power as members of noble or royal families, and in particular as queens.

METALWORK

Amulet is shaped like the hammer of the god Thor.

The Vikings were capable of intricate metalwork, creating jewelery such as amulets, brooches, and arm rings. Many pieces of Viking jewelery and battle armor have been discovered. Some of these have been found buried together—archaeologists call such findings hoards.

The snake represents a giant serpent, a figure in Scandinavian mythology.

AMULET   BROOCH   ARM RING

FACT
Around 930, Viking settlers founded the Althing—a general assembly open to all free men—in Iceland. It remains the national parliament of the country to this day.

EXPLORATION ▶

The Vikings were expert sailors, and from 700 CE, they developed fast boats called longships for their ocean voyages. Longships were flat-bottomed, which meant they could sail along rivers far inland, and were light enough that they could be dragged onto shore.

The back end of the ship (aft) spirals into the shape of a serpent's tail.

Roof made of wooden tiles

▲ LONGHOUSES

Most Viking houses consisted of one large, long room centered around a fireplace, which was used for cooking, heating, and as a source of light. Several generations of the same family would often live in the same house. The image above shows a replica of a Viking longhouse at Fyrkat, Denmark.

Polynesian expansion

From around 1500 BCE, the Lapita people—seafarers from Southeast Asia—started to explore the oceans. Traveling eastward, they settled Fiji and Samoa, and later Hawaii, New Zealand, and many more islands in the Pacific Ocean that are now known as Polynesia. Settlers on each island or group of islands developed their own unique culture over the centuries.

▼ **THE MOAI**
A row of large stone statues, called Moai, stand on Rapa Nui (Easter Island), facing inward toward land. Built between the 11th and 17th centuries, the 887 statues are believed to represent the ancestors who watch over and protect the island.

STAGES OF MIGRATION

1500 BCE

The Lapita people begin their travels across the Pacific Ocean using canoes called outriggers and navigating with the help of the stars, birds, winds, and tides.

MODEL OF A POLYNESIAN
OUTRIGGER CANOE

c. 1500–1000 BCE

Lapita people arrive in Fiji and soon continue further to Tonga, Samoa, and other islands. They take plants and animals with them to establish small villages on new islands.

800–1000 CE

A second stage of eastward expansion takes place, and Polynesian explorers from Tahiti, Tonga, and Samoa travel to and settle Rapa Nui, the Cook Islands, and Hawaii.

c. 1280 CE

The Lapita people reach what they call "Aotearoa" (modern-day New Zealand) and their society flourishes and develops into the Māori culture.

Medieval eastern Europe

Eastern Europe—which stretches from the Baltic Sea to the Black Sea, and includes western Russia—changed dramatically during the medieval period. Some areas were settled by tribes from the east, and across the region different peoples came together to form new countries. Christianity spread, and soon became eastern Europe's major religion.

Much of the region came under the sway of the Eastern Orthodox Church, which was based in the capital of the Byzantine Empire, Constantinople (modern-day Istanbul). The religious influence of the Byzantine Empire led to cultural influence as well. For example; Byzantine missionaries adapted the Greek alphabet into the Cyrillic script, still used in Russia and parts of southeastern Europe today. The Byzantine Empire had less influence over Poland, however, which adopted the Catholic faith in the 10th century, and developed closer links to western Europe.

Various states and kingdoms emerged in eastern Europe during the medieval period, including Poland, Bulgaria, Serbia, Hungary, and the Kievan Rus (the ancestor of present-day Russia, Belarus, and Ukraine). They traded with the growing Byzantine Empire, and some of them, including Bulgaria, formed part of it for a time.

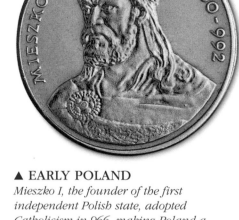

Image of Mieszko I on a Polish coin

▲ **EARLY POLAND**
Mieszko I, the founder of the first independent Polish state, adopted Catholicism in 966, making Poland a Christian country. Under his successor, Bolesław the Brave, Poland became a major European power, but it broke apart again into smaller states in the 12th century.

Árpád, head of the tribes, founded the Hungarian nation.

OLEG OF NOVGOROD

The Viking warrior Oleg of Novgorod (c.845–912) is believed to have founded Kievan Rus, the first Russian state. He attacked the mighty Byzantine Empire in 907, and threatened to destroy the city of Constantinople unless he was paid. In 911, he negotiated a lucrative trade agreement with the empire.

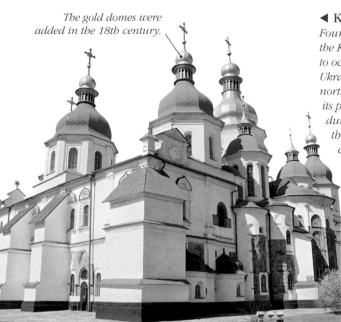

The gold domes were added in the 18th century.

◄ KIEVAN RUS

Founded in the 9th century, the Kievan Rus was the first state to occupy lands in modern-day Ukraine and Belarus, and northwestern Russia. It reached its peak in the 11th century, during the rule of Yaroslav the Wise, who ordered the construction of St. Sophia's Cathedral in Kyiv, Ukraine.

▼ THE BULGARS

The semi-nomadic Bulgar tribe arrived in eastern Europe in the 5th century. Around 630, they united, forming Old Great Bulgaria. Their influence rose in the 9th century under Boris I (below) who expanded their territory and converted his people to Christianity.

▼ THE MAGYARS

The Magyars were tribes from the Ural mountains in western Russia. By the end of the 9th century, chieftains of the seven Magyar tribes (below) moved their people west and settled in what is now Hungary.

FACT

In 1054, the Eastern Orthodox Church formally split from the Roman Catholic Church after years of disagreements. This became known as the East–West Schism.

▼ DUŠAN'S CODE

Under Stefan Dušan (reigned 1331– 1355), Serbia flourished culturally and emerged as a major power in southeastern Europe. Dušan issued a collection of laws, known as Dušan's Code (below), which covered everything from marriage contracts to how to settle disputes between peasants.

African empires

The continent of Africa was filled with many flourishing kingdoms and empires between the 5th and 15th centuries. It was rich in natural resources, so the cities of these empires bustled with trade. From the 7th century, the new religion of Islam began to spread across Africa, influencing the culture of many of these empires.

Despite Africa's huge size and varied lands and cultures, its civilizations were connected by important trade networks. Several kingdoms grew around the coastal areas or large rivers that served these trade routes, and became wealthy. Camels were used to transport goods such as gold across the Sahara Desert from sub-Saharan Africa to North Africa, where they were traded. In West Africa, the empires of Ghana and Mali grew incredibly rich, trading gold and ivory for salt and copper

mined in the Sahara. In southeast Africa, Great Zimbabwe was known for its gold, copper, and ivory.

The Islamic empire spread from the Middle East into North Africa during the 7th century and Muslim kings gradually came to rule in several of Africa's powerful empires and kingdoms. Islam had a big impact on African culture and architecture. Construction began on many palaces and mosques, and Muslim scholars founded places of learning, such as schools, libraries, and universities.

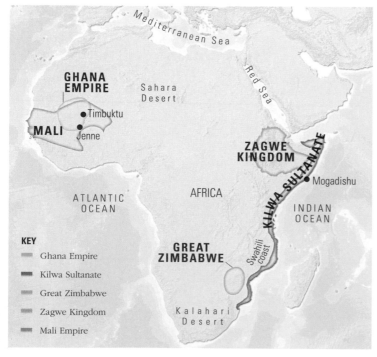

▲ MAJOR AFRICAN EMPIRES
There were hundreds of different African cultures during this period, but some of the largest were the empires of Ghana and Mali in West Africa, Great Zimbabwe in the southeast, and the Zagwe Kingdom and Kilwa Sultanate on the eastern coast.

▼ KILWA SULTANATE
The Kilwa Sultanate was centered on Kilwa, an island off the coast of modern-day Tanzania. At its height between the 12th and 15th centuries, the Sultanate traded as far as China, India, and Sri Lanka. The gold trade and its strategic position made Kilwa the most powerful place on the Swahili coast.

KILWA COINS

◀ **GREAT ZIMBABWE**

The city of Great Zimbabwe was the capital of the mighty Kingdom of Zimbabwe, which flourished between the 11th and 15th centuries. The city grew rich from the gold trade, and its ruins are some of the oldest and largest in Southern Africa. The impressive Great Enclosure (left) is thought to have been the royal palace.

MANSA MUSA

The Mali Empire reached its height during the reign of Mansa Musa I (reigned 1312–1337) who developed cities such as Timbuktu and transformed the kingdom into an important center of learning. Musa was known for his incredible wealth.

▲ **ZAGWE DYNASTY**

The Christian Zagwe Dynasty ruled northern parts of modern-day Ethiopia and Eritrea between the 12th and 13th centuries. The kingdom was centered around Roha (now called Lalibela in Ethiopia), where they built rock-hewn churches, including the church of Bet Giyorgis (St. George).

FACT

Griots originated in the empire of Mali in the 13th century. They told tales of births, marriages, deaths, and battles and still keep traditions alive today as storytellers, musicians, and oral historians.

MALI EMPIRE ▼

The vast empire of Mali in West Africa was established around 1235. It became famous for the immense wealth of its rulers. The original Great Mosque of Djenné, a symbol of the empire's importance, was allowed to fall into ruin after the fall of the empire in the 17th century. It was rebuilt in 1907.

Djenné's mosque is the world's largest mud-brick structure.

Castles and fortresses

Defensive fortifications have been built throughout history all over the world. Most now lie in ruins, but some still stand today. Castles and fortresses protected against invaders, but they were also built as symbols of power and dominance.

Japanese castle
Himeji Castle

Where Hyōgo, Japan
When 14th–17th centuries

In feudal Japan, the *shiro* (castle) was both a fortress and a residence for the regional *daimyo* (lord) and his army of samurai. Himeji Castle—also known as the White Heron Castle due to its elegance and height— is the largest castle in Japan.

Moated castle
Bodiam Castle

Where Sussex, England
When 14th century

The tall towers, thick walls, and wide moat of Bodiam Castle make it an impressive statement of power. It was built by a wealthy English knight, Sir Edward Dallingridge, who made his fortune during the Hundred Years' War against France (see p.77).

Inca citadel
Sacsayhuamán

Where Cusco, Peru
When 15th century

This citadel (hill fortress), built above the Inca capital of Cusco, was also an important temple complex. Its massive walls were made by quarrying vast stone slabs and pounding them so they fitted tightly together without mortar.

Ethiopian fort
Fasil Ghebbi

Where Gondar, Ethiopia
When 17th century

The fortress-city of Fasil Ghebbi was built by the 17th-century Ethiopian emperor Fasilides to be his permanent capital. Inside the fortress are palaces, churches, monasteries, and libraries. The architecture is a mix of Arab, Hindu, and European styles.

Arab-style dome

The castle has seven floors.

Indian hill fort
Gwalior Fort

Where Madhya Pradesh, India
When 15th century

This formidable fort sits on top of a 328-ft- (100-m-) high sandstone hill. Built by the Tomar Dynasty, which ruled parts of central India, the fort changed hands many times over the following centuries. It was even used as a prison by the Mughal emperor Akbar.

Domed towers line the fort walls.

Star fort
Fort Bourtange

Where Groningen, Netherlands
When 16th century

Fort Bourtange was built during the Dutch War of Independence against Spanish rule. The defenses at each corner (bastions) jutted out from the central fortress in the shape of a star, giving guards a good view of an attack. Converted to a village in 1851, the fort is now a museum.

Moroccan kasbah
Telouet Kasbah

Where Morocco, Africa
When 19th century

Kasbah is the Arabic word for a citadel or fortress. High up in the Atlas Mountains of North Africa, the Telouet Kasbah was strategically located on the caravan route between the Sahara Desert and the cities of Morocco. It was built by the head of a local tribe, the Glaoua, who had grown rich from trading in salt and saffron.

The Mongol Empire

The Mongols were made up of many nomadic tribes who lived in the grasslands of Central Asia. They were often at war with each other. In the early 13th century, these tribes were united under the leadership of the Mongol chief Genghis Khan. He formed a powerful army and conquered vast areas of Asia and Europe, creating one of the largest empires in history.

For centuries before the empire was established, the Mongols raided towns and villages in northern China. After uniting the Mongols, Genghis Khan had a huge and powerful army under his command. Turning his attention back to China, in 1211 Genghis launched a campaign against the Jin Dynasty, and by 1215, he had captured Beijing. Soon the Mongol army began pressing west, conquering territory across Central Asia and into Eastern Europe.

While their conquests were violent, the Mongols brought peace and stability to the regions they controlled. This was known as Pax Mongolica ("Mongol Peace"). The Mongols did not rule directly. The conquered kingdoms had to pay large taxes to the empire and in return were allowed to rule their own territories. The Mongol Empire reached its greatest extent under Genghis Khan's grandson, Kublai Khan. After his death in 1294 the empire went into decline.

GENGHIS KHAN ▲
Born as Temüjin in modern-day Mongolia, Genghis Khan (reigned 1206–1227) took his name (which means "universal ruler") after uniting the Mongols in 1206. He was a fearsome warrior and brilliant military tactician who often succeeded in battle even when his armies were outnumbered.

SIEGE OF BAGHDAD
Led by Genghis Khan's grandson Hulagu Khan, the Mongols attacked Baghdad (in modern-day Iraq), the capital of the Abbasid Caliphate, in 1258. In a 13-day siege, the Mongol army killed hundreds of thousands of residents. Baghdad's famous library, the House of Wisdom, was also completely destroyed.

THE EMPIRE ▶

At its peak, the Mongol Empire covered an area of 9 million sq miles (23 million sq km). The empire was divided into four parts by the end of the 13th century—the Yuan Dynasty, which ruled China, the Khanate of the Golden Horde in eastern Europe, the Chagatai Khanate comprising modern-day Afghanistan and northwest India, and the Il-Khanate, which covered Persia (modern-day Iran). Extending west to east across the empire was the important trade route known as the Silk Road.

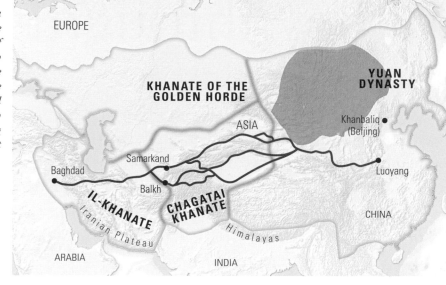

EUROPE

KHANATE OF THE GOLDEN HORDE

YUAN DYNASTY

ASIA

Khanbaliq (Beijing)

Baghdad

Samarkand

Luoyang

IL-KHANATE

Balkh

CHAGATAI KHANATE

CHINA

Iranian Plateau

Himalayas

ARABIA

INDIA

KEY

Mongol homeland c. 1206 ▬

Greatest extent of Mongol Empire c. 1294 ▬

Khanate borders ▬

The Silk Road ▬

◀ MONGOL WARRIORS

The Mongol army was made up of skilled warriors who fought on horseback, and were taught from a young age how to use a bow and arrow. They were known for their speed and aggression and attacked in large groups, overwhelming their enemies with ease. Riders could travel many miles a day across deserts and mountains.

▼ KUBLAI KHAN

Kublai Khan (reigned 1260–1294) completed his grandfather's conquest of China and founded the Yuan Dynasty (1271–1368), making Khanbaliq (modern-day Beijing) his capital. He encouraged trade along the Silk Road and was tolerant to foreign religions such as Buddhism and Islam.

SORGHAGHTANI BEKI

The youngest daughter-in-law of Genghis Khan, Sorghaghtani (1190–1252) served as an advisor to his successors and became one of the most powerful women in the empire. She encouraged the expansion of trade, and influenced decisions so that all four of her sons eventually came into power.

TIMUR THE CONQUEROR ▼

Timur (reigned 1370–1405) was a ruthless military leader from Central Asia who dreamed of rebuilding Genghis Khan's vast empire. After gaining control of the Chagatai Khanate, he founded the Timurid Empire in 1370, and went on to conquer a vast area that stretched from modern-day Turkey to northern India. He is buried in the Gur-e-Amir tomb (below) in his capital city of Samarkand, Uzbekistan.

The roof of the mausoleum is covered in a mosaic of blue tiles.

Money through the ages

From shells and grain to paper notes and credit cards, money has taken many different forms during the thousands of years that humankind has been using it. Even today, money continues to evolve, with brand new digital currencies on the rise, and electronic payments starting to overtake physical cash in many parts of the world.

Early banking
Grain bank

Where Mesopotamia
When c. 3000 BCE

The Mesopotamians devised an early form of banking. Grain, precious stones, and other items of value were kept at temples and royal palaces for safekeeping. These items could then be "withdrawn" at a later time.

Barter system
Direct exchange of goods

Where Mesopotamia (modern-day Iraq)
When c. 6000 BCE

Before the invention of money itself, people often directly exchanged items of the same value. For example, if one tribe had more grain than they needed, they could swap it with another that had cloth to spare. Evidence suggests that Mesopotamian tribes used barter systems 8,000 years ago.

Early currency
Shells

Where China
When c. 1500 BCE

Long before the introduction of coins, people in ancient China used cowrie shells as currency. They were ideal because of their small size, which made them easy to transport, and their strength. Replicas made from other materials such as bone, lead, copper, or stone were also used.

Early coins
Lydian coin

Where Lydia (modern-day Turkey)
When c. 600 BCE

The earliest known coins were minted by people from the ancient kingdom of Lydia. The coins were made from a mixture of gold and silver called electrum and depicted a lion's head.

Paper currency
Song paper money

Where China
When 11th century CE

Under the Song Dynasty, China issued *jiaozi*—the world's first paper money. Though the paper had no value in itself, people were willing to use *jiaozi* as money because they could be exchanged for coins, made of gold or silver, at any time.

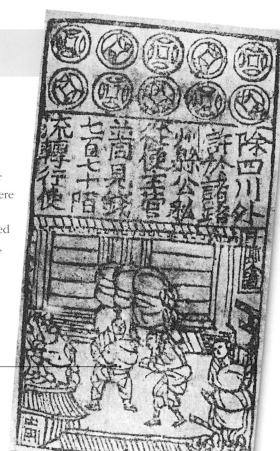

Three men carry sacks of grain in this modern copy of a Song-era jiaozi.

Global currency
Pieces of eight

Where Spain
When 16th century

The Spanish dollar was the first international currency, thanks to the reach of the extensive Spanish Empire. Made from soft silver, Spanish dollars were known as "pieces of eight" because they could be cut up into eight pieces to make smaller change.

Cryptocurrency
Bitcoin

Where Worldwide
When 2009

A type of digital-only money, cryptocurrency such as Bitcoin is controlled by its users and an algorithm (a set of computer rules) rather than by governments. It allows users to safely make payments or store money without using a bank.

Borrowed money
Credit card

Where US
When 1946

The first bank-issued credit card was the Charg-It in 1946. Credit cards allow people to purchase goods but pay for them at a later date. It was only after banking was computerized that debit cards, which took money from the users' bank accounts instantly, were introduced.

The Aztecs

Starting out as a nomadic tribe, the Aztecs settled in the Valley of Mexico in the 1300s and went on to conquer a vast empire. They did not rule conquered lands directly. Instead, they forced the people to send annual tribute (payment in goods) to the Aztec capital, Tenochtitlán. The Aztecs called themselves *Mexica*, which is how Mexico got its name.

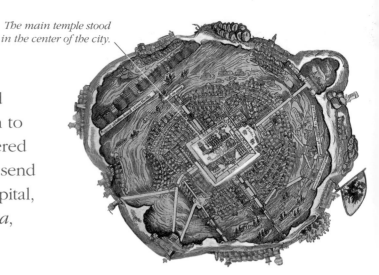
The main temple stood in the center of the city.

The Aztecs built Tenochtitlán on marshy islands in the middle of Lake Texcoco (in central Mexico). They created *chinampas* (plots of fertile land) on the shallow lake where they grew maize and beans.

Warfare was an important part of Aztec culture, and they fought partly for economic reasons. The tribute from captured areas supplied their city with wealth, such as jade, gold, and animal skins. War also had a religious purpose, as the Aztecs practiced ceremonial human sacrifice. Prisoners were sacrificed to the god of war, Huitzilopochtli (Blue Hummingbird).

Between 1519 and 1521, the Aztecs were conquered by the Spanish (see pp.112–113), who built a new capital, Mexico City, on top of Tenochtitlán.

▲ CAPITAL CITY
Tenochtitlán was the largest city of the Americas before the arrival of Europeans. It had hundreds of temples and a palace said to have 300 rooms. The Aztecs built causeways to connect its islands to the mainland, and created a network of canals, which they navigated by canoe. The above plan of the city was made by the Spanish in 1524.

Headgear made of feathers from a quetzal bird

RELIGION ▶
The Aztecs worshipped many gods. As farming was vitally important, they prayed to nature deities to ensure rich harvests every year. Xipe Totec (right) was the god of spring. His clothes represent the new layer of vegetation that arrives in spring.

◀ WARFARE
Most men in the Aztec Empire were trained to become ferocious warriors. They used javelins and bows and arrows as long-range weapons, and a wooden club called maquahuitl *(left) for close combat. These clubs were fitted with razor-sharp blades made from a rock called obsidian along their sides.*

The Incas

In the 12th century, the Incas established their kingdom in the highlands of modern-day Peru. The Inca Empire grew from around 1430 to cover a vast portion of the Andes mountains. At its peak, it extended for 2,200 miles (3,500 km), and included 12 million people. Between 1532 and 1572, the Inca Empire was gradually conquered by Spanish invaders.

Rich civilizations existed in Peru long before the Incas, including the Chimú Empire, who made beautiful pottery and metalwork. They were conquered by the Incas in the 1460s.

The Inca Empire was ruled by an emperor, who was called the *Sapa Ina* (sole lord). Beneath him, society was highly organized with thousands of officials and, under them, millions of common people, who were weavers, farmers, and builders. The Incas built great structures out of enormous blocks of stone that were so well made, they could withstand earthquakes. They built flat terraces for farming on mountainsides, and dug water channels to irrigate them. Llamas were used to carry soil up from the valley to fill the terraces.

The Incas also built a network of stone roads around 24,000 miles (40,000 km) in length. As well as transporting armies and goods, they were used by official messengers called *chasquis* (fast runners who traveled in relay). Many of these roads are still in use today.

KEEPING RECORDS ▲

The Incas had no written language, but kept records on a device made of lengths of knotted string called a quipu. *The colors of the string, and the position, size, and number of knots provided details such as livestock figures and tax payments.*

MACHU PICCHU ▼

No other people built settlements as high up in mountains as the Incas. At 7,972 ft (2,430 m) above sea level, the ancient city of Machu Picchu was built around 1450 for the emperor, Pachacuti. It was abandoned around a century later, after the Spanish invasion, and only rediscovered in 1911.

Flat terraces for growing crops

TAKE A LOOK

Despite the Spanish conquest, many features of Inca daily life continue today. Many Indigenous communities still weave colorful textiles from alpaca and llama wool using a traditional loom, as they have for thousands of years.

PERUVIAN WEAVER

1450–1750

From the 15th century, Europeans were inspired by a newfound curiosity that led to major scientific discoveries and developments in art. Europeans embarked on voyages of exploration, and eventually built overseas empires to rival older civilizations that continued to flourish in the Middle East, China, and India. These new empires were built on the exploitation of Indigenous people that lived in these regions, as well as millions of enslaved Africans.

Ming China

The Ming Dynasty came to power in China in 1368, ending almost a century of rule by Mongol invaders. The new dynasty set about reviving ancient Chinese customs and traditions, and is known for its encouragement of the arts and culture as well as its large-scale building projects.

Under the Ming, the empire was largely peaceful, helped by a smooth transition of power from one emperor to the next. However, Ming rulers were always under threat of invasion. Hongwu, the first Ming emperor, built up an army of more than one million soldiers and set up the world's largest naval dockyards in Nanjing. From the mid-1400s onward, renewed threats of a possible Mongol invasion from the north encouraged the Ming emperors to rebuild the ancient Great Wall.

Although the Ming rulers were distrustful of their neighbors, they allowed increasing contact with European powers. Traders brought new crops from the Americas, such as maize and potatoes, as well as chile peppers.

By the start of the 16th century, the Ming faced a new threat from the Manchu people to the northeast, who had united and threatened to invade. Widespread famine, floods, and plague seriously weakened support for Ming rule. In 1644, an army of peasant rebels seized Beijing. The Ming took help from the Manchus to fight the rebels. But the Manchus captured Beijing for themselves, and established a new dynasty—the Qing.

◄ MING PAINTING
Painting in the Ming era revived the style of the earlier Song Dynasty but with more use of color and calligraphy. Landscapes, flowers, and birds were all popular subjects.

ZHENG HE

Zheng He (1371–c. 1433) was an explorer who led seven expeditions to Southeast Asia, India, and along the East African coast. He commanded up to 30,000 soldiers and his vast wooden ships were among the largest ever built at the time.

Blue dragon design on a Ming era porcelain jar

◄ PORCELAIN
In an effort to bring back old traditions, the first Ming emperor reestablished the imperial porcelain factory in 1369, which had been founded by the Song Dynasty. The factory refined old techniques and styles, especially the blue-and-white porcelain. This distinctive pottery became famous across the world and was often given away by the imperial family as gifts.

THE FORBIDDEN CITY ►
In 1406, Emperor Yongle ordered the construction of a new palace complex in Beijing, which was to become his new capital. The complex was divided into two parts: the inner court was used by the imperial family, and the outer court was used by the emperor and his officials. As access to the complex was restricted, it became known as the Forbidden City.

The northern gate, or "Gate of Divine Might"

MAJOR EVENTS

1368	1402–1424	1425–1435	1449	1644
Zhu Yuanzhang seizes power from the Mongols and establishes the new Ming Dynasty, reigning as Emperor Hongwu.	Emperor Yongle orders the reconstruction of China's Grand Canal. Once the Forbidden City is complete, he moves the capital to Beijing.	Emperor Xuande puts down rebellions in the empire and tries to stop corruption among officials. His reign sees a high point in making blue-and-white porcelain.	Emperor Zhengtong is captured by the Mongols after defeat in battle. The event leads to the rebuilding of the Great Wall.	Emperor Chongzhen, the last Ming ruler, dies in 1644. The Ming Dynasty is overthrown by the Manchus.

Great African kingdoms

Between the 15th and 18th centuries, great kingdoms continued to flourish across Africa. The expansion of trade networks brought considerable wealth, and the architecture and artworks that survive from this time are evidence that the continent was home to many rich cultures.

Several African kingdoms grew rich as a result of the continent's booming trade networks, which expanded as far as Europe, Asia, and the Americas. The trading strategy in each kingdom was different. Some rulers focused on controlling regional trade, while others dominated the growing international networks. There was the centuries-old trade across the Sahara Desert as well as the emerging Atlantic trade with Europeans, which included the exchange of gold, ivory, salt, and enslaved people (see pp.132–133).

The great wealth of these African kingdoms meant that money could be spent on improving the kingdom itself. Some kingdoms used their wealth to equip, organize, and train their military forces, to allow them to conquer neighboring countries and extend the boundaries of their empires. This greater military might also protected them from attempts at colonization, as Europeans began to take more of an interest in the resources of the continent.

FACT
Timbuktu, the capital of the Mali Empire, was an important religious, educational, and trading center. In 1500, its population of 100,000 included scholars, artists, and scientists.

Small brass soldiers surround the central figure of military commander Ehenua.

BENIN EMPIRE ▶
Art flourished in the Kingdom of Benin and these round "ikegobo" (altars to the hand) were made to celebrate a person's chievements. This one was created to honor the heroism of Ehenua, an 18th-century military commander who served under Oba Akenzua I.

QUEEN MOTHER IDIA

Queen Mother Idia was an important figure in the wealthy Kingdom of Benin, in modern-day Nigeria. She was the mother of the Oba (king) and she helped her son defeat his enemies.

SONGHAI EMPIRE ▲

The Songhai Empire was one of West Africa's most powerful states. This tomb was built by Emperor Askia Mohammed in his capital Gao, in modern-day Mali. Gao's location on the Niger River allowed the empire to take control of the gold trade across the Sahara Desert.

KINGDOM OF KONGO ▶

At its height, the Kingdom of Kongo, in present-day Angola, was the most powerful state in western Central Africa. The Kongo formed an alliance with the Dutch. Here the King of Kongo can be seen receiving Dutch ambassadors in 1642.

A 17TH-CENTURY MAP OF THE
KINGDOM OF MUTAPA, ALSO
KNOWN AS MONOMOTAPA

◀ KINGDOM OF MUTAPA

The vast southern African Kingdom of Mutapa spanned present-day Zimbabwe, Zambia, Mozambique, and South Africa. The kingdom grew wealthy trading gold and ivory to Islamic merchants on the East African coast, but civil wars led to its decline and the Portuguese took control in 1629.

ASANTE EMPIRE ▶

Located in what is now modern-day Ghana, the Asante Empire was a thriving center of art and trade. The empire grew rich trading gold, ivory, and enslaved people. It was so rich that it earned the title "Kingdom of Gold," and gold dust was even used as currency.

99

The Ottoman Empire

Named after its founder, a warrior named Osman Ghazi, the Ottoman Empire began as a small state in Anatolia (in modern-day Turkey) in around 1300. From the 14th to the 16th centuries, it was one of the most powerful kingdoms in the world, extending into the Arabian Peninsula, North Africa, and across large parts of Europe. It was known for its military might and advancements in science and arts. The Ottoman Empire lasted until the early 20th century.

GREAT SULTANS

1362–1389	Murad I expands the Ottoman Empire by capturing most of the Balkans, a region in southeastern Europe. He moves the empire's capital city to Adrianople, which he renames Edirne. In 1389, he is killed by a Serbian knight after the Battle of Kosovo.
1451–1481	Under Sultan Mehmed II, better known as Mehmed the Conqueror, the Ottoman army captures Constantinople in 1453, ending the Byzantine Empire. Constantinople is now known as Islambol (later Istanbul), and becomes the Ottoman capital.
1512–1520	Selim I, also known as Selim the Grim, forces his father to give up the throne, and kills his brothers to become sultan. He then defeats the Safavid Empire in Persia and the Mamluk Sultanate of Egypt. The Ottoman Empire becomes the most powerful empire in the Islamic world.
1520–1566	The empire reaches its fullest extent under Suleiman I, also called "the Magnificent." He promotes science, literature, art, music, and architecture, and brings the whole of his empire under a single system of law.

SULEIMAN I

JANISSARY GUARDS ▶

The Janissary were elite soldiers who came out of the Devshirme system set up by Sultan Murad I. In this system, young Christian boys from conquered territories were converted to Islam and then trained as soldiers. Janissaries were loyal only to the sultan and formed his protective guard. They also protected frontier towns from outside attacks.

▲ GYEONGBOKGUNG PALACE
Gyeongbokgung was the largest and most important of five royal palaces built in the city of Seoul, then known as Hanseong, during the Joseon Dynasty. Built in 1395, the palace was home to Joseon kings as well as the government. It was destroyed during the Imjin War with Japan, but was restored and rebuilt in the 19th and 20th centuries.

Korea's Joseon Dynasty

The Joseon Dynasty ruled over the Korean Peninsula (modern-day North Korea and South Korea) from 1392–1910. During this time, Korea went through a golden age of culture and learning as well as significant social change.

FACT
Joseon Korea had a strict class system. People were born into one of four classes— *yangban* (landowner), *chungin* (middle class), *sangmin* (commoner), or *cheonmin* (lowborn).

SEJONG THE GREAT

Sejong the Great (reigned 1418–1450) was the fourth Joseon ruler. He created the Hangul script that made it easier for everyone to read and write Korean. He also promoted science and technology, which led to many inventions.

From 57 BCE until 668 CE, ancient Korea was ruled by three kingdoms. Then, one of the three kingdoms, Silla, gained control over the entire peninsula, and stayed in power until 935. The kingdom then briefly split, before being reunified under the Goryeo Kingdom for a period of 470 years.

The Goryeo Kingdom was overthrown by General Yi Seong-gye, who named his dynasty Joseon and became its first king, taking the title Taejo. The new dynasty expanded its boundaries and moved its capital from Kaesong (in modern-day North Korea) to the city of Hanseong

(modern-day Seoul, the capital of South Korea). Over the next 500 years, the Joseon Kingdom went through great changes. Neo-Confucianism—a philosophy based on the traditional teachings of the Chinese philosopher Confucius—was promoted, and a strict social class system was put in place. The period also saw many important advancements in literature, science, and astronomy.

After several invasions from China and Japan in the 16th and 17th centuries, the kingdom entered a period of isolation for nearly 200 years, and declined in the late 19th century as Japan gradually took over control of Korea.

The wooden dragon head hid a cannon or burner that released fire or smoke.

◀ TURTLE SHIP
The geobukseon *(turtle ship) was designed by the Korean admiral Yi Sun-sin in the 16th century. These armored warships had a protective roof, like a turtle shell, which was covered with spikes. They were also equipped with cannons.*

Powered by up to 70 oarspeople, the ship could turn quickly and achieve bursts of high speed.

▼ HANGUL

Until the mid-15th century, the Korean language was written using classical Chinese characters, but these were difficult to learn and only the educated knew them. In 1446, the Hangul script became the official Korean alphabet. It contained just 28 letters and was much easier to learn.

Each quarter of this wooden seal features a Hangul character.

A ruler was dipped into the funnel to measure rainfall.

◀ RAIN GAUGE

During the reign of Sejong the Great, the cheugugi rain gauge was invented and distributed all across the kingdom. This instrument helped people keep accurate records of rainfall, which helped them predict the weather and therefore improve crop harvests.

SHIN SAIMDANG ▶

Shin Saimdang was one of the most famous artists, writers, and calligraphers under the Joseon dynasty during the 16th century. She painted nature scenes, particularly flowers and insects. Two of her poems still survive, but most examples of her calligraphy have been lost over the years.

IMJIN WAR

Japan twice invaded the Joseon Kingdom in the 1590s, in a conflict known as the Imjin War. Early in the conflict, the Japanese laid siege to the fortress at Busan (below), killing 8,000 Koreans. The war ended when the Japanese withdrew in 1598.

The European Renaissance

In the late medieval period, dramatic changes took place in European society, which had remained relatively unchanged for hundreds of years. New ways of thinking led to a great blossoming of culture and art. This period, lasting from the 14th to the late 16th centuries, is known as the Renaissance (meaning "rebirth").

In the 14th century, contact with other cultures and the rediscovery of ancient texts influenced artists and thinkers. They reacted against the narrow teachings of the Church and developed a new philosophy called humanism, which valued knowledge gained through learning and experience.

The Renaissance began in Florence and other city-states of northern Italy. Painters and sculptors abandoned the flat style of medieval art in favor of depicting subjects in a more lifelike way. Rich people, eager to show off their status, began sponsoring works of art in these new styles. This led to advances in architecture, literature, science, and other areas.

By the 15th century, Renaissance ideas had spread across Europe, helped by the development of the printing press, which introduced both new works and the writers of the ancient world to many more people. The Renaissance movement marked the end of the medieval world, and laid the foundations for the modern world.

◄ NEW ARCHITECTURE
Renaissance architects found inspiration in the buildings of ancient Greece and Rome, which often had elegant domes and columns. Designed in 1418, the dome of Florence Cathedral was the largest to be built in western Europe since Roman times.

RENAISSANCE WOMEN ▼
Despite the new ways of thinking, Renaissance women were expected to stay at home. They were given little opportunity to study, though some who had privileged backgrounds became poets and writers. An Italian noblewoman, Sofonisba Anguissola, was one of the few successful female Renaissance artists. She painted this portrait of her sisters playing chess in 1555.

LORENZO DE' MEDICI

Lorenzo de' Medici (1449–1492) was the most powerful man in Florence at the height of the Italian Renaissance. Known as "Lorenzo the Magnificent," he used his vast wealth, earned from banking, to support great artists such as Michelangelo and Sandro Botticelli.

▲ USING PERSPECTIVE

Renaissance artists developed new techniques to make their paintings appear more natural, including the use of perspective to give the illusion of distance. This view of a city, called The Ideal City, *is painted on a flat surface, but it appears to have depth as the buildings in the background become smaller and seem further away from the viewer.*

The arm span is the same as the figure's height.

▲ VITRUVIAN MAN

The notebooks of Italian Renaissance artist and scientist Leonardo da Vinci were filled with brilliant sketches and designs for inventions ahead of their time, such as a helicopter-like flying machine. He made this drawing, called Vitruvian Man, *to illustrate the "perfect" proportions of the human body.*

FACT
In 1543, Polish astronomer Nicolaus Copernicus proved that Earth revolves round the sun, rather than the other way around— a major breakthrough in our understanding of the universe.

DECORATIVE ARTS

Artists and craftworkers produced beautiful objects to decorate the villas and palaces of the wealthy, including bronze and marble sculptures, ceramics, jewelery, and fine metalwork. Decorative objects were often displayed in cabinets to show off the taste of the collector.

GOLD VESSEL FOR HOLDING SALT

JAR FOR MEDICINES

Neck carved entirely out of ivory

LUTE

TERRA-COTTA WALL DECORATION

▲ THE RENAISSANCE SPREADS

From Italy, the Renaissance spread out across northern Europe. Monarchs such as King Francis I of France (reigned 1515–1547) invited Italian artists to work for them. The Château de Chambord (above) was built by Francis I to display his wealth and power. It included Renaissance features in its design, some of which may have been the work of Leonardo da Vinci.

The written word

Humans have used spoken language for hundreds of thousands of years, but it was only around 5,000 years ago that writing was invented. Since then, people have created writing systems such as alphabets, as well as tools that allow us to write things down.

Picture words
Egyptian hieroglyphs

Where Egypt
When c. 3300 BCE to c. 394 CE

Ancient Egyptian hieroglyphics (see p.20) used around 1,000 different pictures to represent words, sounds, and objects. They fell out of use around 400 CE and remained a mystery until the discovery of the Rosetta Stone in 1799. This stone contained a text written in three languages: ancient Greek, hieroglyphics, and an ancient Egyptian script. Scholars used the Greek to work out the meaning of the hieroglyphs.

Record taking
Cuneiform

Where Mesopotamia (modern-day Iraq)
When c. 3200 BCE to c. 75 CE

The Sumerians of southern Mesopotamia (see p.16) invented a writing system to keep track of business transactions. They used a sharpened reed to make indents of different shapes on a tablet made of wet clay. This writing system is now known as "cuneiform," meaning "wedge-shaped."

Lost symbols
Indus script

Where Indus Valley, modern-day Pakistan
When c. 2600–c. 1900 BCE

Discovered at archaeological sites in modern-day Pakistan, the Indus script was created by the Indus Valley Civilization (see p.32). The meaning of the script has been lost, but experts think that it was written from right to left and had around 400 signs, representing syllables or whole words.

Early alphabet
Phoenician alphabet

Where Phoenicia (modern-day Lebanon)
When c. 1200–c. 900 BCE

While earlier civilizations invented writing systems that had hundreds of symbols and signs, the Phoenicians (see p.36) developed a simple alphabet, in which each symbol represented a single sound. It had 22 letters, which stood for consonants, and was the ancestor of all modern European alphabets.

Writing material
Paper

Where China
When c. 105 CE

By the 2nd century CE, papyrus (made from a reedlike plant) and parchment (made from animal skins) had long been used as writing materials, but they were expensive and decayed over time. The Chinese invented a writing material made from the pulp of plants, such as bamboo. The new material, paper, was cheap and strong, and could be mass produced easily.

3. Mashing it to a pulpy paste
5. Drying out the paper
1. Collecting bamboo
2. Cutting bamboo
4. Laying the paste out on a board
Fire

Printing
Woodblock printing

Where China
When 7th century CE

The Chinese first used woodblock printing to print on paper during the Tang era (see pp.68–69). Wooden blocks were carved with images or words and then ink was applied. A print was made by brushing thin paper onto the block. In the 11th century, Chinese artisan Bi Sheng created moving type by carving letters onto clay. After being baked hard, they were then arranged on an iron frame and pressed against an iron plate.

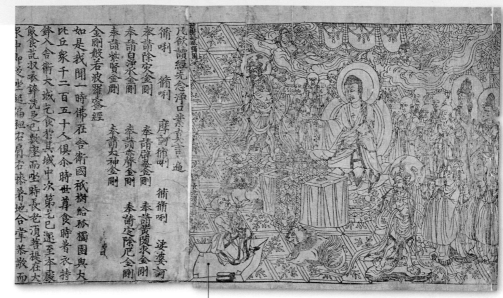

Details from a page from the Buddhist Diamond Sutra *from 868 CE, the earliest-known printed manuscript*

Movable type
Printing press

Where Germany
When 1450

German inventor Johannes Gutenberg's printing press was a huge leap forward for communication. The machine perfected the technique of using movable type originally developed by the Chinese and Koreans. It allowed whole books to be printed incredibly quickly, compared to scribes writing each one out by hand. The printing press caught on across Europe and its success meant that knowledge and new ideas could be shared far faster than ever before.

2. Paper is placed here and pulled over the letters.

3. The press pushes the paper down onto the letters.

1. Ink is applied to letters with ink balls.

Writing machines
Typewriter

Where US
When 1868

The first modern typewriter was created by inventor Christopher Latham Sholes and mechanic Carlos S Glidden. Typewriters were faster than writing things out by hand, and they remained popular for over a century until they were eventually replaced by electronic word processors and computers.

European expansion

Since ancient times, Europeans had been aware of the regions surrounding the Mediterranean, as well as parts of Asia and North Africa. But in the 15th century, they began to set their sights on places farther afield, taking to the open seas to find what lay beyond the edges of their maps.

There were many reasons for the European yearning for exploration, but, at least to begin with, seizing foreign lands was not one of them. Expensive goods such as silk and spices arrived overland from Asia, and the first European expeditions aimed to establish a faster, safer sea route in order to expand trade.

However, as explorers began to realize the abundance of resources in the lands they visited, they started seizing territory by force, often using their superior weapons to kill or enslave Indigenous people living there.

The first expeditions in the mid-15th century began a centuries-long campaign of European expansion and colonization. By the start of World War I in 1914, European nations had conquered more than 80 percent of the land on the planet, and the effects of this violent colonization are still felt across the globe today (see pp.172–173).

▲ **HENRY THE NAVIGATOR**
Prince Henry of Portugal earned himself the nickname "Henry the Navigator," despite never setting off on any voyages himself. He funded expeditions from Portugal to explore the West African coast, which was then unknown to Europeans. For them, these journeys kick-started the era sometimes called the Age of Exploration.

SAILING ESSENTIALS

New inventions and technologies made the Age of Exploration possible. The Portuguese developed small, fast, and powerful ships called caravels to explore the vast oceans. Navigational instruments such as the astrolabe and backstaff helped sailors figure out their location while at sea.

Triangular sails allowed the ship to "tack" (zigzag into the wind).

ASTROLABE

BACKSTAFF

MODEL OF CARAVEL

VOYAGES TO AFRICA ▶
During his exploration of East Africa, Portuguese navigator Diogo Cão discovered that the continent was bigger than Europeans had previously thought. He erected stone pillars called padrãoes (right) to mark his progress and claim land. Later explorers to Africa continued this custom.

▲ **COLUMBIAN EXCHANGE**
Between 1492 and 1504, Italian explorer Christopher Columbus made four voyages to the Americas, establishing the first links of a connection between Europe and the Americas. Fruits and vegetables such as pineapples and sweet potatoes were shipped to Europe, while livestock and crops such as wheat were introduced to the Americas—as were deadly diseases such as smallpox. The early trade of goods, ideas, and diseases between the two regions was known as the Columbian Exchange.

◀ REACHING BRAZIL

While sailing around Africa to reach India in 1500, Portuguese explorer Pedro Álvares Cabral's fleet was carried by the wind further west than intended, and stumbled upon the coast of South America. He claimed the land—now part of Brazil—for Portugal before proceeding to India.

TRAVELS OF DA GAMA ▶

Europe and India had traded with each other since ancient times but the overland journey between them was long and expensive. At the turn of the 16th century, Portuguese explorer Vasco da Gama established a new sea route from Portugal to India, sailing around Africa, and then north across the Indian Ocean to reach Calicut (modern-day Kozhikode) in India.

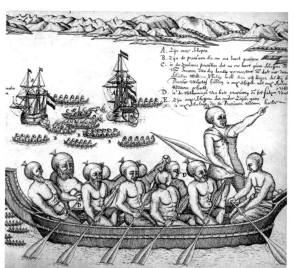

◀ REACHING AUSTRALASIA

Europeans first arrived in Australia in 1606, when Dutch explorer Willem Janszoon set foot in the north of what is now Queensland. In 1642, fellow Dutchman Abel Tasman became the first European to reach New Zealand, Tonga, and Fiji. His crew drew sketches of the Māori warriors they encountered (left).

VOYAGES OF EXPLORATION

Thanks to their location on the western edge of Europe close to Africa, many European voyages of exploration set sail from either Spain or Portugal. Sailors would be at sea for years at a time, traveling through uncharted and unpredictable waters.

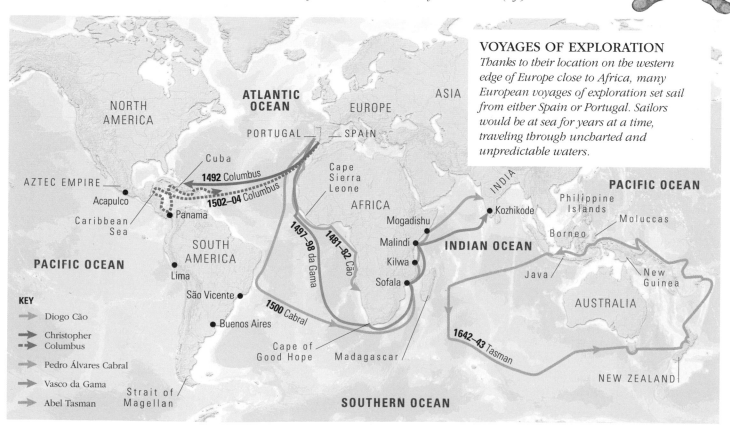

HENRY VIII'S SIX WIVES

1509–1533
Catherine of Aragon, Henry's first wife, gives birth six times but only one child—Mary (later Mary I)—survives infancy. Henry annuls (cancels) their marriage in search of a male heir.

1533–1536
While Henry's marriage to Anne Boleyn produces the future Queen Elizabeth I, he has her executed when she does not produce a son.

ANNE BOLEYN

1536–1537
Jane Seymour bears Henry a male heir to the throne, and is the only queen to do so. She dies shortly after their son Edward is born.

1540
The fourth woman to marry Henry is German-born Anne of Cleves. Their marriage is annulled after just six months.

1540–1542
Catherine Howard, Henry VIII's fifth wife, suffers the same fate as Anne Boleyn. She is beheaded after she fails to bear him children during the two years of their marriage.

1543–1547
Catherine Parr outlives Henry but dies soon after him in 1548. She writes a prayer book, becoming the first woman in England to publish a book in English under her own name.

CATHERINE PARR'S *PRAYERS OR MEDITATIONS*

The Tudors

The rule of the Tudor Dynasty began in 1485 when Henry Tudor seized the throne of England by defeating King Richard III of the rival Yorkist Dynasty in battle, and became Henry VII. The Tudors reigned for more than a century, until the death of Elizabeth I in 1603. During this period, England grew in power and influence, becoming richer than ever before, and enjoyed an unprecedented flowering of culture and the arts.

The Tudors introduced important changes that impacted all areas of life in England. Wary of Yorkist rebellions, Henry VII (reigned 1485–1509) seized their lands and strengthened the power of the monarchy.

His successor, Henry VIII (reigned 1509–1547) removed the authority of the Catholic Church, appointing himself the leader of a new Church of England, which preached a form of Christianity known as Protestantism. He also built up the Royal Navy to become one of the most powerful naval forces in English history. Henry was succeeded by three of his children in turn—Edward VI in 1547, Mary I in 1553, and Elizabeth I in 1558.

Elizabeth I was a strong ruler, and during her reign England emerged as a major power, rivaling Spain for dominance in Europe. Elizabeth's reign was also an age of international expansion, as explorers and merchants ventured to the Americas and set up colonies. Education improved and the arts flourished, too, especially the theater. Despite this, many people lived in poverty and struggled to afford food and clothing.

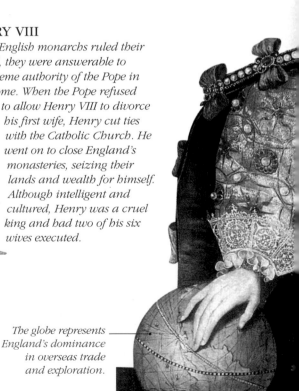

◀ **HENRY VIII**
Although English monarchs ruled their own land, they were answerable to the supreme authority of the Pope in Rome. When the Pope refused to allow Henry VIII to divorce his first wife, Henry cut ties with the Catholic Church. He went on to close England's monasteries, seizing their lands and wealth for himself. Although intelligent and cultured, Henry was a cruel king and had two of his six wives executed.

The globe represents England's dominance in overseas trade and exploration.

MARY I ▶

The eldest daughter of Henry VIII, Mary I (reigned 1553–1558) married Spain's Catholic king, Philip II, and restored the Catholic faith in England. Her reign was marked by violence and bloodshed, and after ordering the execution of leading Protestants she became known as "Bloody Mary."

▼ ELIZABETH I

Dedicated and shrewd, Elizabeth I (reigned 1558–1603) established herself as a powerful monarch who was highly respected by her subjects. She reinstated Protestantism but was a much more tolerant ruler than her sister Mary. Her reign was considered a golden age in England. She never married, and without an heir to the throne, Elizabeth's death in 1603 marked the end of the Tudors.

Coin depicting Mary I, commemorating her marriage to Philip II of Spain

▲ DEFEAT OF THE SPANISH ARMADA

In 1588, King Philip II of Spain sent a fleet of 130 ships—the Spanish Armada—to invade England and overthrow Elizabeth I. This was the biggest threat England had faced for centuries, yet the English fleet triumphed after just an eight-hour battle. This remarkable victory showcased the country's naval strength to the rest of Europe.

WILLIAM SHAKESPEARE ▶

Still widely agreed to be the greatest figure of English literature, William Shakespeare wrote almost 40 plays, including Hamlet, Macbeth, and Romeo and Juliet. Many were performed at the open-air Globe Theatre in London (right). It burned down in 1613, but was reconstructed in 1997 and still puts on performances today.

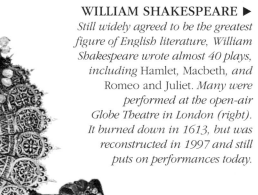

CHILD IN TIME

After King Henry VIII died in 1547, his only son Edward VI took to the throne at the age of nine. The "Boy King" suffered with ill health and died seven years later in 1553.

▲ THE AZTECS AND CORTÉS

Spanish conquistador (conqueror) Hernán Cortés arrived in Mexico in 1519. He made alliances with Indigenous people, such as the Tlaxcala, and with their help was able to capture the Aztec capital of Tenochtitlan (see p.92) after a 79-day siege in 1521. He renamed the former center of the Aztec Empire as Mexico City.

▲ CONQUEST OF THE MAYA

When the Spanish reached Central America in the 16th century, instead of a single Maya kingdom, they found an alliance of multiple cities scattered around the Yucatán Peninsula. This meant that the invaders had to fight individual strongholds to bring the Maya under their control. The conflict lasted 170 years and only ended in 1697 when the last Maya city—Tayasal in modern-day Guatemala—was defeated.

Conquest of the Americas

When Europeans first traveled to the Americas in the late 15th century, Indigenous cultures thrived in modern-day Mexico and Central and South America. Stories of their wealth soon reached Europe, and Spanish explorers flocked to the new lands. They invaded these territories, ultimately leading to the collapse of the Indigenous civilizations.

By the 16th century, Indigenous cultures such as the Aztecs and Inca (see pp.92–93), and Maya (see pp.38–39) had developed sophisticated civilizations. However, they were not prepared for the European invaders, who arrived armed with guns, wearing armor, and riding horses. An even bigger threat came from new diseases brought into the Americas from Europe, such as smallpox, that killed hundreds of thousands.

The Spaniards made use of internal rivalries to conquer Mexico and other parts of the Americas with Indigenous support. Once the native populations had been defeated, the Spanish set about colonizing the conquered lands. The Spanish government introduced a system called *encomienda*, in which conquered Indigenous laborers worked for the settlers, and were taught the Christian faith. Spanish settlers took advantage of this arrangement, treating the Indigenous workers horribly. The system only lasted a few decades in some places, but was not abolished throughout the Spanish Empire until the late 18th century.

BARTOLOMÉ DE LAS CASAS

A Spanish missionary and historian, Bartolomé de las Casas (c. 1474–1566) was shocked at the cruel treatment of the Indigenous people by Spanish colonists. Determined to stop this exploitation, he documented it in a report to the Spanish king, Charles V. As a result the government made laws that gave some protection to Indigenous people.

▼ NEW DISEASES

Spanish invaders and settlers carried many new diseases, such as smallpox, influenza, measles, chickenpox, and typhus, that spread quickly among the Indigenous people of the Americas. Since they had no natural immunity to these diseases, many who got sick died. Almost 80 percent of the Aztec and Inca population died from such diseases, which allowed the Spanish to conquer the rest easily.

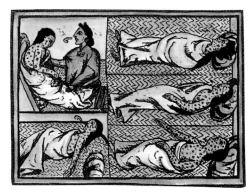

▲ ATAHUALPA

The last Inca emperor Atahualpa (reigned 1532–1533) was deeply respected by his people in Peru. In 1532, he agreed to hold an interview with Spanish conqueror Francisco Pizarro, at which the Spaniards launched an unexpected attack. Atahualpa was taken prisoner and later killed.

◄ SPANISH SILVER

Although the Spanish came seeking gold, they discovered the world's largest supply of silver in the mountains of Potosí (in modern-day Bolivia). Huge quantities of silver were taken to Spain to cover the cost of the country's wars in Europe. The silver from Potosí was used to mint Spanish dollar coins (left) called "pieces of eight."

▼ PORTUGAL AND BRAZIL

Portuguese explorer Pedro Álvares Cabral was on his way to India in 1500 when he accidentally found Brazil and claimed it for Portugal (see p.109). This marked the start of extensive colonization of Brazil by Portuguese settlers. In 1549, the city of Salvador (below) was established by the Portuguese as the first capital of Brazil.

▲ CHRISTIANITY

The colonization of the Americas involved bringing the native people into the fold of the Catholic Church. Indigenous practices and beliefs were not tolerated. Their temples were either destroyed or replaced with buildings such as this Jesuit church in Cuzco, Peru, built on top of an Inca ceremonial building.

The Safavids

In 1501, a 14-year-old boy called Ismail seized control of Persia (modern-day Iran). Over the next 200 years, the Safavid Dynasty he founded ruled over one of the greatest empires to emerge from the region. At its height, the Safavid Empire controlled large parts of Turkey, the Caucasus region between Asia and Europe, and parts of western Asia.

The Safavids were followers of a branch of Islam called Shia. This set them at odds with the followers of other branches of Islam, most notably the Sunni rulers of the Ottoman Empire, their rivals in the region. Rivalry between the two empires led to a series of wars.

The Safavid Empire was located along the Silk Road, the trade route that connected the Far East and Europe. The empire developed busy ports and markets and grew rich by charging foreign traders to use them.

Art and architecture flourished under Safavid rule. The shahs (kings) ordered the building of grand cities,

with large mosques covered in calligraphy and multi-colored tiles. Craftworkers and artists produced fine metalwork, ceramics, and textiles, which were in great demand in markets across Asia and Europe.

The empire reached its peak under Shah Abbas I, but began declining after his death in 1629. A century later, in 1736, Shah Tahmasp II was deposed by one of his military commanders and the dynasty's rule came to an end.

WARS WITH THE OTTOMANS

1532–1555	A land dispute leads to war between the Ottomans and the Safavids. The Ottomans emerge as victors, and gain large parts of western Asia.
1578–1590	The Safavids are in chaos after the death of the shah. Taking advantage, the Ottomans attack and capture Safavid territories in the Caucasus.
1603–1618	Led by Shah Abbas I, the Safavids attack and regain territories in the Caucasus and western Iran that had been lost to the Ottomans.
1623–1639	In the final war between the two empires, the Ottomans gain complete control over the region now known as Iraq.

◀ SHAH ABBAS I
After its formation, the Safavid Empire was frequently at war. The reign of the fifth shah, Abbas I, brought stability. He set up a permanent army, reclaimed lands lost in previous wars, encouraged trade, and welcomed foreigners into his court.

SHAH MOSQUE ▶
In 1590, Abbas I moved the capital of his empire to the city of Isfahan. The new capital was rebuilt and filled with buildings that displayed the empire's wealth. At its center was the beautifully tiled Masjid-e-shah, *or Shah Mosque, which was the tallest building in the city.*

Mosaics of colored tiles

▲ THE SHAHNAMA

Safavid artists produced some of the finest illuminated manuscripts of the period. These hand-decorated books often contained detailed paintings of scenes from folk or historical stories. Tales from the Shahnama (Book of Kings), an epic poem by the 10th-century Persian poet Ferdowsi, were very popular. The illustrations for these stories linked the Safavid shahs to ancient Persian rulers to make them appear as heroes.

▲ PERSIAN RUGS

During the Safavid period, carpet weaving expanded to become an important industry. Carpets woven from silk and gold contained a combination of flower and geometric patterns. They were exported to markets all over Europe, and even as far as China.

FACT
Coffeehouses were important gathering places in Safavid Iran, where ordinary folk met to smoke hookahs (water pipes), drink coffee, and listen to poets reciting their work.

Metal decorated with gold

GOLD AND METAL JUG

ART AND CRAFTS

Safavid arts and crafts were inspired by the work of the Ottomans and the Chinese. The most well known are tiles decorated with beautiful calligraphy or using the *haft-rangi* ("seven-color") technique. Also popular were Chinese-inspired blue and white ceramics, woven carpets, and intricate metalwork.

CERAMIC DRINKING VESSEL

Honeycomb-like ceiling design

CALLIGRAPHY ON THE MASJID-E-SHAH, ISFAHAN

GLAZED DECORATIVE TILE

Playing games

Throughout history, humans have devised ways to entertain themselves using objects such as cards, counters, boards, and dice. Over millennia these have evolved into the games we know today, from traditional sets with simple rules and basic pieces, all the way to modern electronic consoles with advanced technology and lifelike interactive graphics.

Pit and pebble game
Mancala

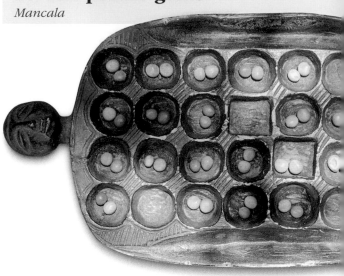

Strategy game
Chess

Where Asia
When c. 600 CE

Many countries claim to have invented chess but one forerunner of the game appeared in India in the 7th century. Over the centuries chess has evolved and spread across the globe, becoming one of the most popular strategy games. It is played with two players who take turns to move 16 pieces to attack each other's king. The aim is to trap the king into checkmate, so that it cannot move to safety.

Card game
Chinese playing cards

Where China
When 9th century CE

The earliest known playing cards are believed to have originated in China during the Tang Dynasty (see pp.66–67), though how games with these cards were played is not known today. The modern pack of 52 playing cards, with hearts, spades, diamonds, and clubs, developed much later, in France during the 15th century.

Decorative cards were made of flexible cardboard.

Word game
Crossword

Where US
When 1913

The first crossword puzzle was published in the Sunday supplement of the *New York World* newspaper. A series of written clues help the player complete a grid of horizontal and vertical missing words. Crosswords are not only entertaining, but also expand vocabulary and aid brain development.

Ancient board game
Royal Game of Ur

Where Africa and Asia
When 3000–1000 BCE

Among the world's oldest games, mancala is a fast-paced, two-player game of skill and strategy in which pebbles are moved across a board pitted with holes. The aim of the game is to capture the opponent's pebbles. Different versions of this game exist and the rules and number of players can vary across regions.

All seven of these pieces need to move across the board.

Where Mesopotamia (modern-day Iraq)
When c. 2600 BCE

Also known as the Game of Twenty Squares, the Royal Game of Ur has players competing to move their pieces to the other side of the board first, based on rolls of a four-sided dice. Many versions of this board game have been discovered across eastern Europe, the Middle East, and North Africa.

Tile-laying game
Mahjong

Where China
When c. 1850

The classic game of mahjong challenges four players to make sets out of tiles engraved with symbols depicting Chinese characters, circles, bamboo stalks, dragons, winds, seasons, and flowers. The winner is the person who scores the most points based on their final hand of tiles.

Modern board game
Monopoly

Where US
When 1904

US author Elizabeth Magie created The Landlord's Game to explain the unfairness of the property system, and the game later inspired Monopoly. The aim is to move around a board buying up properties, while trying to make opponents go bankrupt. Modern versions of Monopoly feature famous street names from major cities.

Role-playing game
Dungeons & Dragons

Where US
When 1974

The fantasy role-playing game of Dungeons & Dragons invites players to create fantastic stories using their own imaginations. One player is the Dungeon Master, who runs the game and creates the world of the story, while the other players take on the role of heroes to go on quests, battle monsters, and find treasures.

Video game console
PlayStation

Where Japan
When 1994

The first generation of home computer consoles appeared in the 1970s, but gaming technology vastly improved over the next few decades. In 1994, Sony released the PlayStation in Japan. It made history as the first console to sell more than 100 million units, bringing the joy of video games to more people than ever before.

The Reformation

In 1517, Martin Luther wrote his *Ninety-Five Theses*—a list of complaints against the Catholic Church—and sent them to the Archbishop of Mainz. Luther was a German monk and professor of theology, and his act of protest launched the Reformation, a movement of religious change that permanently divided Christianity in Europe.

In the early 1500s, the Catholic Church was the only branch of Christianity in western Europe, as it had been for 1,000 years. At its head was the Pope in Rome, and under him were bishops, priests, and monks. The Church had religious power over all men and women, from kings to peasants. Some people, however, were beginning to challenge the Church's authority. They accused the Pope and other Church leaders of greed and questioned their right to decide how people worshipped God. Printed copies of the *Theses* spread quickly across Europe, winning widespread support. As the Reformation grew, the Church split in two, with Catholics on one side and the reformers, who called themselves Protestants, on the other. Religious differences divided the Protestants, too. For more than 100 years, a series of devastating religious wars raged through much of Europe.

ULRICH ZWINGLI

Ulrich Zwingli (1484–1531) was the leader of the Reformation in Switzerland. He wanted to simplify worship and taught that the Bible was God's law. His ideas were very influential.

◀ **SELLING INDULGENCES**
In his Theses, *Martin Luther accused the Church of abusing the practice of selling "indulgences," certificates that were supposed to reduce punishment for sins in the afterlife. Luther is said to have nailed the* Theses *to a church door in Wittenberg, Germany.*

King Henry VIII hands out copies of his authorized version of the Bible in English.

▲ **TRANSLATING THE BIBLE**
The early reformers translated the Bible— believed to be the direct word of God— from Latin into the common European languages to make it available to all. A copy of an English translation of the Bible was placed in every church in England.

◀ PEACE OF AUGSBURG

In Germany, Holy Roman Emperor Charles V, a devout Catholic, led the attacks against Luther. But many German princes became Protestants. In an attempt to end this religious conflict, the Peace of Augsburg (1555) agreed that each German prince was free to decide which religion his subjects should follow.

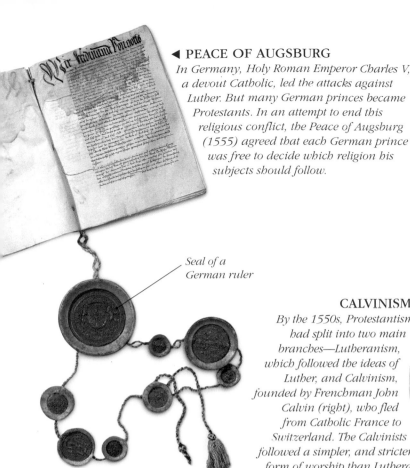

Seal of a German ruler

COUNCIL OF TRENT ▲

Alarmed by the spread of Protestantism, Pope Paul II gathered Catholic leaders to meet several times between 1545 and 1563. This "Council of Trent" launched the Counter Reformation to strengthen the loyalty of Church members. Churches were built in an ornate style and music was encouraged to make worship more attractive.

CALVINISM ▶

By the 1550s, Protestantism had split into two main branches—Lutheranism, which followed the ideas of Luther, and Calvinism, founded by Frenchman John Calvin (right), who fled from Catholic France to Switzerland. The Calvinists followed a simpler, and stricter, form of worship than Lutherans.

WARS OF RELIGION

Both Catholics and Protestants carried out violent acts during the religious wars that followed the Reformation. The wars were mainly fought in Germany, France, and the Netherlands and did not come to an end until 1648. Catholic Spanish soldiers can be seen here sacking the Protestant city of Antwerp in the Netherlands in 1576.

The Mughal Empire

When a warlord from Central Asia named Babur invaded northern India in the early 1520s, he set the stage for one of the greatest empires the world had ever seen. Over the next 300 years, the Mughal Empire he established conquered much of modern-day Afghanistan, Pakistan, India, and Bangladesh. By the 18th century, however, Mughal power had begun to decline.

Armed with matchlocks (early guns) and powerful cannons, Babur and his army had arrived in India searching for a new kingdom. He overthrew the unpopular Lodhi Sultanate in Delhi in 1526 and established the rule of the Mughals. After Babur's initial victories, his descendants extended their empire across much of the Indian subcontinent.

Under the Mughals, Islamic art and culture flourished. Many of the grandest monuments still standing in India and Pakistan today date from Mughal times.

After the death of the sixth Mughal emperor Aurangzeb in 1707, the empire began to crumble. Shivaji, ruler of the rival Marathas, was the first to defeat the Mughal armies. Then came the East India Company, a powerful British trading corporation, with its own private army. The British slowly grabbed territory as their own until they overthrew the last Mughal emperor in 1857.

FACT
The official language of the Mughal court was Persian. Arabic was used for religious prayer and ceremonies while Urdu came to be spoken by the intellectual elites, poets, and saints.

NUR JAHAN

Royal women did not hold much power in the Mughal court, but Nur Jahan (1577–1645), was an exception. The wife of Emperor Jahangir, she was a poet, a skilled hunter, a diplomat, and an art lover. She advised her husband and might have even made political decisions on Jahangir's behalf.

◀ **MUGHAL ARCHITECTURE**
The Mughals built many majestic forts and beautiful tombs. Made of red sandstone and white marble, Humayun's Tomb in Delhi is one of their most elegant early monuments. Its architectural style, with domes and arches, was copied in later buildings, such as the magnificent Taj Mahal, a tomb built by Shah Jahan for his wife Mumtaz Mahal.

MAJOR EMPERORS

1526–1530	1530–1556	1556–1605
After defeating the last Sultan of Delhi at the first Battle of Panipat, Babur goes on to gain more territory in northern India. But his rule is unstable, and when he dies he leaves a kingdom of fighting tribes.	Soon after taking the throne, Babur's son Humayun loses much of his kingdom and is forced into exile in Persia. After 15 years, he reclaims his empire with the help of the Persians, but dies within a year of doing so.	Akbar is considered the greatest Mughal emperor. He restores Mughal rule in the territories lost by his father, promotes art and culture, and encourages harmony between Hindus and Muslims.

◄ MUGHAL TERRITORY

The Mughals expanded into neighboring independent kingdoms. The rulers of these lands were either defeated in battle, given a place in the Mughal government, or made to sign peace treaties (agreements). By the time of Babur's great-great-great-grandson, Aurangzeb, the empire stretched from present-day Afghanistan to southern India.

KEY
- ▮ Mughal Empire under Babur
- ▮ Mughal Empire under Aurangzeb

SHAH JAHAN ▲

The fifth Mughal emperor, Shah Jahan came to power in 1628. Music, art, and architecture thrived under his rule, in a golden age for Mughal culture. In this painting, Shah Jahan sits in his durbar (court), with his son Aurangzeb saluting him on the left.

◄ FLORAL ART

Colorful designs showing flowers and animals were very popular in Mughal art, and were also used in architecture, textiles, and even jewelery. This 18th-century pendant, worn around the neck, is inlaid with gold, pearls, and precious stones.

1605–1627	**1628–1658**	**1658–1707**
Jahangir focuses on managing the empire. He permits the British to trade in India, which leads to the eventual fall of the Mughals.	Shah Jahan executes his brothers to win the throne. His reign is peaceful, and his passion for building leads to the creation of some of the empire's finest monuments.	During Aurangzeb's reign, the Mughal Empire expands to its greatest extent. However, it is plagued by rebellions, and begins to decline after Aurangzeb's death.

AURANGZEB

The Scientific Revolution

In the 16th and 17th centuries, groundbreaking scientific discoveries and developments revolutionized our understanding of the world. The Scientific Revolution got underway when European thinkers—mostly men as women were barred from studying—began to challenge the opinions of ancient philosophers and the accepted beliefs of Christianity. This gave rise to a new "scientific method," based on the principle that ideas need to be tested with experiments to see if they are true.

Copernican revolution
Nicolaus Copernicus

Where Poland
When 1543

Our understanding of the universe was transformed by Polish astronomer Nicolaus Copernicus, who argued that the planets rotated around the sun. His revolutionary ideas were published in the book *On the Revolutions of the Celestial Spheres*, which sparked a lot of controversy because they challenged the belief supported by the Christian Church that Earth was the centre of the universe.

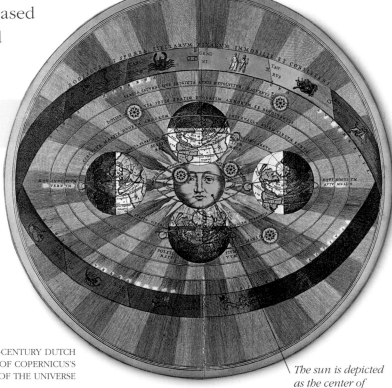

17TH-CENTURY DUTCH ENGRAVING OF COPERNICUS'S MODEL OF THE UNIVERSE

The sun is depicted as the center of the universe.

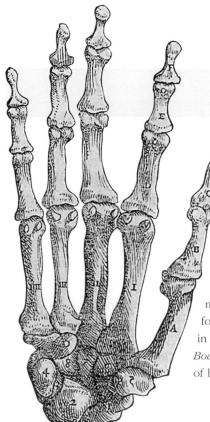

Human anatomy
Andreas Vesalius

Where Switzerland
When 1543

Physician Andreas Vesalius thought that the only way to understand the human body was to see inside it. While studying in Italy and Switzerland, he spent a lot of time dissecting (cutting up) the bodies of executed criminals and made accurate drawings of what he found. His illustrations were published in *On the Structure of the Human Body*, which revolutionized the study of human anatomy.

Compound microscope
Hans and Zacharias Janssen

Where Netherlands
When early 1590s

Dutch father and son Hans and Zacharias Janssen found that looking through lenses placed at both ends of a tube made objects appear bigger. Although the magnification of their pioneering compound microscope (a microscope with more than one lens) was limited, it was the first step in opening up the invisible world of microorganisms.

Galileo's telescope
Galileo Galilei

Where Italy
When 1593–1610

Italian astronomer Galileo Galilei was the first person to use a telescope to study the night sky. His observations revealed spots on the sun, mountains on the moon, and three of Jupiter's largest moons. They also proved beyond doubt that Copernicus's theories were correct.

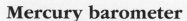

Scientific method
Francis Bacon

Where England
When 1620

An influential politician, English philosopher Francis Bacon was also a keen scientist. In his book *New Method*, he argued that scientific knowledge was key to improving human life, and that the way to establish scientific facts was by careful observation. His thinking was the basis of the modern scientific method, which uses experiments to make new discoveries.

Mercury barometer
Evangelista Torricelli

Where Italy
When 1643

Italian physicist Evangelista Torricelli invented the mercury barometer, the first device that could accurately measure atmospheric pressure—the weight of all the air around us in the atmosphere. Since this pressure changes in different weather conditions, the barometer paved the way for future scientists to develop accurate weather forecasts.

Boyle's law
Robert Boyle

Where England
When 1662

Irish scientist Robert Boyle developed an air pump (right) to study the behavior of gases. This led him to discover Boyle's law, which explains how adding pressure to gas decreases its volume. Boyle's many discoveries, reached through experimentation, helped confirm his status as the first modern chemist.

Laws of motion
Isaac Newton

Where England
When 1687

Celebrated English scientist Isaac Newton was the first to explain how gravity—the invisible force that pulls everything toward the center of the planet—works after watching an apple fall from a tree. He described it in his book *Mathematical Principles of Natural Philosophy*, along with his three laws of motion, which explain the forces that make things move.

The Czardom of Russia

When the Grand Prince of Moscow Ivan IV came to power in 1547, he took the title of "Czar of all Russia"—"czar" meaning "supreme ruler." Over the next two centuries, Russia expanded its borders and by the time Peter I was proclaimed the first emperor of Russia in 1721, it covered a vast area that stretched across Asia to the Pacific Ocean.

Ivan IV was one of the last monarchs of the Rurik Dynasty, who had established themselves as the rulers of the region surrounding Kiev in 882 CE and gradually expanded its territory. When Ivan IV came to power, he reformed local governments and continued to grow the territory of the Duchy of Moscow through military campaigns. The Rurik Dynasty ended when Ivan IV's son Feodor I died in 1598. A period of chaos followed, which ended when Mikhail Romanov was crowned czar in 1613.

Though the Czardom of Russia was large, it was effectively landlocked, with access to the Baltic Sea controlled by Russia's enemy Sweden. Successive czars sought to expand Russian territory to the sea to allow them to develop a powerful navy and provide access to international trade. In 1581, Russia began the slow conquest of Siberia in the east, and in the early 18th century, military victories during the reign of Peter I ("Peter the Great") and Catherine the Great gained Russia access to the Baltic, Black, and Azov Seas, greatly increasing the power of the czardom.

▲ **IVAN THE TERRIBLE**
Ivan IV reigned from 1547 to 1584. In the early days of his rule, he carried out much-needed reforms such as setting up the first parliament, the Zemsky Sobor, and revising the code of law. But later, he became increasingly violent, massacring thousands he suspected of being disloyal to him and even killing his eldest son.

FACT
In 1698, in an effort to modernize society on the lines of Western Europe, Peter the Great introduced a tax on beards and robes to get his courtiers to dress like Europeans.

EVERYDAY LIFE

In czarist times, the majority of Russians were serfs—unfree people who worked on the land for their lords in return for a small amount of produce. Like enslaved people, serfs had very limited rights. Serfdom was abolished in Russia in 1861.

▼ **EXPANSION OF RUSSIA**
From its heartland in eastern Europe, the Russian czardom expanded east into Siberia from around 1600 onward, reaching the Pacific coast in 1649. It also pushed south into Central Asia and the Caucasus, and west into Swedish- and Polish-held territories.

SWEDEN
Baltic Sea
POLAND
St. Petersburg
Moscow
Azov Sea
Black Sea
Caspian Sea
PERSIA
AFGHANISTAN
Tashkent
Altai Mountains
MONGOLIA
Beijing
QING EMPIRE
Ural Mountains
SIBERIA
RUSSIAN EMPIRE
Arctic Ocean
Wrangel Island
Bering Strait
Pacific Ocean
Vladivostok
Sea of Japan
KOREA
JAPAN

KEY
Russian territory c.1600
Expansion, 1600–1725

▲ THE TIME OF TROUBLES

After Feodor I died childless in 1598, Russia entered a period of disorder called the "time of troubles." A terrible famine in 1601–1603 killed about one-third of the population, while a series of impostors tried to take the throne, claiming to be Feodor's half-brother Dmitri. One such "false Dmitri" gathered an army on the edge of Moscow (above) but his planned attack on the city failed.

GOLD CROWN
OF MIKHAIL I

ROMANOV DYNASTY ▶

The Romanovs were a family of nobles whose first link to the Russian throne came when a young Romanov woman married Ivan IV in 1547. The Romanovs became the ruling royal family when a reluctant 16-year-old Mikhail Romanov accepted the crown in 1613, starting a new dynasty that was to rule Russia until 1917.

PETER THE GREAT

Peter I (reigned 1682–1725) was the first czar to travel widely in western Europe. Influenced by Western ideas, he reformed the military and built new roads, slowly transforming Russia into a major European state.

◀ ST. PETERSBURG

Founded by Peter the Great in 1703, the city of St. Petersburg became the capital of Russia in 1712. The czar intended the city to be a "Window on the West"—a major center for trading with European countries. The city has many fine palaces and beautiful buildings. Like many of these landmarks, the Summer Palace (left) of Empress Elizabeth, daughter of Peter the Great, was built in the Baroque style, then very popular across Europe.

▲ DUTCH EAST INDIA COMPANY

In 1602, a group of Dutch businesses came together to form the Dutch East India Company, which was given sole right to trade with Mughal India (see pp.120–121) and the Moluccas (Spice Islands) of Southeast Asia. Within a few years it had set up its headquarters in Batavia (modern-day Jakarta), Indonesia, from where its vast fleets carried spices and other goods to Europe. It was also involved in the international trade of enslaved people. The company quickly grew into the largest in the world, with the power to raise armies, start wars, and establish new colonies in several parts of the world, including Sri Lanka, Malaya (Malacca), and South Africa (Cape Town).

The Dutch Golden Age

In the late 16th century, the Netherlands—then part of the Spanish Empire—began a long fight for independence. The Dutch Republic was founded in 1588 and, based on its people's unrivaled shipbuilding expertise and clever business skills, soon became a leading economic power. This prosperity brought in a golden age of Dutch culture.

The largely Protestant Dutch had first revolted against the rule of Catholic Spain in 1568. The war lasted on and off for 80 years until the Dutch finally gained their independence in 1648.

By this time, the Dutch Republic had become a formidable seafaring power with a strong navy, and a massive

◀ DUTCH PAINTING

Artists such as Rembrandt and Johannes Vermeer experimented with new techniques to paint realistic portraits, landscapes, and domestic scenes. Vermeer's "Girl With A Pearl Earring" (left) has inspired poems, novels, and films.

merchant fleet trading spices and other rare goods around the world. Dutch merchants created the first central bank and stock exchange, and set up vast international trading companies.

The Dutch used their newfound wealth to build beautiful canal-side houses, and commissioned paintings from some of the finest artists in the world. This was also a period of scientific and intellectual discovery, with advances in astronomy, biology, engineering, international law, and philosophy.

◀ SCIENTIFIC PROGRESS

Dutch scientists made groundbreaking scientific discoveries and inventions in the 17th century. In 1608, Hans Lippershey invented the first telescope, and in the 1670s Antonie van Leeuwenhoek became the first person to study microscopic life using an advanced microscope he'd designed (left).

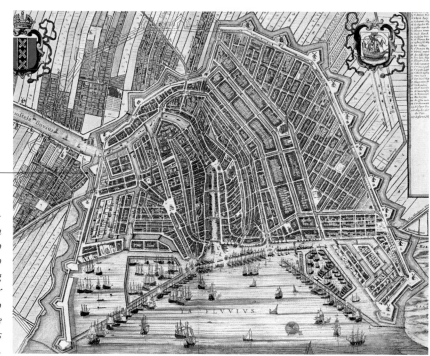

Zig-zag shaped outer canal

RINGS OF CANALS ▶

Now the Dutch capital, Amsterdam was the leading city of the Dutch Republic. As it grew in the 17th century, three major canals were dug in rings around the medieval center (shown on this map partway through construction). Overlooking them, fine townhouses were built for the city's wealthiest inhabitants to live in.

DUTCH INDEPENDENCE

1568
The 17 provinces of the Spanish Netherlands rise in rebellion against their Spanish Catholic rulers, starting the Eighty Years' War for independence.

1581
Seven northern Dutch provinces—all Protestant—formally announce their independence from Spain.

1588
The United Provinces of the Netherlands—the Dutch Republic—is established as a federal republic (a union of states joined together under an elected government).

1648
The Dutch Republic is recognized as an independent country by the Peace of Münster, a treaty signed between the Netherlands and Spain.

1672
The Dutch Republic has to fight for its independence when it finds itself at war against France and Britain—a period known as the *Rampjaar* (Disaster Year).

Red and white "broken tulips" were the most valuable during "Tulip Mania."

◀ TULIP MANIA

As new and rare objects were introduced to Dutch society, they were traded on the stock market. In the 1630s, an obsession with trading tulip bulbs—then an exotic new import from Turkey—gripped Amsterdam's middle classes, increasing their price sharply. Some people even sold their homes to buy bulbs. Then, in 1637, the price of tulip bulbs suddenly crashed, and many of those who had got involved lost a fortune. It was the first stock market crash.

▼ STOCK EXCHANGE

The economic system known as capitalism first emerged in the Netherlands in the early 1600s. The world's first central bank was set up in Amsterdam in 1609, and the first stock exchange (below) was built in the city in 1611. It was a place for traders to buy and sell stocks (shares of ownership) in the newly created trading companies.

UKIYO-E

The Japanese art form of ukiyo-e, *which means "pictures of the floating world," flourished between the 17th and 19th centuries. These prints depicted everyday life in Edo Japan, such as this market street scene.*

▲ KABUKI

Kabuki was a type of theatrical performance with extravagant costumes, makeup, wigs, and masks. Originally women played all the roles, but they were soon banned from the stage and performances became all-male.

Edo Japan

Japan's Edo period was a time of peace, when art and culture flourished and the economy boomed following centuries of war and unrest. Even when the country closed itself off from the wider world, Japan continued to thrive, and many innovations that developed during this time, from *ukiyo-e* art to sumo wrestling, are still part of Japan's modern cultural identity.

The Edo period began in 1603 when Tokugawa Ieyasu moved his capital to Edo (modern-day Tokyo) after reunifying Japan and becoming shogun (see p.74). The Great Peace followed—a marked change after years of warfare between competing *daimyo* (feudal lords).

Right from the start, the shogun was extremely wary of foreign influences. Christianity was rising rapidly in popularity, spurred on by Portuguese missionaries, and this was seen as a threat to the Buddhist way of life. Christianity was banned in 1614 and its followers were tortured, executed, or both.

Shortly after, in 1635, *sakoku* came into effect—a policy that isolated Japan from the rest of the world. Limited trade with a small number of nations continued, but hardly anyone was allowed in or out of the country. This policy remained in place until the Meiji Restoration (see pp.168–169) in 1868, which brought the Tokugawa shogunate and the Edo period to an end.

SUMO WRESTLING ▶

While sumo wrestling had existed for more than 1,000 years, its popularity soared during the Edo period. Tournaments were originally organized by temples that built huge temporary stadiums to host large crowds. It is now Japan's national sport.

EDO CRAFTS

The Edo period saw a boom in craftwork such as *imari* porcelain, which featured delicate decorations. Also popular were small cases known as *inro*, which were worn around the waist of a kimono (robe), and miniature sculptures called *netsuke*.

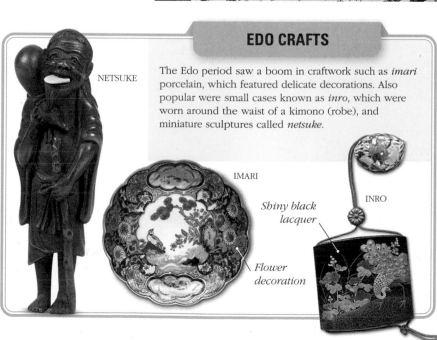

NETSUKE

IMARI

INRO

Shiny black lacquer

Flower decoration

▶ SKILLED ENTERTAINERS

Geishas are female performers who go through strict training to become skilled in a number of art forms, including dancing, singing, and poetry. Known for their traditional costumes and eye-catching white makeup, geishas still perform today.

Colonial North America

After the voyages of Christopher Columbus to the Caribbean, and Central and South America, Europeans began to become interested in the vast landmass to the north. The first explorers mapped the coasts and rivers of North America. But they were soon followed by Europeans looking to settle on the continent, seeking riches and a fresh start.

As settlements and trading posts grew, more and more Europeans began to sail across the Atlantic Ocean, lured by stories of gold or fertile lands. Many also came in search of a better life, to earn a living, as well as maintain their identity—most notably the English settlers known as the Pilgrims, who set up the Plymouth colony in modern-day Massachusetts in 1620.

But North America was home to many Indigenous communities. As the Europeans began taking native people's land for their colonies, conflict arose between the two. The deadliest war, fought between English settlers and Indigenous groups led by the Wampanoag people, ended with the colonists killing about 3,000 native people and burning their towns. There were also conflicts between European powers for control over regions.

Despite this, the colonies prospered by trading furs and other products with Europe and growing tobacco, cotton, rice, and grain for export.

▲ **EARLY EUROPEAN EXPLORERS**
The first European explorer to reach the continent after Columbus was John Cabot. An Italian navigator sent by the king of England, Cabot reached the east coast of Canada in 1497. Later, French explorer Jacques Cartier became the first to map the St. Lawrence River (above) in Canada after making three voyages to the region between 1534 and 1542.

▲ **COLONIAL SETTLEMENTS**
Over five centuries after the Vikings first made their way to North America, the Spanish set up a trading colony in Florida in 1565. The English set up colonies along the east coast after 1584, while the French began to colonize Canada in 1608. The Dutch colony of New Amsterdam (above), set up in 1626, was captured by the English in 1664. They renamed it New York.

POCAHONTAS

Daughter of a chief of the Powhatan people, Pocahontas (c.1596–1617) was captured by colonists from Jamestown. She later married John Rolfe, an English tobacco planter, and became an ambassador and translator between the two peoples. In 1616, Pocahontas travelled to England where she met King James I and became famous, but she died before the return home.

▼ EARLY INTERACTIONS

The Indigenous peoples of North America had advanced civilizations. They had mastered farming and traded furs, animal skins, and precious stones. Despite conflicts with the European colonizers, some Indigenous peoples traded with the newcomers and taught them how to farm and survive.

Thatched cottage in a reconstruction of Jamestown

▲ THE THIRTEEN COLONIES

Jamestown in modern-day Virginia was the first permanent English colony in North America, established in 1607. The English had established 12 more colonies along the coast by 1733, and these settlements gradually extended inland. The Thirteen Colonies, as they came to be known, developed into strong trading and agricultural communities, and even established their own laws.

◄ EUROPEAN CONFLICTS

In the first half of the 18th century, North America became a battleground for European powers as colonists from France, Britain, and Spain fought to seize each other's lands, often supported by rival native peoples (left). By 1763, after the French had suffered a succession of major losses, Britain came to control almost all of North America.

▲ ROAD TO REVOLUTION

After the costly battles against the French, the British government forced their North American colonies to pay heavy new taxes. Matters came to a head in 1773 when colonists in Boston threw chests of tea into the harbor (above) to protest a tea tax. The government's attempts to punish those responsible resulted in a popular rebellion against Britain, leading to the American Revolution (see pp.150–151).

◀ **FORTS OF ENSLAVEMENT**
Enslaved Africans were brought to the coast of West Africa. Here, they were held in captivity in forts or castles, such as the Cape Coast Castle in Ghana (left). For most of them, these buildings were their last memories of Africa before being shipped off to the colonies.

The transatlantic slave trade

The settlement of new European colonies in the Americas led to the horrific enslavement of Africans. From the 16th to the mid-19th century, more than 12 million Africans were bought or kidnapped from their homes to be sold into a lifetime of hard labor. This has become known as the Ma'afa, a Kiswahili term meaning "great tragedy."

Ravaged by war, plague, and famine in the 15th century, Europe needed fresh resources and found them in their newly established colonies in the Americas. But to gather these resources, labor was needed that could work the fields and mines.

Traders from Portugal, soon followed by other European countries, found a grim solution to this problem in Africa, and began buying human beings from Africa's western coast.

People were enslaved and shipped off to the colonies, and those who survived the journey were sold at auctions into a life of misery.

The riches extracted from the colonies made the West incredibly wealthy. Meanwhile, generations of enslaved Africans—and their descendants—struggled to fight for their rightful place in society as human beings worthy of dignity.

Up to 600 enslaved people had to lie on their backs to fit into the cramped space.

THE MIDDLE PASSAGE ▶
Once bought, captured Africans were chained in the lower deck of a ship for transport to the Americas. Called the "middle passage," this journey could take up to 11 weeks and there was limited food, water, and sanitation available. Many did not survive the harsh journey.

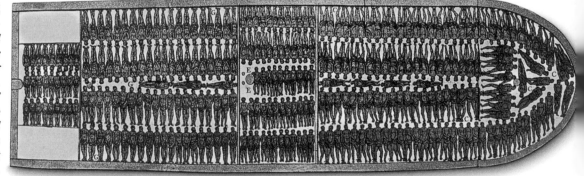

◀ PLANTATIONS

Enslaved Africans were sold in large numbers to work on sugar plantations (left). Jamaica was one of the main sugar-producing islands in the Caribbean, and by the mid-18th century, it held more than 100,000 enslaved Africans. As the population of the enslaved workers grew, so did the size and numbers of plantations in the Americas.

Heavy iron bars made the collar hard to move.

▲ ENSLAVED LIFE

The working day for an enslaved person lasted from dawn till dusk. During harvest periods, they would be forced to work 18-hour days. Those who tried to escape were often brutally beaten and many were shackled with an iron collar (above) around their neck.

▲ MAROON RESISTANCE

Maroons were communities of formerly enslaved people in the Caribbean islands who managed to escape. They lived deep in mountains or forests to hide from those who hunted them. They would raid plantations and help other enslaved people escape, and often fought against colonial forces.

OLAUDAH EQUIANO

Born in the Kingdom of Benin (in modern-day Nigeria), Olaudah Equiano (1745–1797) was enslaved around the age of 11. He bought his freedom at 21 and settled in Britain where he became a leading voice against slavery.

FIGHTING FOR FREEDOM ▶

From the West African coast to plantations in the Americas, there are many recorded instances of rebellions by enslaved Africans. In 1839, a group of kidnapped Africans sailing on a ship called the Amistad *took control of it and killed the captain (right). They reached the US, where they won a legal case against their enslavers, and were sent back home to Africa.*

1750–1900

Between the 18th and 19th centuries, the world was transformed through different kinds of revolutions. The United States of America was born as settlers rebelled against colonial rule, the first of many political revolutions that took place during this period. The Industrial Revolution saw people moving from the countryside to towns and cities to work in factories, while the discovery of electricity transformed daily life for people around the world.

The European Enlightenment

The Enlightenment was a period from the mid-17th to the early 19th centuries in which writers and thinkers from Europe questioned traditional beliefs about nature, religion, and society. Its aims were summed up in the words of German philosopher Immanuel Kant—"Dare to know!"—meaning that people should have the courage to think for themselves.

The European Enlightenment, sometimes called the Age of Reason, was influenced by the ideas of 17th-century French thinker René Descartes (see p.139), who argued that reason (logical thought) is the source of all knowledge, and that everything should be doubted until it could be proven. This inspired a new scientific approach to solving problems, and through devising experiments into natural phenomena, scientists such as Isaac Newton made breakthroughs that changed our understanding of the world.

Political thinkers, meanwhile, argued about the way people live and how they should be governed. New ideas emerged about people's rights and equality, especially in politics and religion. They spread rapidly through coffeehouses and reading clubs, where people met to read newspapers and exchange views. In due course, some of these ideas would go on to inspire great changes and revolutions in some parts of the world.

LANGUAGE OF SCIENCE ▼

Swedish biologist Carl Linnaeus created a binomial (two-name) classification system to describe every living creature, so that scientists writing in different languages could use the same names for plants and animals. Linnaeus presented his new system in his book Systema Naturae *in 1735, and it is still in use today.*

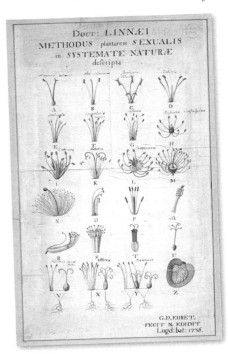

CHILD IN TIME

Even as a child, Wolfgang Amadeus Mozart (1756–1791) amazed audiences across Europe with his extraordinary musical skills. He went on to become the greatest classical composer of the era.

▼ FREE SPEECH

French writer Voltaire was famous for his fearless defense of people's right to speak freely without being punished, and for opposing slavery. He used to meet other thinkers at his house to discuss ideas (below). Voltaire often poked fun at the Church and the government, and as a result was imprisoned twice, and spent nearly 30 years in exile.

Voltaire raises his hand to make a point.

LISBON EARTHQUAKE ▶
When an earthquake destroyed the city of Lisbon in Portugal in 1755, many people believed that the devastation was God's way of punishing wrongdoers. Portuguese reformer Marquis de Pombal disagreed, and after helping rebuild the city to make it earthquake proof, he went on to modernize Portugal using Enlightenment ideas.

▲ FIRST ENCYCLOPEDIA
French thinker Denis Diderot was the chief compiler of the Encyclopedia, *one of the most influential books of the Enlightenment. It aimed to gather together all human knowledge, including Enlightenment ideas. The first volume was published in 1751.*

ELECTRIFYING EXPERIMENT
American politician Benjamin Franklin was also an enthusiastic scientist. Some people believe that in 1752 he flew a kite in a storm to prove that lightning carries an electric charge. A prolific author and publisher, Franklin helped spread Enlightenment ideas.

▲ WOMEN'S RIGHTS
In her book A Vindication of the Rights of Woman, *English writer Mary Wollstonecraft argued that girls should have the same education as boys, and that women deserved equal rights with men. She is regarded as one of the first feminists.*

Great thinkers

The pursuit of knowledge has inspired and influenced people since ancient times. The first philosophers wanted to understand the world around them and sought ways to make it a better place. Over the centuries and across the continents, new concepts and powerful theories have developed our understanding, expanded our learning, and encouraged ideas about equality, justice, and freedom.

China's great teacher
Kong Fuzi (or Confucius)

Where China
When 551–479 BCE

Ancient Chinese philosopher and politician Confucius ran a school out of his own home. His teachings were based on "Five virtues"—*Ren* (benevolence), *Yi* (righteousness), *Li* (right behavior), *Zhi* (knowledge and wisdom), and *Xin* (trustworthiness)—each crucial for a happy life. His belief system is called Confucianism, and it eventually became the state religion of China in c. 202 BCE.

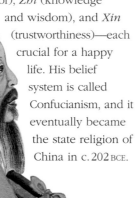

Ancient Greek thinkers
Plato and Aristotle

Plato is holding his book Timaeus.

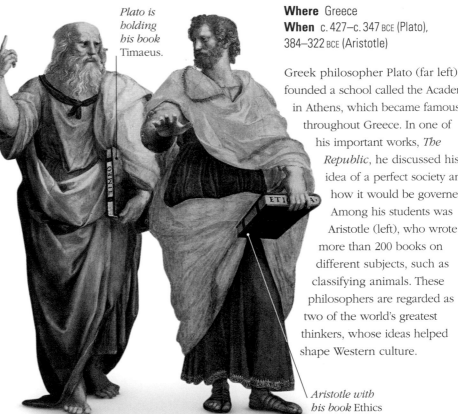

Where Greece
When c. 427–c. 347 BCE (Plato), 384–322 BCE (Aristotle)

Greek philosopher Plato (far left) founded a school called the Academy in Athens, which became famous throughout Greece. In one of his important works, *The Republic*, he discussed his idea of a perfect society and how it would be governed. Among his students was Aristotle (left), who wrote more than 200 books on different subjects, such as classifying animals. These philosophers are regarded as two of the world's greatest thinkers, whose ideas helped shape Western culture.

Aristotle with his book Ethics

Arab polymath
Abu Yusuf Ya'qub ibn Ishaq al-Sabbah al-Kindi

Where Abbasid Caliphate (modern-day Iraq)
When c. 800–870

A great scholar, al-Kindi transformed philosophy and science in the Islamic world. His extensive writings included books on the nature of God, a mathematical work about parallel lines, and a set of four books about the Indian number system. He also led a team of translators to convert the works of Greek philosophers into Arabic.

French philosopher
René Descartes

Where France
When 1596–1650

Often called "the first modern philosopher," French thinker René Descartes broke away from the ancient philosophies and took a new, scientific approach. His statement *"I think, therefore I am"* explains how his ability to think was proof of his own existence. Descartes' ideas form a starting point for much of later philosophy, but he also wrote on scientific subjects as well. His mathematical ideas inspired physicist Isaac Newton's theories on the laws of motion.

American sociologist
W. E. B Du Bois

Where US
When 1868–1963

Du Bois was a pioneer in the field of sociology. For more than a decade, he studied discrimination against Black Americans. His findings drove him to become a civil rights campaigner who fought racism and injustice. He encouraged the Black community to fight for equality through political agitation.

French feminist
Simone de Beauvoir

Where France
When 1908–1986

A great philosopher and teacher, de Beauvoir is widely regarded as the pioneer of feminism. Her best-known book, *The Second Sex* (1949), states that society tells women how to behave and controls them by ranking them lower than men. She encouraged women to choose their own path instead of conforming to society's idea of what they should be.

British philosopher
Philippa Foot

Where England
When 1920–2010

One of the leading 20th-century philosophers, Philippa Foot focused on the area of ethics (how we should behave). She was influenced by the teachings of Aristotle and shared his belief that what mattered most in people was their moral character and essential virtues. Her writings are an essential part of modern moral philosophy.

Qing China

The Qing Dynasty was the last dynasty of imperial China. It was established by the Manchu people from the modern-day region of Manchuria. In 1644, generals of the Ming dynasty asked for Manchu support to crush rebels. After defeating the rebels, the Manchu took power for themselves, occupying Beijing and establishing a new dynasty. Under Qing rule, the empire grew in strength and tripled in size.

The Manchus made up only a small percent of the entire Chinese population, so in order to rule peacefully they kept the Ming style of government but filled key posts with Manchu officials. Three remarkable emperors—Kangxi, Yongzheng, and Qianlong—ruled over a period of 134 years between 1661 and 1796. They extended Qing rule over modern-day Mongolia and much of Central Asia, and established political control over present-day Southeast Asia. These rulers also provided stability and prosperity at home.

Highly successful at first, the Qing gradually lost power during the 19th century. The empire was forced to make compromises with foreign nations, lost a war against Japan in 1895, and was rocked by two major uprisings. Eventually, revolution broke out in China and the Qing Dynasty was overthrown in 1911.

FACT
Almost all the tea in the world was grown in China until British colonizers first brought tea to the hills of northern India in the 1830s.

◀ **COMMERCIAL SUCCESS**
In the 18th century, imperial China enjoyed a booming economy. The kingdom was at peace, and its population doubled to around 300 million. It exported tea, cotton, silk, porcelain, and furniture to Southeast Asia and Europe.

Chinese workers processing tea leaves in a factory

◀ **ARTS AND CRAFTS**
Under the Qing, arts such as painting and calligraphy flourished, while Chinese craftsmanship reached new peaks. Emperor Kangxi ordered the publication of a dictionary, while Emperor Qianlong sponsored a library of Chinese writings. The Qing also produced beautiful examples of porcelain and glassware.

◀ **FOREIGN INFLUENCE**
The Qing lost a war with the British army in 1842, which forced them to hand Hong Kong Island to Britain and open up their ports to foreign traders. After another war in 1856, more ports were opened. Foreign traders were allowed to travel throughout China, bringing the whole country under increasing influence from the West.

EMPRESS DOWAGER CIXI

After the death of Emperor Xianfeng in 1861, his widow, Cixi, became regent for her son Tongzhi and then, in 1875, for her nephew Guangxu. She controlled the country for 47 years until her death in 1908. The Empress resisted Western influence, supporting the Boxer Rebellion against foreign domination, but attempted to reform Qing China during its difficult final years.

WARS AND REBELLIONS

1661–1722	The second Qing emperor Kangxi reestablishes Chinese dominance over Mongolia and Tibet. He also conquers the Kingdom of Dongning in present-day Taiwan.
1839–1842	The Qing are defeated in the First Opium War with Britain. Under the terms of the Treaty of Nanking that followed, foreign-run treaty ports open up China to international trade.
1850–1864	The long-running Taiping Rebellion to overthrow Manchu rule weakens the Qing Dynasty. Around 50 million people die during this period.
1899–1901	The Boxer Rebellion, a revolt by a peasant rebel group against foreign and Christian influence in the Qing Empire, breaks out. An international force invades Beijing to suppress it.
1911–1912	Frustrated by the slow pace of change in China, revolutionaries start uprisings across the country, leading to the fall of the Qing Dynasty.

EVERYDAY LIFE

In 1645, the Qing government ordered that all men had to wear their hair in a style called a queue. Hair on top of the scalp had to be grown long and then braided, while the front portion of the head was shaved.

▲ WAR AGAINST NAPOLEON
French emperor Napoleon I invaded Russia in 1812, but suffered heavy losses due to harsh winter conditions and food shortages. After defeating French forces at the Battle of Leipzig, Russia and its allies marched into Paris, the French capital, in March 1814, forcing Napoleon to go into exile.

CATHERINE THE GREAT

Catherine the Great (reigned 1762–1796) was a German princess who overthrew her husband, Peter III of Russia, to rule the empire in her own right. Intelligent and cultured, she promoted women's education, and established institutions for learning in Europe.

Imperial Russia

Russia became an empire in 1721 (see pp.124–125), and over the next 200 years expanded its territory and slowly emerged as a major European power. Despite this, the people of Russia were largely illiterate and poor, and by 1917 they had risen up in revolt against their rulers.

Imperial Russia was ruled by a single family, the Romanov Dynasty. Though the empire slowly industrialized, the czars failed to modernize their government and introduce reforms. The country was largely rural, and right up until the mid-19th century many ordinary people working the land were serfs—unfree people with few rights (see p.124).

Jews were forced to live in a poor region known as the Pale of Settlement. In the late 19th century, violent massacres forced many Jews to migrate to the West.

The pace of industrialization picked up in the mid-19th century, which created more jobs for people. Aware of the wide gap between rich and poor, workers began to demand more rights, leading eventually to the downfall of the Romanovs. Yet this social unrest overlapped with great artistic developments in Russia. Writers such as Leo Tolstoy and Alexander Pushkin wrote fine novels and poems, while composers like Pyotr Tchaikovsky and Igor Stravinsky created musical works that drew worldwide fame.

ROYAL REGALIA

Russian rulers were crowned in elaborate ceremonies. From the coronation of Catherine the Great in 1762 onward, all monarchs used the Great Imperial Crown, which was decorated with more than 5,000 gemstones. The last czar, Nicholas II, had the jeweled Imperial Coronation egg made for his wife, Czarina Alexandra, to celebrate his coronation.

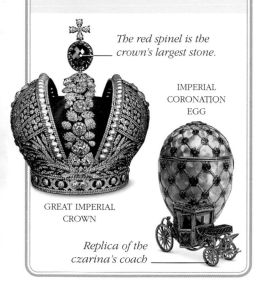

The red spinel is the crown's largest stone.

IMPERIAL CORONATION EGG

GREAT IMPERIAL CROWN

Replica of the czarina's coach

▲ THE CRIMEAN WAR

In 1853, war broke out between Russia and an alliance of France, Britain, and the Ottoman Empire. Most of the fighting took place in the Crimean Peninsula in eastern Europe. The war was one of the first to use modern technologies such as railroads to transport ammunition, but ended in defeat for Russia.

IMPERIAL RULERS

1762–1796 During the reign of Catherine the Great, the Russian Empire expands to the Black Sea coast, and takes in parts of Poland and Alaska.

1801–1825 Czar Alexander I comes to the throne after his father, Paul I, is killed. Early in his reign, he introduces many reforms that he overturns later in life.

1825–1855 Czar Nicholas I takes the throne after surviving a military revolt against him. During his reign, Russia expands its borders further and develops industry.

1855–1881 Alexander II is a liberal ruler who brings in many reforms in Russia, including freeing the serfs in 1861. He is killed in 1881.

ALEXANDER II

1881–1894 Alexander III opposes any reform that limits his power and reverses many of the new laws introduced by his father.

1894–1917 After military losses, Nicholas II quickly loses popularity and is forced to leave the throne after the revolution of 1917.

FACT
The House of Romanov was the last imperial dynasty to rule Russia. Their reign had lasted almost 300 years.

THE LAST CZAR ▼

Nicholas II was a weak ruler, who refused to modernize his country and led Russia disastrously in World War I. He was overthrown during the revolution of 1917, and along with his family (below), killed in 1918.

GRAND DUCHESS MARIA

CZARINA ALEXANDRA

GRAND DUCHESS OLGA

CZAR NICHOLAS II

GRAND DUCHESS ANASTASIA

GRAND DUCHESS TATIANA

CZAREVITCH ALEXEI

The Industrial Revolution

The invention of new technology in mid-18th-century Britain led to a period of rapid development and social change called the Industrial Revolution, which quickly spread around the world. The Industrial Revolution brought about a shift from a traditional agricultural way of life to one in which most people worked in mills, factories, and mines.

▲ COTTON PRODUCTION

The first mills were equipped with machines such as the spinning "mule," which spun fiber into thread and sped up the production of cotton. Early mills were set up by fast-flowing rivers to drive the water wheels they used for power. Later mills were powered by steam and located near coalfields. Workers—including children—spent long hours working the machines.

GEORGE STEPHENSON

Railroad pioneer George Stephenson (1781–1848) designed his first steam locomotive in 1814 to haul coal wagons. He oversaw the construction of the first public railroad in 1825, devised the standard railroad gauge (a fixed spacing between tracks), and built railroads all over Britain.

The Industrial Revolution originated in mines and in the cotton industry. New inventions such as the spinning jenny and the flying shuttle, which sped up the process of making textiles, made it possible to replace human labor with machines. Within a few decades, steam engines were being used to power machines in large factories. These engines required coal for fuel, so mines were dug deeper to meet the growing demand. Newly constructed railroads and canals carried raw materials and goods around the country, while large ships were built to export them

worldwide. Industrialization quickly spread beyond the borders of Britain. By the 1850s, the US and Germany were beginning to overtake Britain in industrial production. The Great Exhibition, held in London in 1851 to showcase industry, contained exhibits not just from Britain but from all over the world.

4. The rocking beam causes the flywheel to turn.

THE STEAM ENGINE ▶

The first steam engines wasted a lot of energy because the cylinder that powered them had to be repeatedly heated and cooled. James Watt made them more efficient by making sure the cylinder stayed hot continuously. These machines could now be used to drive machinery. Watts patented his engine in 1769 and supplied it to mills and factories.

MACHINE WRECKERS ▶

In the 1810s, put out of work by the new textile factories, gangs of traditional hand spinners and weavers began breaking into factories to destroy the machines that had deprived them of their livelihoods. They were called Luddites after their supposed leader, Ned Ludd.

▲ THE IRON BRIDGE

In the 18th century, engineers discovered ways to make iron tougher as well as easier to work with. It could then be used to construct buildings and other structures. In 1779, the world's first cast iron bridge (above) was built across the Severn River in Shropshire, England. Demand for high-quality iron soared with the success of the bridge.

◀ INDUSTRIAL SECRETS

Despite a British law banning industrial designs being taken abroad, Samuel Slater (left), an apprentice at a cotton mill, memorized the plans of an early spinning machine before sailing to the US in 1789. He used his knowledge to kick-start the US's Industrial Revolution.

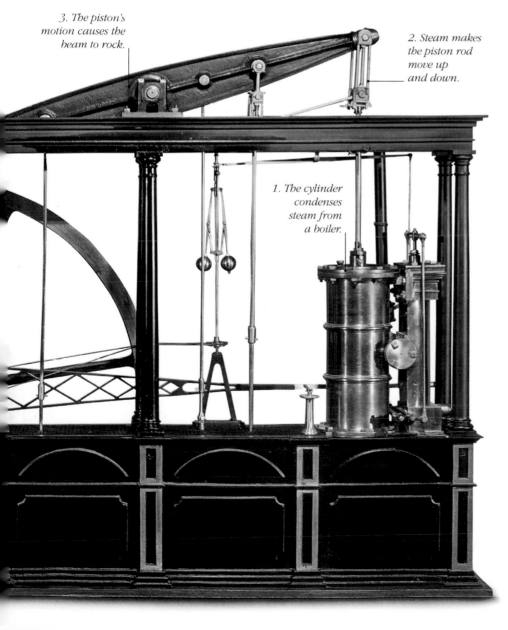

3. The piston's motion causes the beam to rock.

2. Steam makes the piston rod move up and down.

1. The cylinder condenses steam from a boiler.

THE STORY OF STEAM

1712 British engineer Thomas Newcomen builds the first engine able to harness the power of steam. It is used for pumping water out of mines.

1765 Scottish inventor James Watts improves Newcomen's design by condensing steam, which makes the engine far more efficient.

1769 Nicolas-Joseph Cugnot, a French military engineer, designs a steam-driven, self-propelled road vehicle for carrying cannons.

1804 British engineer Richard Trevithick mounts a small steam engine on wheels to create the world's first steam locomotive.

1807 In the US, Robert Fulton builds the first commercial steamboat to carry passengers on the Hudson River.

▲ RAILROAD BOOM

In 1830, the world's first railroad running services solely powered by steam locomotives opened in northwestern England. Five years later, the Ludwigs-Eisenbahn company opened the first steam-operated train line in modern-day Germany (above). By the 1840s, railroad construction was booming all over Europe, making long-distance travel quicker and easier.

LIVING IN THE CITY

The rapid industrialization of Europe, North America, and parts of Asia in the 19th century had a huge impact on society and the environment.

During the Industrial Revolution, many people moved to towns and cities from the countryside in search of work. As a result, urban areas became crowded. Factories hired more workers, including women and children—who were paid much less than men—to increase production and profit. Workers often spent long hours in cramped, dirty, poorly lit factories for very little money.

From the mid-19th century, things began to change. Workers around the world started to organize themselves into unions to demand better pay and working conditions from factory owners. They often went on strike, which sometimes led to violent riots. At around the same time advancements in technology, improved sanitation, and the development of electric power led to improvements in city life.

▼ CHILDREN AT WORK

During the industrial period, children were often employed by factories and mines to do jobs adults could not. For example, only children were small enough to squeeze between working looms to tie up broken threads or untangle fine threads. Conditions were often dangerous and serious injuries were common. In the 1830s, Prussia and Britain passed the first laws restricting working hours for children, and other countries soon followed.

THE STORY OF ELECTRICITY

1800	Italian scientist Alessandro Volta discovers that sinking two metals into acid can produce a steady electric current. This leads to his invention of the voltaic pile, the first reliable battery.
1876	Alexander Graham Bell, a Scottish-born inventor, experiments with turning sound waves into electric currents that could be sent through the wires of a telegraph—inventing the first telephone.
1879	US inventor Thomas Edison creates a long-lasting electric light bulb. It stays lit for 13½ hours.
1881	The world's first electric tram line, built by German engineer Werner von Siemens, opens in Lichterfelde near Berlin, Germany.
1882	Black American scientist Lewis Latimer invents a carbon filament that makes light bulbs cheaper and long-lasting.

LIVING CONDITIONS

City life was harsh for many people in the 19th century. The air was filled with smoke from factory chimneys, and layers of soot covered everything. The poor lived in crowded slum areas, where houses were badly built and the lack of clean water and proper waste disposal meant that infectious diseases, such as cholera and typhoid, could spread rapidly.

BETTER EDUCATION ▶

Most children born into poverty didn't go to school and grew up not knowing how to read or write. In New Lanark, Scotland, a textile manufacturer called Robert Owen built good-quality housing for his mill workers and set up a school (right) to provide their children with an education.

CHARLES DICKENS

Charles Dickens (1812–1870), was the most popular novelist of 19th-century Britain. His books were entertaining but also focused on the social problems of the day, such as the terrible conditions in city slums, bad treatment of children, and unfair laws that punished the poor.

WENTWORTH WORKS

▲ **WORKHOUSES**

Unemployed poor people, including widows, orphans, and the old or sick, were forced into workhouses (known as poorhouses in the US). Most were expected to work for their shelter and food. Some workhouses were well run, but in many the conditions were terrible. Families were split up and people were often treated no better than prisoners.

▲ **IMPROVED SANITATION**

In the 19th century, it was common for human waste to end up in rivers, which caused disease because rivers were also used for drinking and washing. In 1858, British engineer Joseph Bazalgette (center) designed a groundbreaking new sewage system in London, which diverted filthy water into underground brick tunnels and away from where people lived.

CHANGING CITIES ▶

By the late 19th century, advances in the use of electricity helped improve life in cities. Electricity powered streetcars, and bright electric street lighting helped make city streets safer. In London, the first underground rail line was opened in 1863, providing transportation to a larger number of people.

Inventions of the Industrial Age

The Industrial Revolution (1760–1840) was a period of great innovation as groundbreaking technologies and inventions transformed the way humans lived and worked. Not all these new machines improved the lives of ordinary workers—some required operators to labor for long hours in dangerous conditions. But others, such as the automobile, offered a glimpse of a new freedom.

Seed separator
Cotton gin

Where US
When 1793

US inventor Eli Whitney created the cotton gin to remove unwanted seeds from cotton fibers. Before this, the seeds were picked out manually or with handheld rollers, a slow and laborious process. This made large-scale cotton production possible, and by 1850 it had become the US's main export. But since most cotton workers were enslaved Black people, it guaranteed them a life of backbreaking drudgery.

Automatic pattern weaver
Jacquard loom

Where France
When 1804

Named after its French inventor Joseph Marie Jacquard, the Jacquard loom pioneered the mass production of woven patterned cloth. Previously, skilled workers wove patterns into cloth by adjusting threads by hand. Now anyone could change the threads simply by following instructions from cards punched with holes.

Holes indicate where to put the threads.

Mechanical reaper
McCormick Reaper

Where US
When 1831

US inventor Cyrus McCormick designed a horse-drawn mechanical reaping machine. A rotating wheel pulled and cut the crops, which then dropped into the fields ready for collection. Crops could now be harvested quicker than ever before using fewer farmhands to help.

Electric telegraph
Cooke and Wheatstone telegraph

Where England
When 1837

The world's first commercial electric telegraph was designed by British inventors William Cooke and Charles Wheatstone. Electric signals sent along a wire moved a needle to point to letters on a grid, which spelled out the message to the receiver.

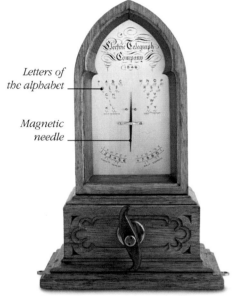

Letters of the alphabet

Magnetic needle

Steel furnace
Bessemer furnace

Where England
When 1856

English inventor Henry Bessemer's furnace greatly sped up the process of turning molten iron into steel, which was stronger and longer-lasting than iron. Steel was used to make railroads and ships, and soon the first steel-framed buildings began to appear on city skylines.

Safe elevator
Passenger hydraulic elevator

Where US
When 1857

Fitted with a device that would stop it tumbling even if the cable broke, the first safety elevator was installed by US engineer Elisha Otis in a New York City department store. As elevators could now carry passengers quickly to previously impossible heights, skyscrapers began to be built to save space in busy cities.

Cooling system
Portable refrigeration system

Where Germany
When 1873

The first modern refrigeration system was designed by German scientist Carl Von Linde for a brewery in the city of Munich. His invention soon became an essential part of the food and drink industry, allowing easily spoiled goods to be stored and transported safely.

First automobile
Benz Patent-Motorwagen

Where Germany
When 1885

The first car to be powered by an internal combustion engine was designed by German engineer Karl Benz. In 1888, his wife Bertha drove their two sons on a 75-mile (120-km) trip in the Benz Patent-Motorwagen. News of the journey's success quickly spread and automobile sales took off.

Steering lever

Brake lever

Engine in the rear

Hollow, tube-shaped steel frame

149

American independence

In the 18th century, the American Revolution began when the Thirteen Colonies in North America staged an uprising against British colonial rule. The British had introduced new taxes on goods imported to the colonies, such as sugar and tea, which the colonists felt were deeply unfair. Tensions escalated, and war broke out on April 19, 1775, with the battles of Lexington and Concord, both victories for the colonists. The following year, on July 4, the colonists declared their independence from Britain, forming the United States of America. After eight years of warfare, in 1783 the British were finally defeated, and the fight for independence was won.

CROSSING THE ICY DELAWARE
On the night of December 25–26, 1776, American general George Washington (center) secretly led his troops by boat across the Delaware River near New Jersey. On reaching the other side, they targeted unsuspecting German troops who had been hired to help the British. The surprise attack was a success, and gave the Americans an early advantage, and helped raise the American troops' morale.

▲ SIGNING THE CONSTITUTION
Following the Revolutionary War, people from the thirteen newly independent states gathered to create an official Constitution for the new country. This groundbreaking document was agreed upon and signed in 1787. It laid the foundations for law and government in the United States, while also protecting the freedoms of white male American citizens.

The colonization of Australia and the Pacific

European explorers first set sail to the Pacific Ocean in the 16th century. They encountered lush lands occupied by Indigenous communities who had lived there for 65,000 years. In the late 18th century, European powers began to seize control of Pacific lands, starting centuries of oppression.

The Indigenous peoples of the Pacific islands and Australia had built complex civilizations, with unique traditions and ways of life (see pp.80–81). Despite this, many Europeans considered these lands *terra nullius* ("lands belonging to no one"), to be used as they saw fit.

Colonizing Australia began in earnest in 1770 when Captain James Cook claimed it for Britain. By 1788, the British had set up a colony for exiled convicts, and an increasing number of free settlers arrived from the 1820s. In New Zealand, the first official colony was set up in 1840.

The arrival of Europeans had a devastating impact. Local populations were harmed by new diseases and violent conflict with the colonizers, who took their lands and tried to eliminate their cultures in order to increase their dominance.

Iron shackles used to keep prisoners from escaping on the journey to Australia

THE FIRST COLONISTS ▲
Most of the early colonists in Australia were convicts sent there to serve their time. They built roads and settlements, and prepared the new colonies for future settlers. After they finished their prison sentences, some people were allowed to buy land in the region, marry, and settle down.

◄ CAPTAIN COOK
The British explorer James Cook made three journeys to the Pacific between 1768 and 1779. He visited Tahiti, Australia, and New Zealand, where he became the first recorded European to meet the Māori people (left). His reports of these journeys played an important part in the European understanding of the inhabitants of these islands.

TAKE A LOOK

In the 20th century, the Australian government took many First Nations children from their communities and placed them with white families. Although they claimed this would improve the lives of the children, the purpose was to destroy Indigenous culture. The First Australians call these children the "Stolen Generations."

Large gold nugget discovered in Victoria in 1853

▲ SPREAD OF CHRISTIANITY

From the 17th century onward, European missionaries traveled to the Pacific islands to convert the Indigenous peoples of these islands to Christianity. Conversion gathered pace during the colonization of these territories by European countries. To this day, Christianity is the main religion on many of the islands.

▲ TREATY OF WAITANGI

In 1840, about 540 Māori Rangatira (chiefs) signed the Treaty of Waitangi with Britain. The treaty gave Britain the right to buy Māori lands in exchange for defending them from attacks by other colonizing powers. However, arguments over the treaty's exact meaning led to future conflicts, and settlers at times ignored its terms to claim new lands.

◄ GOLD RUSH

In 1851, coal miners in the Australian colonies (now states) of New South Wales and Victoria found gold. The following year, prospectors arrived from Europe, the US, and China in the hope of making a fortune. Within twenty years, the Australian population had grown threefold to 1.7 million.

COLONIZING SAMOA

In the 19th century, the US, Germany, and Britain battled for control of the Samoan islands. In 1899, without consulting the Samoans, Germany and the US divided the islands between them. New Zealand took control of the west in 1914 but years of misrule led to growing demands for independence. In 1962, Western Samoa became the first Pacific nation to become independent. The eastern islands remain in US hands.

The French Revolution

In the late 18th century, a revolution began in France that would lead to dramatic changes in society. In this violent period, the French people overthrew the monarchy before executing its members, and replaced it with a new type of government that pushed to give people greater freedom and equality.

In 1789, the gap between rich and poor in French society was huge. King Louis XVI and the aristocracy, who paid no taxes, held all of the political power as well as most of the wealth. At the same time, a series of bad harvests had led to food shortages and the price of basic essentials such as bread rose so high that many poor people—who were forced to pay taxes—couldn't afford it.

The people's anger built toward a king who didn't seem to care about his people. By June 1789, the people claimed power by forming a National Assembly (a government by the common people), which demanded more rights, but when the king failed to give it his support violence erupted on the streets of Paris.

Desperation pushed the French people toward the abolition of their monarchy much sooner than any other country in Europe. The revolution's slogan—"Liberty, equality, fraternity!"—summed up what they were fighting for, and this remains the motto of France today.

▼ RIGHTS OF MAN

The Declaration of the Rights of Man and of the Citizen *was published in 1789 and expressed the aims of the new revolutionary government. The document stated that all men were equal under the law. Despite protests, the declaration was not amended to give women these same rights.*

STORMING THE BASTILLE

In July 1789, rumors that the king planned to shut down the National Assembly enraged Parisians. On the 14th, they stormed the Bastille, a royal fortress and prison, and freed seven prisoners held captive there. The revolution had started. This day is celebrated in France each year as Bastille Day.

Inspired by the women, many men joined the protest in support.

◄ THE WOMEN'S MARCH

On October 5, 1789, a group of around 7,000 protesters—most of them women—marched on the royal palace of Versailles to protest the high price of bread. The numbers swelled and the king was forced to meet some of their demands. The march's success helped weaken royal power.

MAXIMILIEN ROBESPIERRE

Robespierre (1758–1794) was an influential leader of the French Revolution who campaigned to end the monarchy and to give equal rights to all men. He led the new parliament established after the revolution but soon became the brutal architect of the "Reign of Terror" (see below). He was executed by his political rivals in 1794.

EXECUTION OF LOUIS XVI ►

In August 1792, King Louis XVI was imprisoned, and soon afterward the French monarchy was abolished. Louis was charged with treason and on January 21, 1793, he was executed by guillotine. Queen Marie Antoinette was executed nine months later.

The sharp, heavy blade of a guillotine would drop on the victim's neck, killing them instantly.

NAPOLEON BONAPARTE ►

A leading military general during the revolution, Napoleon Bonaparte seized control of France in November 1799, later declaring himself the emperor. Between 1803 and 1815, he led France into a series of wars against other European powers, briefly conquering much of western Europe.

THE REIGN OF TERROR ►

Known in French as La Terreur, the Reign of Terror was a period of ruthless brutality that started after the king was beheaded and lasted until mid-1794. During this time the revolutionary government, led by Maximilien Robespierre, imprisoned thousands of aristocrats and other "enemies of the revolution" and executed them by guillotine.

The expansion of the US

After the Thirteen Colonies in British North America gained independence in 1783, many believed that their new nation was destined to expand across the continent. Land was stolen from Indigenous nations through war and treaties that were not upheld, or acquired from other European colonial powers.

Settlers rapidly expanded US territory westward from the east coast. The land they moved into was already occupied by Indigenous peoples, who endured great losses of life as they fought hard to protect their territory and lifestyles. But they were overcome by soldiers and settlers with superior firepower. Indigenous nations in the eastern US were forced to move from ancestral homelands into a designated "Indian Territory." Many people died on the journey, which became known as the Trail of Tears (see p.173).

The discovery of gold in California in 1848 sparked a "gold rush" that attracted thousands more settlers to move to the west coast to make their fortunes, and the opening in 1869 of the first transcontinental railroad—connecting the Atlantic coast to the Pacific—drew in many more.

By 1898, the US had acquired its present shape, although not all the new lands immediately became states. Alaska and Hawaii, the final two territories to join the Union, were given statehood in 1959.

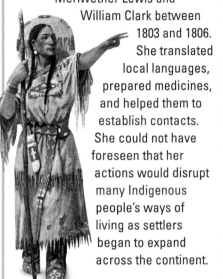

SACAGAWEA

An Indigenous American woman of the Shoshone nation, Sacagawea (c.1788–1812) scouted for explorers Meriwether Lewis and William Clark between 1803 and 1806. She translated local languages, prepared medicines, and helped them to establish contacts. She could not have foreseen that her actions would disrupt many Indigenous people's ways of living as settlers began to expand across the continent.

◀ LOUISIANA PURCHASE

In 1803, President Thomas Jefferson bought the Louisiana Territory from France, doubling the size of the US. This purchase had not been approved by the Indigenous American nations. He then sent Meriwether Lewis and William Clark—whose compass is shown here—on an expedition to explore it all.

SETTLING THE LAND ▶

A series of trails built by pioneers across the US led settlers to a new life in the west. People took all their belongings with them in horse-drawn covered wagons, traveling together in long convoys for safety. Some went to farm new lands, others to find work.

THE HOMESTEAD ACT ▶

In 1862, the US government passed a law that encouraged new settlers to move westward by offering them land for free if they agreed to live and farm on it for at least five years. This was another blow to Indigenous nations, whose stolen lands were traded in this way. More than 250,000 sq miles (650,000 sq km), or nearly 10 percent of the total area of the US, was given to homesteaders under this law.

▼ TRANSCONTINENTAL RAILROAD

After years of construction, in 1869, two cross-country railroads—the eastern Union Pacific Railroad and the western Central Pacific Railroad—were finally linked at Promontory Point in Utah (below). The coasts of America were now joined together by rail. This event was symbolic of the permanent settlement of the US across North America.

KEY
- Thirteen Colonies 1776
- Added to US by 1818
- Added to US by 1898

▲ THE CHANGING FRONTIER

After the Thirteen Colonies won independence from Britain in 1783, the US rapidly gained new territory from France, Spain, Britain, and Mexico, and added the independent republic of Texas. In 1867, it bought Alaska from Russia for $7.2 million, before taking over the former Kingdom of Hawaii in 1898.

INDIGENOUS RESISTANCE ▼

Throughout this period of expansion, settlers faced fierce resistance from the Indigenous peoples, who fought for their lands and their livelihoods. An Apache war leader and healer, Geronimo (below), held out against US invasions for decades, but his capture in 1886 weakened the resistance considerably.

The conquest of Africa

From the 1880s, European nations began campaigns to take over large parts of Africa. They claimed they were trying to stamp out slavery in Africa, but in truth they wanted to exploit the resource-rich continent to feed the growing industries in Europe and the US.

By the 19th century, many countries in Europe had grown wealthy by using enslaved people from Africa as free labor (see pp.132–133). But as these nations became more industrialized, there was a shift in demand—instead of workers, they now needed raw materials for their factories.

Most European countries had created coastal trading posts in Africa by 1600, but 200 years later they had barely started exploring the interior of the continent. Reports of vast untapped resources in the heart of Africa resulted in a race to colonize

the land. The nations involved were Britain, Spain, France, Belgium, Italy, Portugal, and Germany. Each tried to grab lands through pacts with local chiefs or kings, battling other colonial armies, or forcing native communities off their lands.

At the time, Africa was home to more than 10,000 different states and societies, and the colonists were met with fierce opposition. Countless battles ensued over the last quarter of the 19th century. However, by 1900, most the continent was under the control of colonial powers.

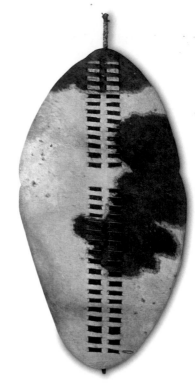

▲ BATTLE OF ISANDLWANA
In January 1879, the British began their invasion of Zululand in southern Africa. Zulu warriors armed with iron spears, cow-hide shields (above), and just a few rifles crushed the British in the Battle of Isandlwana. The British forces had suffered their worst defeat against an Indigenous force, but six months later, they returned to defeat the Zulu Kingdom, turning the region into a colony.

KEY

Belgium		Italy
Britain		Portugal
France		Spain
Germany		Independent

FACT
In 1884, Anglo-American inventor Hiram Stevens Maxim created the first automatic machine gun—the Maxim gun. It played a major role in the colonial invasion of Africa.

◀ COLONIAL EMPIRES OF AFRICA
By the end of the 19th century, most of Africa was under European rule. France, Britain, Germany, Belgium, Portugal, Italy, and Spain had each claimed regions for themselves. Britain and France controlled the largest portions of the continent.

SHAKA ZULU

King Shaka Zulu (reigned 1816–1828) was a powerful warrior who founded a large Zulu Empire in southern Africa. He is credited with inventing a stabbing spear and creating new battle attack formations. Both of these were used by the Zulus in their wars against the British.

ETHIOPIA ▶
In 1889, the Kingdom of Ethiopia signed a treaty with Italy, handing over some territories in a bid to maintain its independence. In 1896, Italy invaded Ethiopia but was defeated by the African kingdom's military might at the Battle of Adwa. Italy retreated, and Ethiopia remained one of only two independent countries in Africa.

THE IMPACT OF COLONIALISM ▶
The Europeans stripped African states of their political power and identity. They also disregarded the differences between the various ethnic groups, establishing their own boundaries and states. In some places colonists had to approve the rulers chosen by Africans, while in others they put in power rulers who would not challenge their authority, such as Daudi Chwa (right) of Buganda, in present-day Uganda.

◀ THE RESISTANCE
African empires fought hard to keep their territories. In West Africa, the female warriors of the Kingdom of Dahomey, called the Mino ("our mothers"), faced the French in 1890. Although known for their courage and ferocity, the Mino were defeated by the modern firepower of the Europeans.

Medical milestones

In the 18th and 19th centuries, technological innovations and the growing scientific approach taken to medicine led to many important advances in the field. During this period, new inventions, treatments, and methods of diagnosis laid the foundation for modern medical care.

▲ **GERM THEORY**

French biochemist Louis Pasteur discovered that microorganisms in the air made wine turn sour. He then looked at how microorganisms affected the human body, and, in 1861, he published his findings that germs invading human bodies caused many diseases. German microbiologist Robert Koch later identified many specific bacteria that caused individual diseases.

Some of the new knowledge was used to improve on current methods of treating disease. In parts of Asia, Africa, and the Middle East, a process called "variolation," in which a mild form of a disease was introduced into a healthy body to immunize it, had been used for centuries against smallpox. However, this was unreliable. In 1796, the first safe and reliable vaccine for smallpox was created in Britain.

New discoveries about the natural world led to an improved understanding of human biology. Some tiny microorganisms, such as varieties of bacteria, were found to be capable of causing disease. These organisms became known as germs. Antiseptics—substances that kill germs—were developed, and as a result nursing methods improved significantly.

In 1901, Austrian biologist Karl Landsteiner's discovery of the four types of human blood groups A, B, O, and AB was crucial to improving the success of blood transfusions, and would change medical surgery forever.

MARY SEACOLE

When British-Jamaican nurse Mary Seacole (1805–1881) offered her nursing services during the Crimean War (1853–1856), she was rejected because of her skin color. However, she used her own money and traveled to Crimea to tend to the wounded British soldiers.

FACT
British nurse Florence Nightingale established the first-ever nursing school called "The Nightingale Training School for Nurses" at St. Thomas' Hospital in London in 1860.

THE FIRST VACCINATION ▶
In 1796, English doctor Edward Jenner observed that milkmaids who caught cowpox did not catch smallpox (a much more dangerous disease). Jenner injected a boy with cowpox—he fell slightly ill but recovered. Jenner then exposed the boy to smallpox—he suffered only a mild form of the disease. This vaccine eventually led to the complete elimination of the disease.

▼ ANTISEPTICS

Until the 1860s, surgeons did not clean operating tables or equipment because they were unaware of the role of bacteria in causing infections. As a result of these unhygienic conditions, death rates among patients were very high. In 1867, British surgeon Joseph Lister discovered that carbolic acid killed bacteria. He sprayed his medical instruments with this antiseptic and reduced death rates of his patients from 46 percent to 15 percent.

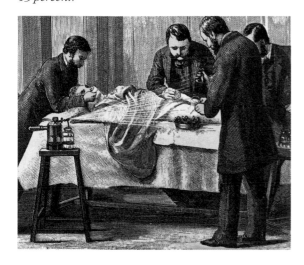

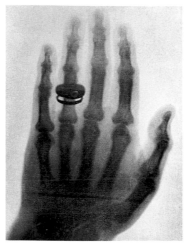

▲ X-RAYS

In 1895, German physicist Wilhelm Röntgen discovered a new form of radiation that could pass through the human body, and produce an image of its interior. Unable to identify it, he called it the X-ray. His discovery revolutionized medical diagnosis, as doctors could now look inside the human body.

Until the 20th century, the people of China relied on traditional Chinese medicine techniques. Acupuncture is one such technique that is still studied and practiced today, where needles are inserted into pressure points in the skin to relieve pain, cure disease, and improve health. Many people in China still opt for traditional medicine treatments, along with Western medicine.

1750–1900

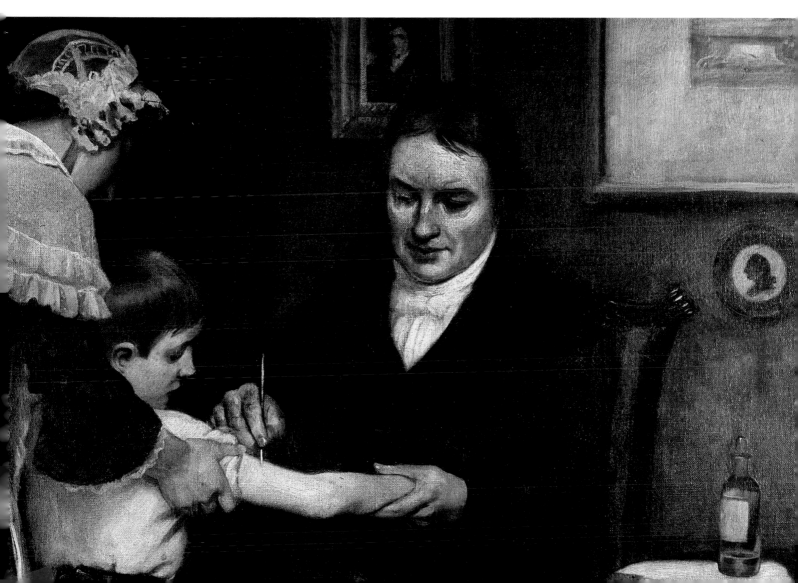

Revolution in Haiti

In the 18th century, Haiti was a colony of France known as Saint-Domingue. In 1791, thousands of enslaved people rose up in rebellion against French colonists, an event that forced the French to abolish enslavement across their empire. In 1804, Saint-Domingue declared its independence from France and became the world's first Black-governed republic.

▲ BURNING PLANTATIONS
During the revolution in Haiti, enslaved workers burned the plantations they were forced to work on to the ground and killed their French enslavers. Within three years, France was forced to end enslavement in all its colonies.

France had established its colony of Saint-Domingue on the Caribbean island of Hispaniola in 1659. Soon, plantations were set up across the colony and enslaved Africans were shipped across the Atlantic to work on them. By the 1780s, Saint-Domingue was the top producer of sugar and coffee in the world.

After the French Revolution in 1789, revolutionaries in France granted free people of color (*affranchis*) French citizenship, but when white plantation owners refused to accept this, fighting broke out. By 1791, thousands of enslaved people had joined the revolt. They found an inspirational leader in Toussaint Louverture, who created a powerful army and gradually took over the island. Saint-Domingue's declaration of independence from France in 1804 inspired others to resist colonial rule, as they learned how the formerly enslaved had liberated themselves.

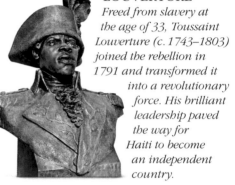

◄ TOUSSAINT LOUVERTURE
Freed from slavery at the age of 33, Toussaint Louverture (c. 1743–1803) joined the rebellion in 1791 and transformed it into a revolutionary force. His brilliant leadership paved the way for Haiti to become an independent country.

TAKE A LOOK

The Vodou religion is derived from West African beliefs, such as those of the Fon people, mixed with Roman Catholicism. It played an important role during the revolution. Enslaved Africans came together at secret Vodou gatherings, and the religion became a symbol of resistance against French rule. Vodou is still an important part of life in Haiti today.

AFFRANCHIS
During their rule, French colonists in Saint-Domingue created a class system, with white elites at the top, affranchis in the middle, and enslaved Africans at the bottom. Affranchis were free people of color or mixed race people who had some legal rights.

▲ MEXICAN INDEPENDENCE
Mexico was one of the oldest centers of Spanish power and its struggle for independence was one of the hardest fought. It began in 1810 with the "Cry of Dolores," an inspirational speech by the criollo *priest Miguel Hidalgo in the small town of Dolores (above), which led to an armed revolt.*

▲ CROSSING THE ANDES
In 1817, Chile still lay in Spanish hands. Argentina's independence leader General José de San Martín led an army on a daring mission across the Andes Mountains. They took the Spanish by surprise and liberated Chile after only a few short battles.

Latin American independence

Inspired by the French and American revolutions, with their calls for freedom and equality, the people of what is now known as Latin America (French-, Portuguese-, and Spanish-speaking countries in the Americas) began to fight for independence from colonial rule in the late 18th and early 19th centuries. By 1826, revolutionaries across Latin America had freed their nations from three centuries of European control.

▲ BRAZILIAN INDEPENDENCE
After Napoleon invaded Portugal in 1808, King João VI fled to Brazil, then a Portuguese colony. The king returned to Portugal in 1821 leaving his son Pedro in charge. The following year, Pedro declared Brazil's independence and became its first emperor.

In the late 18th century, the Spanish introduced new laws, which reduced the power and privileges of the *criollos* (people of Spanish heritage born in the Americas) in their colonies. When Napoleon Bonaparte invaded Portugal and Spain in 1807 to 1808 and put his own brother on the Spanish throne, the authority of both countries over their colonies was severely weakened.

Criollos seized the opportunity to take power into their own hands. Instability spread throughout the region and a wave of revolutions began. The fight for independence in southern South America was led by General José de San Martín, born in Yapeyú in modern-day Argentina, while Simón Bolívar of Caracas in modern-day Venezuela led armies in the north.

By 1826, when Peru gained its independence after a 15-year struggle, Spain and Portugal had lost all of their colonies in the Americas apart from Cuba and Puerto Rico, which remained under Spanish rule until the Spanish–American War of 1898.

SIMÓN BOLÍVAR

Simón Bolívar (1783–1830) was a hero of the revolutions in Latin America. He helped liberate not just his native Venezuela, but also the modern-day countries of Colombia, Panama, Ecuador, Peru, and Bolivia, which was named after him.

The progress of science

Scientific discoveries and developments transformed the world in the 19th century. As the study of science became an admired profession, and not just an eccentric hobby, the pace of scientific progress quickened. Discoveries led to new technologies and inventions, and scientists came up with theories that challenged people's beliefs. Russian chemist Dmitri Mendeleev devised the periodic table, a way of organizing chemical elements that led not only to the discovery of new elements but also helped scientists figure out how atoms—the building blocks of matter—are structured. Polish-French physicist Marie Curie was one of the first to reveal the secrets of radioactivity. An equally important step in the progress of science was English scientist Charles Darwin's theory that life on Earth had developed through a process of evolution—a discovery that changed the way humans saw the natural world.

▲ DARWIN'S THEORY OF EVOLUTION
During a visit to the Galápagos Islands off the South American coast, Charles Darwin noticed differences between the beaks of finches on the various islands. He wondered if this was because the finches had adapted in different ways to the food available in their habitats in order to survive. This led him to the idea that over time plants and animals gradually change and develop into new species—the theory of evolution.

The 1848 Revolutions

In the early months of 1848, a wave of revolutions spread like wildfire across Europe. The first began in Sicily in January. In February, violent protests in France brought an end to the French monarchy. By March, revolutions had broken out in cities throughout present-day Germany and the Austrian Empire, including Hungary and parts of Italy.

One of the main causes of the unrest was a series of poor harvests in the mid-1840s, leading to widespread famine and hardship. In the industrial cities of Europe, unemployment and poverty increased, and the gap between the rich and the poor grew wider. At the same time, harsh governments refused to allow more people the right to vote.

In parts of the Austrian empire, such as Hungary and Italy, people sharing the same language and culture demanded the right to rule themselves. Shaken by the speed and violence of the protests, governments at first promised political change.

A parliament elected to unite Germany met for the first time in May, and in Denmark and the Netherlands greater democratic freedom was allowed. But by the end of the year, the revolutions had mostly been put down by military force, crushing all hopes of political reform for the immediate future.

▼ FRANKFURT PARLIAMENT

Two months after the March revolutions, a parliament for all of Germany—then divided into 39 separate states—met in Frankfurt with plans to unify the country and give it a democratic constitution (set of laws) under the king of Prussia. However, their hopes ended when the king refused to cooperate.

▼ REVOLUTION IN PARIS

On February 23, soldiers in Paris opened fire on people protesting against the banning of political meetings in France. In the riots that followed, King Louis Philippe was forced to give up his throne and protesters declared the Second French Republic.

KARL MARX

German philosopher Karl Marx (1818–1883) published *The Communist Manifesto* with coauthor Friedrich Engels just before the events of 1848. The book predicted revolution in Europe as a result of the "class struggle" between the rich and poor. While Marx's writings did not influence the 1848 protests, they inspired many revolutionary movements in the 20th century.

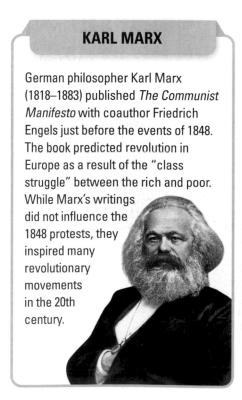

▲ HUNGARIAN DEMANDS

On March 15, a mass protest in Hungary forced the Austrian government to accept reforms, including the abolition of serfdom (forced peasant labor). The protesters were inspired by the poem "Nemzeti dal" (National Song) by poet Sándor Petófi, who is pictured above holding a scroll.

▼ ROMAN REPUBLIC

Italian soldier Giuseppe Garibaldi led the defense of the short-lived Roman Republic, which was set up after protesters forced the Pope to flee Rome in November 1848. Garibaldi later helped to unite Italy in the 1860s, leading an army of "Red Shirts."

Garibaldi was known for his signature red shirt.

▼ BRITISH CHARTISTS

Encouraged by the events in Europe, a British working-class movement called the Chartists held a mass rally in London demanding the right to vote. Fearing revolution, the government called in the army, but the expected violence did not take place.

The Meiji Restoration

In 1867, a group of Japanese nobles toppled the Tokugawa Shogunate that had ruled Japan for more than 250 years, and placed the 14-year-old Prince Mutsuhito in power. Known as Emperor Meiji, Mutsuhito reigned for 45 years during which time Japan changed from a feudal society led by landowners into an industrial nation.

Japan had long been isolated from the rest of the world, but that had all changed in 1854, when the US forced the shogun Tokugawa Iesada to open the country's ports to foreign traders. Many felt the shogun had given in too easily to Western pressure, and resentment grew, leading to Iesada's overthrow and the installment of Emperor Meiji.

Japan's new government ended the dominance of *daimyos* (landowners), and abolished the samurai class

(see p.74). It modernized Japan by investing heavily in industry, especially steel-making, textiles, and building railroads. The Meiji government studied Western technologies and systems of public education and government, hiring 3,000 foreign advisers to teach the Japanese new skills.

Meiji Japan created a national army equipped with guns and expanded its navy, building dozens of battleships. Within three decades, the country had become a major world power.

▼ RAILROAD CONNECTIONS
Railroads were seen as a symbol of Japan's new modernity. By the end of the Meiji period in 1912, Japan had constructed more than 7,000 miles (11,000 km) of railroad track. The first railroad route opened between Tokyo and Yokohama in 1872.

◄ END OF ISOLATION
In 1853, a fleet of four iron warships under the command of Commodore Matthew Perry of the US Navy steamed into Tokyo Bay. Perry carried a letter from the US President Millard Fillmore, demanding that Japan open up trade with the Western world. A year later, he returned with a bigger fleet, and forced Japan to sign an unfair treaty that favored foreign powers.

Gold decoration was popular with Western buyers.

GROWING EXPORTS ►
After Japan opened up, a craze for all things Japanese swept through Europe and the US. Traditional Japanese industries, such as porcelain- and silk-making, were equipped with modern machinery to meet the soaring demand. This Satsuma earthenware tea bowl from the Meiji period was made for export.

◀ FOCUS ON EDUCATION

The Meiji government built schools throughout the country to increase literacy levels and create an educated workforce. All boys and girls had to attend elementary school. The lessons encouraged harmony between people and loyalty to the Japanese nation and to the emperor.

FACT
The word Meiji means "enlightened rule." It was chosen as the name for Mutsuhito's reign to mark the start of a new era in Japanese history.

MILITARY MIGHT ▶

In 1905, Japanese forces drove the Russians out of Manchuria (in northern China), proving that Japan was now a major world power. One of the major clashes of the Russo–Japanese War (1904–1905), the Battle of Tsushima was the first sea battle fought between modern steel battleships.

Japanese battleships

EVERYDAY LIFE

Most workers in Japan's booming textile factories were women and children. The conditions were harsh; they worked long hours for low pay, and slept in crowded dormitories where disease spread quickly.

169

The US Civil War

In 1861, a bitter and bloody war broke out in the US between the northern (or Union) and southern (or Confederate) states. The main cause was slavery. The economy of the South relied on enslaving Black people to work on plantations, while in the industrialized North, public opinion was in favor of ending slavery. The war ended in 1865 with a Union victory.

At the start of the 1860s, almost 4 million out of the US population of 31 million were enslaved Black people. They were forced to do back-breaking work for no wages.

In 1860, Abraham Lincoln won the presidential election on the promise of refusing to extend slavery into the new US territories in the west. Fearing for their future, seven southern states—later joined by four more—left the Union to form the Confederate States of America. When Lincoln refused to hand over military property to the new government, Confederate forces attacked.

Both sides raised large armies, the Confederates winning the early battles due to their superior military leadership. But in 1863, Union forces took control of the Mississippi River and split the states of Texas and Arkansas from the rest of the Confederacy. Their victory soon after at Gettysburg was decisive. Union forces attacked the Confederacy from all directions, wrecking its economy, and finally defeating it in 1865.

CONFEDERATE BREAKAWAY ▶
The US Civil War began in April 1861 when Confederate forces bombarded the Union-held Fort Sumter (right) in South Carolina. Four southern states that had remained in the Union until then joined the Confederacy after this attack.

MAJOR EVENTS

1861	1862	1862
The first major land battle of the war is fought at Bull Run in Virginia, resulting in a huge Confederate victory.	The first-ever battle between ironclad warships—the Union's USS *Monitor* and the Confederate's CSS *Virginia*—takes place at Hampton Roads in Virginia.	Union forces win a narrow victory at Shiloh near Pittsburgh Landing in Tennessee, weakening the Confederacy.

MODERN COMMUNICATIONS ▶

In the Civil War, railroads moved troops around, aerial balloons spied across enemy lines, and the telegraph (right) sent and received instant information. Its receiver machine recorded messages on paper tape in Morse code, which uses dots and dashes to represent numbers and letters of the alphabet.

The paper tape came out of here marked with Morse code.

ABRAHAM LINCOLN

Born into rural poverty in Kentucky, Abraham Lincoln (1809–1865), trained as a lawyer. He was elected president in 1861 and his strong leadership steered the Union to victory in the Civil War. Lincoln was assassinated in April 1865, days after the war ended.

◀ A CONTINENTAL WAR

Most of the fighting in the war took place in Virginia, Maryland, and Pennsylvania in the east. There were also battles in Kentucky and Tennessee in the west and down the Mississippi River to New Orleans. In 1864, General William T. Sherman (left) conducted a major campaign in Georgia and the Carolinas.

▼ RECONSTRUCTION

A process of rebuilding and reconstruction followed the war. In 1870, the US Constitution was amended to allow Black men the right to vote. When Reconstruction ended in 1877, southern states introduced laws that legalized discrimination against Black people. They remained in place for almost a century.

▲ THE ABOLITION OF SLAVERY

On September 22, 1862, President Lincoln issued the Emancipation Proclamation, which freed all enslaved people in the Confederacy from January 1, 1863. In 1865 Congress passed the 13th Amendment (law change) to the US Constitution, making slavery illegal across the soon-to-be reunited country.

1863	1863	1864	1865
The 54th Massachusetts Infantry Regiment—the first Black regiment in US history—is formed in Boston.	Union forces win the Battle of Gettysburg in Pennsylvania, turning the tide of war in their favor. It is the bloodiest battle of the war.	General Sherman leads the "March to the Sea" through Georgia, destroying railroads and towns in an attempt to damage the Confederate economy.	Confederate forces under General Robert E. Lee surrender at Appomattox Court House in Virginia, ending the war.

The effects of colonization

European countries had colonized the Americas, Africa, and Asia to secure power, generate wealth, and create a global trade in cotton, tobacco, and sugar. They enslaved millions of people and oppressed millions more, suppressing local cultures and traditions in the process. The effects of the colonial era can still be felt around the world today.

In the 18th and 19th centuries, powerful European nations, such as France and Britain, continued to expand their territory by invading and colonizing other countries, until by the end of the 19th century their empires included most of Africa, India, Southeast Asia, Australia, and the Pacific Islands. In most colonies, people were forced to convert to Christianity, their rights and ways of life came under attack, and they were exploited and poorly paid, or sold into slavery. Although European powers eventually withdrew or were ousted from the majority of their colonies by the late 20th century, this period of colonialism has had a lasting impact on colonized people, lands, and cultures. European nations are only now starting to fully face the cruelty of their colonial past.

▲ **LOSS OF INDIGENOUS BELIEFS**
European colonizers believed that Christianity was the "true religion." They used their Christian faith to justify claiming land from nonbelievers, taking over from local rulers and exploiting their people. Many Indigenous people were forced to convert to Christianity. These Papuans from New Guinea are burning objects of worship important to their old religion.

SAMUEL MAHARERO

Namibian hero Samuel Maharero (1856–1923) was Paramount Chief of the Herero people. When German colonizers began shooting his people for rebelling against their rule, Maharero bravely led around 1,000 people to safety.

◀ TIPU SULTAN

Between 1782 and 1789, Tipu Sultan ruled the Kingdom of Mysore in south India. He fought to stop the British taking control of India in four Anglo–Mysore wars in the late 18th century. He was killed in the final battle.

◀ LOOTED ARTIFACTS

Priceless treasures were stolen when the British captured Benin in West Africa in 1897. Colonizers wanted control of the land—which is now part of Nigeria—for its oil and rubber, which were in high demand at the time. The "Benin Bronzes" have become symbols of colonialism, and there is a growing call for these looted artifacts to be returned to their rightful home in Nigeria.

▼ TRAIL OF TEARS

In 1830, as American settlers moved west, the Indian Removal Act allowed the government to forcibly remove Indigenous Americans from their lands in the southeast to "Indian Territory" west of the Mississippi River. Thousands died from illness and starvation on the journey, which became known as the Trail of Tears.

FACT

British colonists in Australia brought influenza, measles, and smallpox with them. First Australians had no resistance to these new diseases, and their populations fell dramatically.

THE COMMONWEALTH ▶

The Commonwealth is an organization of 54 countries— nearly all former territories of the British Empire—which was launched in 1949 after World War II. At that time, Europe's empires had been weakened by years of fighting and countries began to call for independence.

TAKE A LOOK

During the worldwide Black Lives Matter protests in 2020, symbols of past colonialism were destroyed, including this statue of a 17th-century merchant and slave-trader that stood in Bristol, England.

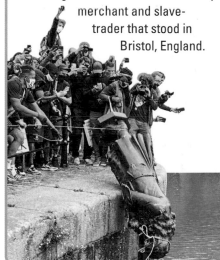
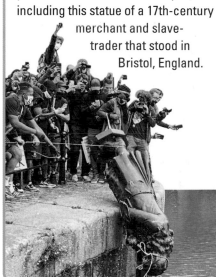

1900 TO PRESENT

The early 20th century was dominated by two world wars, which weakened many European nations. They lost control of their overseas territories in Africa, Asia, and other parts of the world as people fought for and gained independence. The late 20th century saw new conflicts rise, but also new ideas about freedom and equality. The invention of computers led to space exploration and an information age that continues into the 21st century.

The New China

The first half of the 20th century was a period of turmoil for China. The country went through revolutions and civil wars, suffered a foreign invasion, and took part in two world wars. Finally, after decades of conflict that had caused serious hardship and division, a new communist China emerged in 1949.

After the fall of the Qing in 1911 (see pp.140–141), China was thrown into a period of conflict between competing factions known as the Warlord Era. This lasted from 1916 to 1928, when the Nationalist Party reunified China. Soon after, a long struggle for power began between the Nationalists and the Chinese Communist Party (CCP).

In 1931, Japan invaded China. The Sino-Japanese War that followed became part of the wider conflict of World War II, which started in 1939. China joined the Allies, and the war ended with the defeat of Japan in 1945 (see pp.194–195). The fighting between the CCP and the Nationalists, which had halted due to the war, resumed the following year. The CCP won and established their government in 1949.

This new China was led by Mao Zedong, who launched a series of campaigns to reform the economy and society along communist lines. In 1966, he began the Cultural Revolution, an attempt to get rid of old attitudes by advancing communist ideals and solidifying Mao's power. During Mao's rule, China was unstable and largely cut off from the outside world, but after his death in 1976, new reforms turned the country into a superpower.

▲ **XINHAI REVOLUTION**
In October 1911, revolutionaries overthrew the Qing Dynasty and set up the Republic of China the following year. Revolutionary leader Sun Yat-Sen (above) became the first president, but he was soon replaced by the military official Yuan Shikai.

Mao Zedong declares his new government in front of 200,000 people at Tiananmen Square in the capital, Beijing.

CHILD IN TIME

Puyi became the last emperor of China at the age of two in 1908, but was then overthrown in the Xinhai Revolution. He was made a puppet emperor of Manchuria by the Japanese in 1934, without any real power. After their defeat in 1945, Puyi was imprisoned. He died in 1967.

NATIONALISTS AND WARLORDS ▶

After the revolution of 1911, China drifted into chaos, with much of the north and west of the country ruled by rival warlords. A weak Nationalist government ruled the south of the country. In 1926, the Nationalist military leader Chiang Kai-shek led a campaign known as the Northern Expedition to fight the warlords and reunified the country in 1928 under his control.

Smoke rises from buildings after the Japanese bombing of Shanghai.

WAR AGAINST JAPAN ▶

In 1931, the Japanese seized the northern province of Manchuria. They then launched a full-scale invasion of China in 1937, capturing most of the northeast and the east coast, including Shanghai. The Chinese fought back, helped by the US and the Soviet Union, and the war ended with Japan's surrender in 1945.

CIVIL WAR ▶

The Chinese Communist Party (CCP) was formed in Shanghai in 1921, and helped the Nationalist government defeat the warlords, but in 1927 the Nationalists turned on their Communist allies. In 1934, Communist forces retreated to the north—a 12-month expedition known as the Long March (right)—to avoid capture. A truce was agreed between the two sides in 1937, but war broke out again in 1946.

◀ COMMUNIST CHINA

By 1949, Communist forces had captured much of China from the Nationalists. On October 1, CCP leader Mao Zedong founded the new People's Republic of China, setting up a Communist government in the most populous state in the world.

▲ WESTERN FRONT

For most of the war in Western Europe, fighting was deadlocked along a 440-mile (700-km) strip of land that ran from the North Sea south through Belgium and France called the Western Front. Both sides dug deep trenches along the frontier to defend themselves against bombardment.

▼ TANK WARFARE

Tanks were a new weapon of war developed by Britain and France during World War I. They helped troops cross rubble-covered battle grounds and enemy trenches, and could resist light gunfire and shrapnel from exploding shells.

World War I

When war broke out in Europe in 1914, European colonies across the world were soon dragged into the conflict. The results were catastrophic. Over the next four years, towns and cities were destroyed, and national economies were wrecked. By the war's end, more than 20 million people had died.

The origins of the war lay in the two rival alliances that divided Europe: the Central Powers, led by Austria-Hungary and Germany, and the Allies, led by Russia, France, and Britain. In June 1914, a Serbian revolutionary assassinated Archduke Franz Ferdinand, heir to the Austro-Hungarian throne. Austria–Hungary blamed the Serbian government for the attack and declared war, prompting Russia to come to Serbia's aid. Germany then declared war on Russia and France. Germany then invaded Belgium, bringing Britain, which had promised to protect Belgium, into the conflict.

Fighting took place mainly in Europe, but also spread to Africa and Asia. Both France and Britain drew on their colonial empires for troops, many of whom were Asian or Black. For a long time, the war was at a stalemate, with massive casualties in battles that only achieved tiny advances. This changed in 1917 when the US joined the Allies. When the conflict ended in November 1918, it was said to be the "war to end all wars."

▼ EASTERN FRONT

Unlike on the Western Front, the battle line of the Eastern Front moved back and forth as the large German, Russian, and Austrian armies fought to win territory. The Eastern Front stretched from the Baltic Sea in the north to the Black Sea in the south. Fighting continued until Russia left the war after the revolution of October 1917.

▲ WOMEN DURING THE WAR

Women played a major role in the war, many taking on jobs that had previously been denied to them because of their sex. They worked in ammunition factories, on farms producing food, and ran local businesses. On the front, many women served as nurses, ambulance drivers, and support staff to the troops.

◀ HARLEM HELLFIGHTERS

When the US entered the war, hundreds of thousands of troops were shipped across the Atlantic to fight in Europe. Among them were the Harlem Hellfighters, an infantry regiment from the New York Army National Guard. This regiment was made up mainly of Black Americans, because the US Army segregated its troops by skin color.

ARMISTICE AND PEACE ▶

By 1918, Germany was struggling. The US had now entered the war, food was short, and many soldiers had deserted. On November 11, 1918, Germany and the Allies signed an armistice (an agreement to stop fighting). In Britain, many people commemorate those who died by wearing red poppies around this date each year.

MAJOR BATTLES

1914	1915	1916	1917
The German advance into France is stopped in September by French and British troops at the First Battle of the Marne.	The Allies attack the Ottoman Empire (a German ally) at the Gallipoli Peninsula in modern-day Turkey. The assault ends in failure.	In France, the 140-day-long Battle of the Somme, between German and Allied troops, results in more than one million casualties with neither side gaining an advantage.	The Third Battle of Ypres, fought between the Allies and Germany in Belgium, ends in a stalemate with massive loss of life on both sides.

Global pandemics

A pandemic occurs when a disease begins to spread over a large region, or even the whole world. Pandemics have devastated populations throughout history. The 1918 Spanish flu, which is thought to have infected a third of the world's population at the time, was the deadliest of the 20th century. More recent pandemics have included the HIV/AIDS pandemic, which began in the 1980s and has killed around 40 million people; the 2009 swine flu pandemic; and COVID-19, which was declared a worldwide pandemic in March 2020.

MAJOR OUTBREAKS

1918–1920	An estimated 500 million people around the world are infected with the Spanish flu, and between 20 and 50 million die from the disease. To stop the spread, social distancing, quarantine, and mask wearing are all put in place, similar to our response to pandemics today.
1957–1968	Asian flu spreads rapidly and creates havoc, but a vaccine is quickly developed to help control the pandemic. It kills more than a million people in two years, before subsiding. In 1968, another similar flu virus appears and kills a million people worldwide.
1976	The first cases of Ebola are recorded in South Sudan and the Democratic Republic of the Congo. Ebola is one of the deadliest diseases in the world and cases are still being identified today. The virus spreads through body fluids, including sweat.
2000s	Major outbreaks in the 21st century so far include Ebola, SARS, Swine flu, MERS, and COVID-19.

COVID-19 VACCINATION

SOLDIERS WITH THE SPANISH FLU ▶

The 1918 Spanish flu, one of the deadliest pandemics in history, swept across the world, killing millions. Here, sick soldiers can be seen at a hospital in North America. Unusually, most people who became unwell were young and healthy adults, rather than the elderly who are usually more vulnerable to flu.

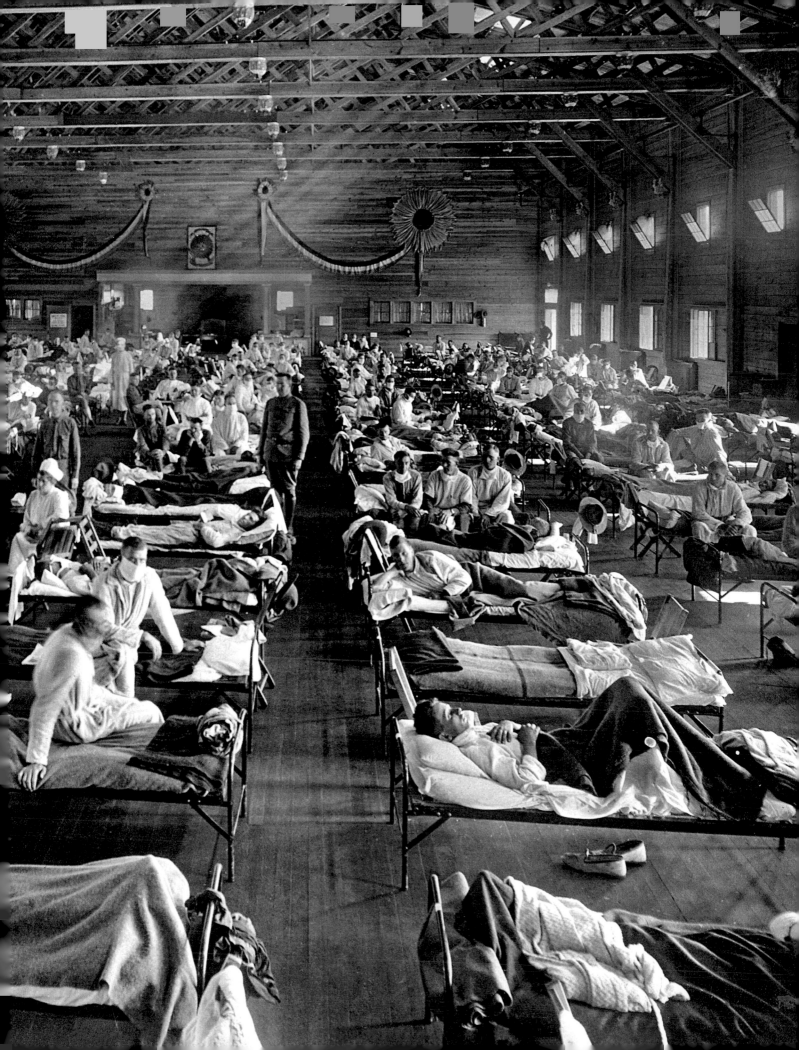

STORMING THE WINTER PALACE
*In October, the Bolsheviks launched the second
revolution of 1917, this time against the unpopular
provisional government. They stormed the Winter
Palace in Petrograd (above), and seized the capital.
The communist takeover of Russia had begun.*

The Russian Revolution

In 1917, at the height of World War I, two violent revolutions broke out in Russia. The first overthrew the czar (emperor) and brought the Russian Empire to an end. The second overthrew the whole government to establish the world's first communist state.

Russia joined World War I in 1914 on the Allied side. The war went badly for Russia and the Russian people grew dissatisfied with their government. When bread rationing was introduced in February 1917, there were riots in Petrograd (modern-day St. Petersburg). The government collapsed, and Czar Nicholas II gave up his throne.

Several revolutionary groups, including the Mensheviks, Kadets, and the Socialist Revolutionaries, formed a new provisional government. Their decision to keep fighting in the war led to people rising up in rebellion, which allowed the Bolshevik Party—led by Vladimir Lenin—to seize power in a second revolution in October. The Bolsheviks managed to suppress all other opposition movements and brought a new political system, known

as communism, to Russia. Communists believed that the country's wealth should be shared equally among its citizens. In 1922, the country was reorganized and renamed the Union of Soviet Socialist Republics (the USSR).

▲ **THE FEBRUARY REVOLUTION**
The first revolution took place in Russia in February 1917 after the country failed to defeat Germany in World War I and bread shortages led to riots in Petrograd. The army refused to suppress the riots and joined the protesters, leading to the downfall of the emperor and his government.

▲ **BUILDING A NEW WORLD**
The Bolsheviks wanted to build a completely new state, where there was more equality between people who lived in urban and rural areas. Revolutionaries went out to educate people, such as these members of the Russian Railway Women Workers, about their new government.

VLADIMIR LENIN

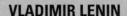

Vladimir Lenin (1870–1924) believed that people should have an equal share of wealth and was the world's first communist leader. He took power in Russia after the second revolution of 1917, but suffered a stroke in 1922 and died in 1924.

▲ **CIVIL WAR**
The new Bolshevik government had to fight a violent civil war after 1918 to stay in power in Russia. The Bolsheviks (also called the Red Army) eventually won the war when the White Army (above) collapsed in June 1923. But fighting in Central Asia continued until 1934.

The hammer and sickle are prominent on communist posters of the period.

▼ **SYMBOLS OF THE REVOLUTION**
After the revolutions, the Communist Party adopted the symbol of a crossed hammer and sickle on a red background. The hammer represented the city workers while the sickle was for the rural farmers. A new Russian flag was also designed based on this, which included a gold star above the hammer and sickle and stood for the Communist Party.

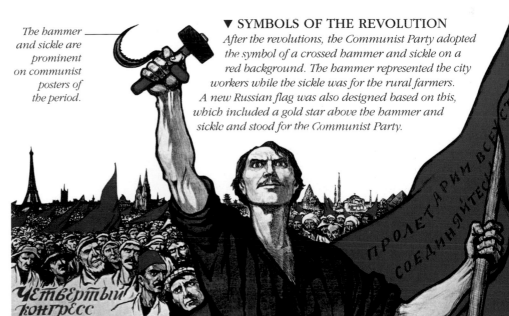

THE RIGHT TO VOTE

1893 After years of campaigning led by the suffragist Kate Sheppard, New Zealand becomes the first country in the world to grant women the right to vote in national elections.

1906 Finland becomes the first European country to grant the vote to women in 1906. It is also the first European nation to allow women to stand as candidates in elections.

1920–1965 In the US, women are granted the right to vote in 1920, but several local measures deny this right to Black voters. The Voting Rights Act of 1965 outlaws this discrimination.

1929 Ecuador becomes the first Latin American country to grant women the right to vote. It adopts a new constitution in 1929 that extends voting rights to literate women above the age of 21.

1956 Egyptian women are given the vote in 1956. Doria Shafik, a women's rights activist, leads the campaign through demonstrations and an eight-day hunger strike.

DORIA SHAFIK

BRITISH SUFFRAGE ▶
In the UK, there were two groups of suffrage campaigners. The Suffragists believed in peaceful methods while the Suffragettes were willing to take direct action. The Suffragettes were led by Emmeline Pankhurst (right). They smashed windows and cut telegraph lines, and were often jailed for their actions. In prison, they went on hunger strikes to protest.

Women's rights

Throughout history, women have been denied rights that men take for granted. In the past two centuries, women around the world have fought for greater equality, whether that means voting in an election, receiving an education, owning property, or getting paid as much as men to do the same job. But the battle is far from over.

Historically, most men who lived in democracies had the right to elect their chosen representatives. Women were not given this right automatically, but had to fight for it. From the late 19th century, women in Western countries began to campaign for suffrage (the right to vote) and today there are very few countries that don't allow women to vote.

Women then focused on other inequalities. In the 1960s, a new movement began in the US, with demands that ranged from equality in pay to more access to birth-control methods. As more women activists from other countries came together to discuss their issues in forums such as the United Nations, the movement spread. Over the years, subsequent campaigns have helped create laws that are more just toward women.

While the movements that began in the West focused on white women, today, there is a growing awareness that women from different cultures and backgrounds may face a variety of challenges, for example, because of their racial identity. It has led to many new movements across the world.

◄ FEMINISM IN THE 1960S

The belief that women should have the same rights and opportunities as men is known as feminism. In the 1960s, the Women's Liberation Movement was formed to fight for the ideals of feminism in the US. Its members were inspired by the book The Feminine Mystique by US feminist author Betty Friedan (left). The book was based on interviews with thousands of American women and argued that women were not satisfied with being just housewives but wanted the choice to have careers as well.

#NIUNAMENOS ▼

In 2016, Argentinian women gathered to protest against rising levels of violence against women. The movement, known as #NiUnaMenos (Not One Woman Less), demanded better laws to be put into place for women's safety. As the campaign grew, it spread to other Central and South American countries, including Mexico, Brazil, Bolivia, and Chile.

MALALA YOUSAFZAI

Pakistani activist Malala Yousafzai (born 1997), grew up in an area where education for girls was banned. When she spoke out against this, she was shot. Malala survived and is now a campaigner for the right to education for girls around the world.

▼ WOMEN'S MARCH OF 2017

Many women in the US were alarmed when Donald Trump became president in 2017, as they felt that his views would undermine the progress of women's rights in the country. On January 21, the day after he officially took office, a nationwide protest was attended by thousands of women and men.

The Roaring Twenties

After the horrors of World War I, the 1920s was a decade of hope and excitement across the US and Europe. Economies flourished, and a new popular culture emerged. People spent money on fashion, music, going to the movies, and luxury items such as cars.

Western economies recovered quickly after World War I. Improvements in technology helped reduce the price of goods. Wages rose steadily, so people had more money to spend. As businesses grew, they needed more office space. In the US, this led to the construction of tall buildings known as skyscrapers, which started to change city skylines.

Movies became extremely popular, and by the mid-1920s, 50 million people went to the movies every week in the US. This was also a golden age for Black American dance, music, and theater.

However, the good times ended abruptly in 1929, when the US stock market crashed, triggering an economic crisis that would eventually spread across the world.

◀ FLAPPERS
The 1920s was a period of newfound freedom for women in the West. After becoming part of the workforce during World War I, many had their own money to spend on fashion and entertainment. Young women who dressed in ways that expressed this new sense of fun and freedom were called "flappers."

BESSIE SMITH

The powerful voice of Bessie Smith (1894–1937) made her the highest-paid Black American musical artist of the 1920s. She was called the Empress of the Blues, a sad, emotional musical style that had its origins in slavery.

GROWTH OF RADIO ▼
In the 1920s, radios became much more affordable. People now had immediate access to news and entertainment. By the end of the decade, up to 40 percent of American households had a radio.

◀ THE JAZZ AGE
Jazz, a new musical style blending African rhythms and European harmonies, emerged in the Black American communities of New Orleans, and soon caught on across the whole country. Jazz artists such as Louis Armstrong and Joe "King" Oliver became celebrities. Jazz became so popular that the 1920s came to be known as the "Jazz Age."

The Great Depression

In October 1929, the US stock market crashed. Billions of dollars were lost, leading to the biggest economic crisis in history, known as the Great Depression. Companies went out of business, and factories were forced to close, causing millions to lose their jobs. Poverty and hunger became widespread, and the impact of the crash was soon felt across the world. It took a decade for the global economy to recover.

▲ SOUP KITCHENS

More than 10 million Americans were out of work by 1932. Private charities and church communities opened soup kitchens for the hungry and unemployed. They served soup and bread for free, and for thousands of people, these were the only places they could get a meal. By the mid-1930s the government had taken over the running of soup kitchens.

NEW DEAL ▶

Franklin D. Roosevelt became president of the US on the promise of a "new deal," which would help the country's economy to recover. From 1933 to 1939, his government introduced policies that helped people find work again. Many projects, such as the construction of the massive Hoover Dam (right), were started to create more jobs.

The economic boom of the 1920s had led ordinary Americans to invest in the stock market. But by 1929, economic growth had begun to slow and companies found they couldn't sell their goods. Share prices dipped, causing investors to sell their shares.

When the stock market crashed, the shares suddenly became worthless. Millionaires became poor overnight, and people who had taken loans from banks to buy houses couldn't pay them back and lost their homes. Hunger and mass unemployment raged, and slums with terrible living conditions emerged.

Meanwhile, the effect of the depression spread across the world. In Germany, poverty and unemployment led people to vote for the Nazi Party, which promised a way out—leading, in time, to World War II (see pp.190–191).

The rise of fascism

In 1919, Italian leader Benito Mussolini named his political party *Fasci Italiani di Combattimento*, which later came to power as the National Fascist Party. A fascist government has a strong leader, often a dictator, who has total control of society and the economy and suppresses all political opposition. By the end of the 1930s, fascist governments took power across southern and Eastern Europe, such as in Portugal, Greece, and Croatia. Small-scale fascist movements also arose in Britain, Ireland, the US, and other democratic countries. In Germany, fascism flourished under the name of Nazism, but, unlike Italy, one of its main features was extreme anti-Semitism (hatred of Jewish people).

◀ **ADOLF HITLER**
In 1919, Austrian-born Adolf Hitler joined the small right-wing German Worker's Party, which later became the National Socialist German Workers'—or Nazi—Party under his leadership. The Nazis took power in Germany in 1933, staging huge rallies, such as this one at Nuremberg, to gain support. Hitler led Germany into World War II in 1939, and died by suicide when Germany was defeated in 1945.

▲ **BENITO MUSSOLINI**
In 1921, Benito Mussolini founded the National Fascist Party to campaign for a fascist state in Italy. After staging a march on Rome in October 1922 in order to seize power, he was appointed prime minister of Italy by the king. Mussolini governed Italy until he was deposed in 1943.

World War II in Europe

Barely two decades after World War I ended in 1918, war broke out across Europe once again in 1939. World War II was the deadliest conflict in human history. Around 70 million people lost their lives, and countries across the world suffered devastation. After six long years, the war finally came to an end in 1945.

World War II began as a result of the aggressive actions of Germany's ruling Nazi Party, led by Adolf Hitler. In September 1939, Hitler ordered the invasion of Poland. In response, France and Britain declared war against Germany. Italy joined forces with Germany in 1940, by which time Germany was in control of large areas of western and central Europe. Both Germany and Italy wanted to create their own empires in Europe and North Africa.

At first, the USSR made a pact with Hitler not to fight Germany, but it joined the Allied forces when Hitler invaded the USSR in June 1941. This invasion started on a massive scale, but German troops were eventually defeated at Stalingrad in February 1943. A year later, boosted by the arrival of US troops, Allied armies landed in German-occupied France and slowly moved toward Germany, forcing it to surrender in May 1945.

EVERYDAY LIFE

When war broke out, governments introduced rationing, a system that limited the amount of food and other items that people could buy. Windows had to be covered at night to prevent light escaping to guide enemy bombers. During bombing raids, people sought protection underground and in specially built shelters. In Britain, children were moved out of the cities to the countryside in case of air attacks (below).

▼ THE BLITZ

In the summer of 1940, Hitler commanded Germany's air force (the Luftwaffe) to attack British planes in the skies in order to prepare for a land invasion. When that failed, he switched to bombing British cities—a campaign called the Blitz (German for "lightning"). For eight months, London and other major cities were ruthlessly bombarded. Up to 43,000 civilians were killed and many more injured before Hitler called off the campaign in 1941.

▲ GERMANY ADVANCES

For the first seven months after the outbreak of war no fighting took place in western Europe, a period known as the "Phony war." Then, in April 1940, Germany suddenly attacked Denmark and Norway and in May moved to invade France, Belgium, Luxembourg, and the Netherlands. German troops marched into Paris (above) on June 14, 1940.

D-DAY LANDINGS

On June 6, 1944, US, British, and Canadian troops launched an attack to free western Europe from Nazi control. More than 150,000 soldiers crossed the English Channel to land on the beaches of Normandy in northern France. The invasion was successful, and by the end of the year almost all of France and Belgium had been liberated.

▼ **GERMANY SURRENDERS**

On April 29, 1945, Soviet troops entered the center of the German capital, Berlin, and a few days later captured the Reichstag, the German parliament building (below). Germany finally surrendered on May 7, bringing the war in Europe to an end.

▲ **OPERATION BARBAROSSA**

Hitler launched Operation Barbarossa on the USSR on June 22, 1941, pouring 3.8 million troops and 3,795 tanks across the border. German troops laid siege to the city of Leningrad for 1,000 days and almost reached the Soviet capital, Moscow, but the harsh Russian winter and food shortages stopped them from taking the city. The USSR then launched a long but successful campaign to push German forces back.

THE HOLOCAUST

Between 1941 and 1945, the Nazis and their collaborators murdered more than six million European Jews. This genocide (a mass killing intended to wipe out an entire group of people) was known as the Holocaust. Millions of others—Poles, Roma, Russians, political protesters, and homosexual people—were killed alongside them.

Adolf Hitler and the Nazis were antisemitic (hated Jewish people) and believed Jews were responsible for Germany's problems. When the Nazis came to power in 1933, they passed laws to strip Jews of their rights as citizens. After World War II began in 1939, the Nazis forced Jews, primarily from occupied Poland and areas of the USSR, inside ghettos—sectioned off city areas. Here, Jews lived in cramped conditions with very little food, and many were murdered by death squads. Jews were also sent to labor camps where they were worked to death, and from 1941 to death camps, where millions of Jews were killed.

Yet many Jews fought against the tyranny of the Nazis. Secret resistance groups performed act of sabotage, or organized armed uprisings from within the ghettos and camps.

◀ THE YELLOW BADGE
After September 1, 1941, all Jews in Nazi-occupied lands were forced to wear a star with the word Jude *(Jew) written on it. These identification badges were meant to be a mark of shame.*

CHILD IN TIME

Anne Frank (1929–1945) was born to a Jewish family in Germany. The Franks moved to Amsterdam when the Nazis came to power, and when Germany occupied the Netherlands they went into hiding. They lived in a small space, constantly in fear of discovery, for two years. During this time Anne wrote about her daily life in a diary. After her capture and death, the diary was found and published. It has been translated into more than 70 languages.

WARSAW GHETTO
The Nazis set up more than 1,000 ghettos to confine and control the Jews. The Warsaw Ghetto in Poland was the largest, with up to 460,000 Jews imprisoned there. From the ghetto, many were sent to their deaths at Treblinka camp.

▲ KINDERTRANSPORT

From 1938 to 1940, a scheme called Kindertransport (children's transport) brought around 10,000 Jewish children from Germany and occupied Europe to live in Britain. They arrived by train and boat, and were cared for by British families. They were often the only members of a family to survive the Holocaust.

▼ THE FINAL SOLUTION

At the beginning of the Holocaust, the Nazis killed Jews by shooting them, or gassing them in mobile vans. But in 1942, Nazi leaders decided on a new method of killing Jews. They came up with what they called the "Final Solution"—the murder of Europe's Jews on a massive scale at death camps. This pile of shoes belonged to just some of the people murdered at the Auschwitz camp in Poland.

◄ THE CAMPS

The Nazis established concentration camps to imprison people, labor camps to make them work for the war effort, and death camps where they were killed. The camp of Auschwitz-Birkenau (left) in Poland acted as all three. Jews were transported to death camps from all over Europe by train, stripped of their belongings, and many were gassed to death shortly after their arrival.

FACT
In the Hebrew language, which is central to Judaism, the Holocaust is known as the *Shoah*, meaning "catastrophe."

LIBERATION ►

As Soviet forces advanced through Poland, the Nazis tried to hide their crimes by forcing prisoners to walk long distances to camps in Germany. Those who survived these "death marches," or were freed from the camps by the Allied armies, were often starving and in bad health. These Polish prisoners were rescued from the Dachau camp in Germany by the US Army in 1945.

World War II in the Pacific

The war between Japan and the United States and its allies, often called the Pacific War, was one of the most intense conflicts of World War II. Fighting spread across a large area from Myanmar (Burma) in the west, across Southeast Asia, and out to the Pacific Ocean to the east. This war in the Pacific saw major sea battles, as well as land campaigns in Myanmar, New Guinea, and the Philippines.

In the 1870s, Japan began building an empire in East Asia, and by 1920 had taken control of Taiwan, Korea, and many Pacific islands. It seized Manchuria in 1931 and invaded the rest of China in 1937 (see pp.176–177).

The US and its allies wanted to protect their colonies in the region, so to stop Japan's expansion into Asia, the US restricted trade with the country. Japan seized French Indochina (modern-day Vietnam, Laos, and Cambodia), which resulted in further restrictions. As tensions increased, Japan attacked Pearl Harbor—a US naval and air base in Hawaii—in December 1941. This immediately brought the US into World War II.

Japan quickly conquered European colonies in Asia. It seemed impossible to halt the Japanese advance until the Allies discovered their secret plans in 1942. After two major sea battles, the Allies began taking control of the Pacific and advanced on Japan island by island. In 1945, the US dropped two atomic bombs on Japan, forcing it to surrender and ending World War II.

FACT
As Japan began to lose the war, suicide pilots known as *kamikaze* crash-dived their planes into US ships to blow them up. More than 2,500 lost their lives in a desperate attempt to avoid defeat and dishonor.

BOMBING PEARL HARBOR ▶
The attack on Pearl Harbor took the Americans by complete surprise. In two bombing missions on the morning of December 7, 1941, Japanese aircraft sank or damaged around 18 US warships, destroyed almost 200 planes, and killed more than 2,400 Americans.

▲ INVADING ASIA AND THE PACIFIC
After their attack on Pearl Harbor, the Japanese launched a series of quick, highly successful invasions of colonies held by the US, Britain, and the Netherlands in the region. Up to 136,000 British troops surrendered to the Japanese in Singapore, then a British colony, in February 1942.

◀ THE WAR ON IWO JIMA

By early 1945, the US had taken back many of the Pacific islands occupied by Japan. They now needed an island base to launch air attacks on the Japanese mainland. They chose tiny Iwo Jima, just 750 miles (1,200 km) south of Tokyo. The five-week campaign to take the island was one of the bloodiest battles in the war in the Pacific. Once captured, the island was used as a base to launch 66 air raids on Japanese cities.

▲ FIGHTING AT SEA

For the first time, battles were fought at sea using aircraft carriers—huge ships like floating airbases—from which planes could take off and land. There were two major aircraft carrier battles between the US and Japan in mid-1942, first in the Coral Sea off the Australian coast, and then off Midway Island in the central Pacific. At the Battle of Midway, Japan suffered heavy losses and lost control of the Pacific. This turned the course of the war.

US Marines raise the American flag over Iwo Jima on February 23, 1945.

▼ DEVASTATING JAPAN

On August 6, 1945, a US bomber dropped an atomic bomb named "Little Boy" on the Japanese city of Hiroshima (below), followed by a second bomb on Nagasaki three days later. More than 195,000 people are estimated to have died in the two bombings. Japan surrendered unconditionally on August 15.

"LITTLE BOY" ATOMIC BOMB

EVERYDAY LIFE

At the outbreak of war against Japan in 1941, around 120,000 Japanese-Americans living in the US were locked up in camps by the US government, fearing they might become enemy agents. People were cramped in small barracks and had to survive in very poor living conditions.

South Asian independence

The struggle for Indian independence intensified during the early 20th century as more people began to protest against British rule. In 1947, India achieved freedom but it was partitioned (divided) into two countries—India and Pakistan. In 1971, East Pakistan broke away to form Bangladesh.

Most of the Indian subcontinent had been under the direct control of the British government since 1858. In the early 20th century, the leaders of the Indian independence movement demanded self-rule from the British government and launched many campaigns to achieve this. In 1920, a leading figure of the independence movement, Mahatma Gandhi, launched the Non-Cooperation Movement, urging people not to buy British goods. He followed it up by calling for all Indians to engage in civil disobedience—a form of nonviolent protest where people refused to obey any unjust laws.

By 1945, British rule had weakened and it was decided that power would soon be transferred to Indians. However, Muhammad Ali Jinnah, a key leader of the freedom struggle, asked for a separate homeland for Muslims. Eventually, the British agreed to do this. On August 14, 1947, the new country Pakistan came into existence, and a day later, India gained independence.

▲ QUIT INDIA MOVEMENT
The slogan "Quit India" was launched by Gandhi on August 9, 1942. His demand for Britain to bring a complete end to its rule in India was met with widespread support. He urged for civil disobedience, inspiring people from across the country to take part in workers strikes and nonviolent marches. The British responded by imprisoning nearly all the movement's leaders.

MAHATMA GANDHI

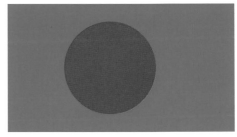

Mohandas K. Gandhi (1869–1948), popularly known as Mahatma Gandhi, was an Indian lawyer and freedom fighter. He championed civil disobedience and nonviolent resistance in India's struggle for independence.

▲ BANGLADESH IS BORN
Twenty years after Pakistan was created, the people of East Pakistan demanded more economic and political powers, and fought for independence. Their victory in the Bangladesh War of Independence led to the creation of The People's Republic of Bangladesh in 1971.

PARTITION OF INDIA ▶
In August 1947, the Indian subcontinent was divided into two countries. In the following months, millions of people moved across the new borders of India and Pakistan on foot, in bullock carts, and on trains. Muslims living in India fled to West and East Pakistan, while Sikhs and Hindus traveled to India. It was one of the largest human migrations in history. Violence and riots broke out between different religious communities. By 1948, more than a million people had died in the riots, and more than 15 million people had become refugees.

◄ THE YEAR OF AFRICA
1960 marked a turning point for the continent, as it was the year when 17 African nations, including Cameroon, Ivory Coast, Senegal, Nigeria, Somalia, and others, gained independence from their colonizers. European rulers, such as King Baudouin of Belgium (right), were obliged to hand over power to African rulers.

African independence

In the mid-20th century, following the end of World War II, African countries successfully gained their freedom from the European countries that had colonized them. Some African independence movements were born from armed struggle, but many involved peaceful handovers when it became clear that foreign rule had to end.

In the 19th century, seven European nations—Britain, France, Spain, Italy, Portugal, Belgium, and Germany—established control over almost the entire African continent (see pp.158–159).

After World War II, the demand for independence from colonial rule in many African nations grew stronger. In various countries, people rose up in rebellion against their European colonizers. In 1952, a group of Kenyan freedom fighters known as the Mau Mau revolted against the British authorities. Between 1954 and 1962, Algerian rebels waged a war against French forces. When it became clear that the European countries would not be able to maintain imperial rule for much longer, the colonies were granted the right to self rule. More than 20 new nations were formed between 1956 and 1960, as former colonies gained independence.

◄ FREEDOM ACROSS AFRICA
A total of 46 African nations gained independence between 1957 and 1980. The first was Ghana and the last was Zimbabwe. The fight for freedom was a shared struggle for all Africans. Today, many people across the continent celebrate the date of their nation's independence with music, dance, and fireworks.

NEW NATIONS

1952
In a revolution that sought to end the British occupation of Egypt, King Farouk is toppled by army officers. The Republic of Egypt is born.

1957
Ghana, under British rule, becomes the first sub-Saharan African nation to achieve independence. The leader of the freedom movement, Kwame Nkrumah, becomes the first Prime Minister of Ghana.

1964-1968
More nations gain independence from colonial rulers including Malawi, Zambia, Botswana, Mauritius, Swaziland, and Equatorial Guinea.

1980
After a 15-year-long civil war, the British colony of Rhodesia gains independence and forms the nation of Zimbabwe.

▲ DIVIDING BERLIN

After World War II, Germany's capital Berlin was split into West Berlin, under the control of the US, France, and Britain, and East Berlin, under the USSR. In 1961, the government of East Berlin built a wall dividing it from West Berlin to prevent East Berliners escaping to the West. Guards and watchtowers monitored the strip of land around the wall.

CHILD IN TIME

In 1982, 10-year-old Samantha Smith from the US wrote a letter to the Soviet leader Yuri Andropov, asking him how he would prevent a nuclear war. Samantha was troubled by news reports of the tensions between the US and the USSR. In response, Andropov invited Samantha to visit the USSR, and she became known as "America's Youngest Ambassador."

The Cold War

The United States and the Soviet Union (USSR) emerged as powerful nations after the end of World War II. But the political differences between these two "superpowers" soon led to a struggle for dominance. Without actually declaring war, between 1946–1991, they fought a "cold war" in which they opposed each other through alliances with other nations and through the threat of nuclear warfare.

Although the US and the USSR had been allies during World War II, tensions quickly escalated during the reorganization and rebuilding of the war-ravaged countries of Europe.

The USSR took control of countries in Eastern Europe, and established communist governments in the region. Meanwhile, the US, Britain, and France supported democracy and capitalism in the countries in Western Europe. As communist influence spread to China and other parts of

Asia, the world became increasingly divided. Both superpowers backed governments in different parts of the world that supported their ideologies. They even sent weapons and troops when wars broke out in other regions— these "proxy wars" became the main battlefield of the Cold War and caused devastation in many countries.

After decades of hostilities, the Cold War came to an end with the collapse of the USSR in 1991 (see p.222).

▼ SPACE RACE
The power struggle between the US and USSR was not limited to politics. Both superpowers also competed to develop technology that would make travel to space possible. In 1961, USSR's Yuri Gagarin became the first man to reach Earth's orbit on board the spacecraft Vostok 1 (below).

▲ CUBAN MISSILE CRISIS
In 1961, the US tried to overthrow Cuba's communist government. In response, the USSR promised to defend Cuba by setting up missiles in the country. The US then tried to block Soviet ships (above), and sent planes to patrol the waters around Cuba. A nuclear war seemed inevitable, but the two sides reached a compromise and the USSR withdrew its missiles from the region.

FACT
Many countries in Asia and Africa did not want to support either of the two superpowers during the Cold War. They formed the Non-Aligned Movement in the 1960s.

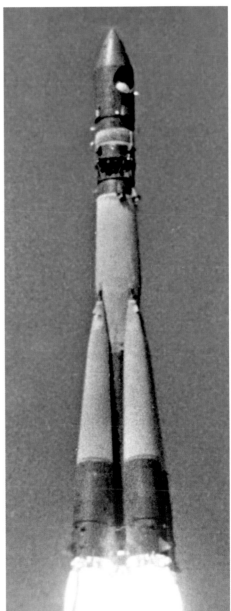

MCCARTHYISM ▲
In the 1950s, many people in the US feared a communist uprising in the country. In reaction to this fear, a US Senator, Joseph McCarthy (above), began accusing some people, from government officials to Hollywood stars, of being secret communists or supporters of the USSR. His anticommunist campaign ruined the careers and lives of many.

THREAT OF NUCLEAR WAR ▶
After the end of World War II, the US and USSR began to develop more powerful weapons. By the 1960s both countries had nuclear weapons, and people lived in fear of nuclear attack. Across the US, schools held drills teaching children to dive under desks and cover their heads to protect themselves in case of a nuclear explosion.

PROXY WARS

1950–1953	1955–1975	1975	1979–1989
War breaks out in the Korean Peninsula as North Korea, supported by China and the USSR, and South Korea, aided by the US, battle to control the region.	Communist North Vietnam attacks South Vietnam. The conflict escalates when the US sends thousands of soldiers to hold back the communists.	Civil war erupts in the African country of Angola. The US sends aid to the anticommunist party, while Cuba sends troops to support the communist fighters.	The USSR sends its army to support the communist government of Afghanistan against anticommunists, who were armed by the US.

Israel and Palestine

After six million Jews died in the Holocaust (see pp.192–193), Jews sought a safe haven in their ancestral homeland. The United Nations voted to separate British-controlled Palestine into two states, one Jewish (Israel) and one Arab (Palestine). But the decision angered Arab states, as the Arab population considered Palestine its home as well. A series of wars began, and the conflict is still unresolved today.

▲ **THE SS EXODUS**
In 1947, 4,500 Jewish refugees set sail for Palestine on board the SS Exodus. They were stopped by the British who decided that they had to return to Germany. Protests around the world eventually led to support for the creation of a Jewish state.

In 1948, as the last British troops left Palestine and the state of Israel was declared, all its Arab neighbors attacked. At the end of this First Arab–Israeli War, Israel had captured more land from the Palestinians, and the Arab nations of Jordan and Egypt occupied the areas known as the

West Bank and Gaza respectively. The occupation of the West Bank stirred religious nationalism in Israel. During the Six-Day War of 1967, the West Bank and Gaza were taken by Israel, who also occupied the Sinai Peninsula in Egypt and Golan Heights in Syria.

The Sinai Peninsula was returned to Egypt after a peace treaty in 1979, and Gaza and parts of the West Bank have been returned to Palestine. But today the two sides remain as far from reaching an agreement about their terrority disputes as ever.

▲ **PEACE NEGOTIATIONS**
The United Nations supports a two-state solution, with an independent state of Palestine alongside the state of Israel. The global community has tried to negotiate several peace deals. One such example was the 1993 Oslo Peace Accords, which initiated peace talks between Israel and Palestine. However, tensions and fighting are still ongoing.

▼ **PALESTINE'S REFUGEE CAMPS**
In 1948, during the First Arab–Israeli War, 700,000 Palestinians were expelled or fled their homes and became refugees in the West Bank and Gaza, as well as Lebanon, Syria, and Jordan. Palestinians refer to this loss of their homeland as their "nakba" (catastrophe).

Conflicts in the Middle East

The Middle East extends across West Asia to Egypt in North Africa. Many of the region's national borders were carelessly created by the British and French when they abandoned their colonies as their empires collapsed. The region has suffered frequent conflicts and upheavals throughout the 20th and early 21st centuries. These have included civil wars, religious conflicts, and invasions by foreign powers.

▲ IRANIAN REVOLUTION
In 1979, the Iranian people were unhappy with the ruling Shah (king) and his dependence on the West, particularly the US. A million people took to the streets to protest, forcing the Shah to step down and bringing Ayatollah Khomeini—an Islamic leader and figurehead of the revolution—to power.

When Britain and France withdrew from the region in the 1940s, borders were haphazardly decided, and leaders loyal to the former rulers put in place. Palestine was divided into Jewish and Arab states and the Israel–Palestinian conflict remains unresolved today (see opposite).

Iraq and Egypt overthrew their kings, and Egypt's ruler Gamal Abdel Nasser provoked a failed British and French invasion after taking control of the Suez Canal. Iran and Iraq have also experienced frequent conflicts. Following the 1979 Iranian Revolution, Iraq invaded Iran in 1980. A million people died during the war before a ceasefire was declared in 1988. On September 11, 2001, Islamic terrorist group "Al-Qaeda" carried out attacks in the US. The US responded with a "war on terror," invading Afghanistan and Iraq to search for weapons that could destroy the West.

▼ ARAB SPRING
In 2010, Arabs across the region took part in uprisings, calling for more democratic rule from their governments. Egypt's President Muharak was toppled, but little else was achieved in the region except more conflict, including the Syrian Civil War.

SADDAM HUSSEIN

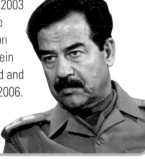

Saddam Hussein (ruled 1979–2003) led Iraq to war with Iran from 1980 to 1988, and in 1990 he invaded Kuwait. Iraq was invaded in 1991 by the US and its allies to liberate Kuwait, and again in 2003 as part of the wider "war on terror." Hussein was captured and executed in 2006.

▲ THE IRAQ WAR
In 2003, the US invaded Iraq with support from the UK, Australia, and Poland. The Iraq War (2003–2011) was linked to the wider "war on terror" and began on the belief that Iraq had weapons of mass destruction which would be used against the West, though no weapons were found.

▲ SEGREGATION
Under apartheid, separate areas were created for each ethnic group. Facilities and areas for "non-whites", such as this public toilet, were always worse than the "white-only" spaces. Black people had to carry passes in white areas and marriages between "whites" and "non-whites" was forbidden.

The struggle against apartheid

A system known as apartheid ("separateness") existed in South Africa from 1948 until the early 1990s. Under this system, Black people were discriminated against—they had fewer rights than white people, and faced restrictions on where they could live, go to school, and work.

FACT
Steve Biko was a key figure in the fight against apartheid. He led several campaigns and founded the South African Students Organization to fight for the rights of Black students.

Although the population of South Africa was mostly Black, the laws of apartheid gave white people control of the country and the power to set and enforce the laws. Black people were forced out of their homes and were not allowed to own businesses or land, live, travel, or work in certain areas. If they broke these laws, they were punished or sent to jail.

Many people were against apartheid and protests were led by the African National Congress (ANC). At first the protests were peaceful but as the government's regime grew more brutal—more than 50 protesters were killed in the Sharpeville Massacre in the 1960s—the protests became more violent, too. But from the 1980s, increasing international pressure

highlighted the need for reform. In May 1994, Nelson Mandela—the leader of the ANC—was elected the first Black president of South Africa in the first elections in which Black people could vote, marking the end of apartheid.

▲ AFRICAN NATIONAL CONGRESS
The African National Congress (ANC), founded in 1912, became the leading group campaigning against apartheid. It was banned by the government from 1960 to 1990 and was forced to operate in secret during this period.

▼ GROUP AREAS ACT
In 1950, the South African government passed the "Group Areas Act," a law that created different areas for each race. Thousands of Black people were later forced out of their homes to live in new areas called "homelands."

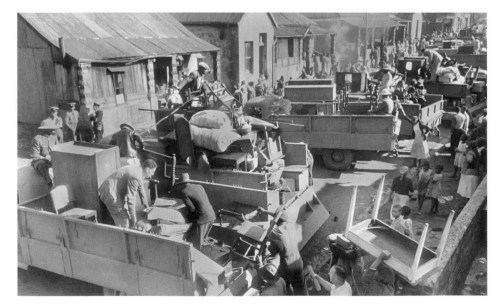

ALBERTINA SISULU

Albertina Sisulu (1918–2011) was one of the most famous activists of the anti-apartheid movement. She was the wife of ANC leader Walter Sisulu, and became known by many as "Ma Sisulu," the mother of the nation.

NELSON MANDELA

1956
Mandela is arrested (along with other members of the ANC) and charged with "high treason" for betraying the government. He is found not guilty in 1961.

1962
Mandela is arrested and sentenced to five years in prison for urging South African workers to go on strike and for leaving the country without a passport.

1964
On June 12, Mandela and seven others are convicted and sentenced to life in prison for plotting to overthrow the government. Mandela is sent to Robben Island prison.

1990
Following calls from around the world to "free Nelson Mandela," on February 11—after spending 27 years in prison—Mandela is finally released at the age of 71. He becomes president of the ANC in 1991.

1993
Mandela works with the president of South Africa, F. W. de Klerk, to put an end to apartheid and introduce equal rights for all South Africans. The pair are awarded a Nobel Peace Prize.

1994
All South Africans are allowed to vote for the first time ever in the general election. Mandela's ANC party wins the election and Mandela becomes the first Black president of South Africa on May 10.

SOWETO UPRISING

On June 16, 1976, thousands of Black students came together in Soweto to protest about a new law that said all pupils must learn Afrikaans in school. They were brutally attacked by police and many were killed in what became known as the "Soweto uprising."

The Vietnam War

In 1955, a conflict began in South Vietnam between communist rebels and the anticommunist government. The US, desperate to stop the spread of communism, supported the South Vietnamese government, and the conflict escalated into a long and bitter war. It ended in 1975, with the defeat of the South Vietnam government.

Vietnam had been split between the communist North Vietnam and the pro-Western South Vietnam in 1954, a year before the conflict began. With support from North Vietnam, communist rebels in the south launched a campaign against the

government aiming to reunite the country under communist rule. Initially, the US sent only military advisors to South Vietnam, but in 1964, following a North Vietnamese attack on a US warship, President Johnson won approval from the US Congress to send in ground troops. The first marines landed in 1965.

Despite heavily bombing in the North, the US was unable to win the war and withdrew all its troops in 1973. Two years later, Vietnam was unified under communist control.

▲ THE TET OFFENSIVE
During the Tet spring festival in 1968, communist forces started a series of attacks on South Vietnamese towns and cities, hoping to trigger an uprising in the country. Although the offensive was beaten back, thousands of soldiers and civilians were killed and the war lost public support in the US.

▼ US INVOLVEMENT IN THE WAR
US military involvement in the war increased from fewer than 1,000 military advisors in 1960 to more than half a million soldiers by the end of the following decade. The US Army used helicopters to transport troops and weapons across Vietnam's jungle terrain.

▲ OPPOSITION TO THE WAR
Opposition to the war in the US grew steadily, particularly among students, and around 50,000 soldiers deserted the armed forces. The killing of four students at a peace rally in 1970 led to massive protests across the nation.

MAJOR EVENTS

1954	1955	1964	1975
After Vietnam wins its freedom from France, the country is divided into two zones—communist-run North Vietnam and anticommunist South Vietnam.	The communist National Liberation Front of South Vietnam, or Viet Cong, starts a rebellion against the South Vietnamese government.	After a naval clash in the Gulf of Tonkin, US President Lyndon B. Johnson massively increases the US military presence in South Vietnam and starts to bomb North Vietnamese cities.	North Vietnam conquers the south following the 1973 Paris Peace Accords and the withdrawal of US forces from Vietnam.

The Cuban Revolution

In 1959, Cuban revolutionary Fidel Castro and a small group of rebels seized control of Cuba, ending the brutal dictatorship of Fulgencio Batista. Their new government made many reforms, improving the health care and education systems in the country.

Fidel Castro was the son of a wealthy farmer, and developed an interest in politics while studying law in Havana, Cuba's capital. He started a campaign to overthrow Batista, but his first attempt to do so in 1953 failed. In 1956, Castro began a second military campaign in the mountains of eastern Cuba, which by 1958 had gained considerable ground. The following January, Castro overthrew Batista and took power.

The Cuban Revolution brought huge social and economic changes to the island. The government transformed the economy and took control of land ownership. Cuba also supported revolutionaries in other

BATISTA'S CUBA ▶
Fulgencio Batista seized power in a military coup in 1952 and ruled until 1959. During this time, 20,000 people were killed and many others tortured. Government corruption was so great that in 1957, even the US government, an ally, withheld military aid, and for a time supported Castro's resistance movement.

Latin American nations and sent troops to fight against colonialism and apartheid in Africa. After the government took over US oil facilities on the island, the US banned trade with Cuba. Following a failed invasion sponsored by the US in 1961, Cuba allied itself more closely with the USSR.

CASTRO'S RETURN ▶
After a year in exile in Mexico, Castro returned to Cuba along with 82 fighters in December 1956. All but 20 were killed in an ambush on arrival but the survivors set up a base in Cuba's Sierra Maestra mountains from which they then began another armed struggle to overthrow Batista.

▲ MONCADA BARRACKS
In 1952, as a young lawyer, Fidel Castro ran for parliament but the elections were canceled after Batista seized power. On May 26, 1953, Castro led an attack by 135 rebels on the Moncada military barracks in the city of Santiago de Cuba. The attack failed and Castro was imprisoned until 1955.

REVOLUTIONARY VICTORY ▶
As leader, Castro converted Cuba into a communist country (one where wealth is supposed to be shared among the people). He improved conditions for the poor, and provided better access to hospitals and schools. Yet Castro also went on ban any opposition to his rule, becoming a dictator himself.

The US Civil Rights Movement

Until the 1960s, laws in many of the southern states of the US allowed discrimination against Black Americans. Activists began a campaign to fight back against this oppression, which gained ground in the 1950s and 1960s. Known as the Civil Rights Movement, it demanded equality for all citizens.

In 1862, US President Abraham Lincoln issued the Emancipation Proclamation. This ended slavery in the US, but it did not ensure equality for Black people.

By the 1870s, laws came into force in some southern states that allowed local authorities to separate people on the basis of skin color, as long as they provided equal facilities for all. This led to separate spaces being created for Black people across the US—different schools and hospitals, and separate seating on buses, trains, and even in restaurants. The facilities created for Black people were always inferior, and many public places and businesses refused to allow Black people to use their amenities at all. This discrimination spread to politics as well, with Black voters being denied entry to voting booths at election time.

In the mid-20th century, Black American activists began using peaceful protests, boycotts, and legal actions to demand equality for Black people. The movement led to the Civil Rights Act of 1964, which outlawed discrimination based on skin color, sex, religion, or national origin.

FACT
It was only in June 1967 that the US Supreme Court abolished a law that banned marriage between people of different races.

◀ BUS BOYCOTT
In the 1950s, Black people had to sit in the back of public buses by law in some areas. In 1955, Black American seamstress Rosa Parks sat in the first row of seats reserved for Black people on a bus in Montgomery, Alabama, and refused to give up the seat for a white person as the bus filled up. Her arrest sparked a year-long bus boycott by Black people, bringing attention to the unfair law.

CHILD IN TIME

In 1960, six-year-old Ruby Bridges became the first Black child to attend a previously all-white school in Louisiana. On her first days at school, Ruby had to be protected by government officials as there were threats against her. She grew up to become a civil rights activist.

MARCH ON WASHINGTON

Dr. Martin Luther King, Jr., was a leading activist of the Civil Rights Movement, known for inspirational speeches and nonviolent protests. In 1963, Dr. King led the largest march of the movement, in which nearly 250,000 people gathered in Washington, D.C. It was here that he gave his famous "I have a dream" speech, which gave hope for a more equal society.

LITTLE ROCK NINE ▶

The US Supreme Court ruled against separate schools for Black people in 1954, but it was difficult to implement. In 1957, the state governor of Arkansas attempted to prevent nine Black students attending school in the city of Little Rock. In response, US President Dwight D. Eisenhower sent in the army to protect them.

◀ BALLOT OR THE BULLET

Like Martin Luther King, Malcolm X was a leading figure in the Civil Rights Movement, but he argued against some of King's ideas. In his "Ballot or the Bullet Speech" in 1963, he encouraged Black people to use their right to vote, but warned that they may have to use violence instead if the politicians in power didn't deliver equality.

🔑 TAKE A LOOK

Black Lives Matter began as a movement on social media in 2013, to express outrage against the use of violence by the police against Black Americans. After the murder of a Black man, George Floyd, by a white police officer captured worldwide attention in 2020, it grew into a global movement supported by millions.

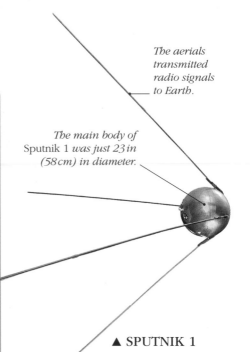

The aerials transmitted radio signals to Earth.

The main body of Sputnik 1 was just 23 in (58 cm) in diameter.

Space exploration

Since the earliest times, humans have been fascinated by the vast dark space that lies beyond Earth. We have wondered what other stars and planets are like, and whether there is life out there. It was only in the mid-20th century that technology advanced enough to allow humans to build powerful rockets and begin the first steps toward space exploration.

▲ SPUTNIK 1

On October 4, 1957, the USSR launched Sputnik 1, *the first human-made object to orbit (travel around) Earth. It stayed in orbit for three weeks, and gathered valuable scientific data about Earth's atmosphere. Today, satellites are sent into space to collect information for weather forecasting, communications, spying, navigation, and other uses.*

During World War II, scientists in Nazi Germany built V-2 rockets that were used as missiles. After the war, the Soviet Union (USSR) developed this technology to launch the world's first artificial satellite into space— *Sputnik 1*. This sparked a "space race" between the two world superpowers of the time, the USSR and the US, with each country trying to outdo the other. While the Soviets were the first to send a human into space in 1961, the US won the race to land astronauts on the moon in 1969.

Since then, astronauts from around 40 countries have explored space, and many more missions have been launched without a crew. Some spacecraft have even left the solar system—the region of space in which Earth sits, along with the sun and seven other planets—to explore deep space and further our knowledge of the universe. Future crewed missions may even try sending humans to Mars!

◀ TO THE MOON

In 1961, after Yuri Gagarin's spaceflight, US president John F. Kennedy promised to land a human on the moon by the end of the decade. On July 20, 1969, two US astronauts—Neil Armstrong and Buzz Aldrin (left)—became the first humans to set foot on the moon's surface. Since then, other astronauts have walked on the moon, and many uncrewed space vehicles have orbited or landed on it.

SPACE MILESTONES

1944	1958	1965	1981
German scientists launch a V-2 rocket—the first human-made object to reach space.	Cosmonaut (Russian astronaut) Yuri Gagarin becomes the first person in space, orbiting Earth for 1 hour and 48 minutes.	Soviet cosmonaut Alexei Leonov performs the first "spacewalk"—getting out of a spacecraft into outer space.	*Columbia,* the first reusable spacecraft, is launched by US space agency NASA. It goes on to fly 28 missions.

LIVING IN SPACE

Space stations are designed to be lived in by teams of astronauts for months at a time while they conduct scientific tests. The first, Salyut 1, was launched by the USSR in 1971, followed by the US's Skylab in 1973. In 1998, the two countries, along with others, came together to build the International Space Station (ISS) pictured here. The ISS can hold a crew of up to six people at a time and is used to study the effects of living in space on plants, animals, and humans.

YURI GAGARIN

Russian pilot Yuri Gagarin (1934–1968) was the first person to travel into space. On April 12, 1961, he orbited Earth in a capsule called *Vostok I*, kick-starting the era of human spaceflight. Gagarin became a huge celebrity in Russia and around the world, and his home town was renamed in his honor.

◄ BEYOND THE SOLAR SYSTEM

Launched in 1977, NASA's twin spacecraft Voyagers 1 *and 2 have journeyed beyond the solar system and are still operating today, sending valuable data about the interstellar universe to Earth. Space telescopes, such as the Hubble (left) and soon the James Webb, observe the deepest reaches of space, and provide incredible images of galaxies and other stellar objects.*

The 25-ft- (7.6-m-) long solar panels generate power from the sun.

China's first rover on Mars, Zhurong, stands 6ft (1.85m) tall.

UNCREWED MISSIONS ►

Several uncrewed spacecraft have been sent to explore the solar system in detail. The first, the Russian craft Venera 1, *flew past Venus in 1961, and since then many have landed on Venus, Mars, and Titan (Saturn's largest moon). The data from the voyages tells us what these objects are made of, their surface, and their atmospheres.*

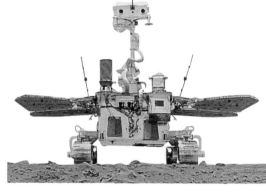

1990	2012	2019	2021
The Hubble Space Telescope becomes the first major telescope to be placed in space.	*Voyager 1* becomes the first human-made object to leave the solar system and travel into interstellar space—the space between stars.	China's *Chang'e 4* rover (robotic vehicle) makes the first successful landing on the far side of the moon.	A robotic helicopter called *Ingenuity*—part of NASA's Perseverance mission to Mars—achieves the first ever powered flight on another planet.

VOYAGER 1

209

Travel and transit

Improvements in transportation, from cars and ships to trains and planes, have radically changed the way we live, work, travel, and trade. Trips that once took months now take hours, and journeys that were once impossible are now a reality, as state-of-the-art spacecraft prove that, for humankind, not even outer space is beyond reach.

Two wheels
Draisienne

Where Mannheim, Germany
When 1817

German inventor Karl von Drais created the first bicycle—the *draisienne*. Riders pushed themselves along with their feet until versions with pedals were developed. Two-wheeled transportation evolved further with the invention of the motorcycle in 1885.

Iron steamship
Aaron Manby

Where Staffordshire, England
When 1822

The *Aaron Manby*, named after the British engineer who built it, was the first steamship made of iron to sail on the sea. The ship completed its maiden voyage from London to Paris in 1822. In 1845, the SS *Great Britain* was the first iron steamer to sail across the Atlantic.

Train travel
Stephenson's Rocket

Where Rainhill, England
When 1829

Although the steam locomotive had been invented in 1803, it was British engineers George and Robert Stephenson who really set the railroad revolution in motion. Their *Rocket* reached a record-breaking speed of 36mph (58kph) in a competition in 1829, and was used on the world's first intercity railroad, which opened the following year.

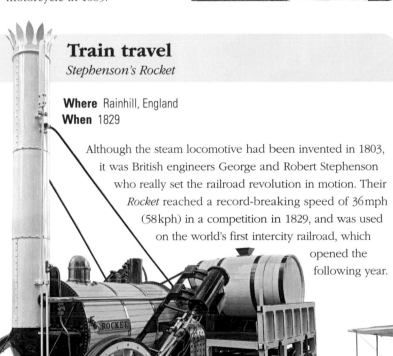

Into the air
Wright Flyer

Where Kitty Hawk, North Carolina
When 1903

US brothers Orville and Wilbur Wright made the first powered airplane flight in their *Flyer*. Though the flight only lasted for 12 seconds, it paved the way for future advances in aviation. Less than 50 years later, the first commercial jet airliner flew from London, UK, to Johannesburg, South Africa, opening up worldwide air travel.

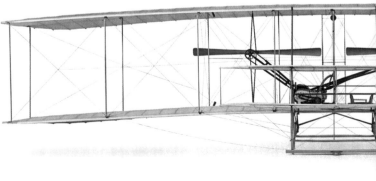

Flying without wings
VS-300

Where Connecticut
When 1939

People had long tried to build helicopters, but it was in 1939 that Russian–American aviator Igor Sikorsky made one that could be kept under control. His *VS-300* featured a rotating part called a rotor attached to the helicopter's tail to stop it from spinning while in flight. This innovation still features on most helicopters.

Cars for all
Ford Model T

Where Michigan
When 1908

Ford Motor Company's Model-T went on sale in the US in 1908. It was the world's first affordable car, and more than 15 million of them were sold. Like the Model T, most cars today still run on gasoline, although more eco-friendly electric cars are growing in popularity.

Only black models were sold after 1914.

Launching into space
V-2 rocket

Where Peenemünde, Germany
When 1944

German scientists invented the V-2 rocket in 1936. It was loaded with explosives and used against Germany's enemies during World War II. In 1944, a V-2 launched vertically and reached a height of 109 miles (175 km), entering space. After Germany's defeat in the war, V-2 technology was further developed by US and Soviet scientists, leading to the creation of space rockets.

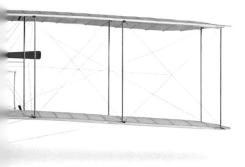

Reusable spacecraft
Space Shuttle Columbia

Where Florida
When 1981

All early spacecraft could only complete one flight because they broke apart on reentering Earth's atmosphere. On April 12, 1981, the US launched its first reusable Space Shuttle, *Columbia*. Reusable spacecraft have allowed humans to establish a permanent presence in space aboard satellites such as the International Space Station.

The shuttle's cargo bay was used to carry supplies into space.

The Swinging Sixties

The 1960s was a decade of optimism, revolution, and glamour, in which young people rebelled against the values of their parents. They fought for freedom and change, and embraced new styles of fashion, movies, music, and art.

Teenagers in the 1960s wanted to have more freedom and fun than their parents, many of whom had been teenagers during World War II. As this younger generation watched the horrors of war—particularly the Vietnam War—play out on the new TVs in their homes, they wanted their lives to be different. The 1960s saw young people reject violence; campaign for nuclear weapons to be abandoned; and start the hippie movement, which stood for world peace and universal love.

Young people also began to challenge the authority and laws of previous generations. They called for an end to discrimination and fought for equal rights for women and people of color.

People also searched for happiness, and experimented with exciting new forms of art, music, and fashion. This was a colorful and creative period of experimental art, revolutionary pop music, and clothing made to shock. The decade ended with an air of optimism when in 1969 the first humans landed on the moon, showing that anything was possible.

▼ TEEN FASHION
Young people in the 1960s wore bright colors, miniskirts, and shift dresses with bold geometric prints to show off their new-found freedoms. They wanted to be different and used their clothes to rebel and make a statement.

BEATLEMANIA ▶
The Beatles were at the center of the pop music explosion in the 1960s. By 1964, "Beatlemania" had swept the globe and the "Fab Four" had become huge international stars. They went on to sell 600 million albums worldwide and to inspire countless other musicians.

◀ HIPPIES
Young people who had rejected mainstream life and wanted to experiment with new ways of living were known as hippies. They cared about the environment, and believed in nonviolence. Volkswagen Buses became popular vehicles among hippies, and were decorated with symbols of peace.

CND ▶

Alongside the growing peace movement in the 1960s, there were growing concerns about the use of nuclear weapons. Fears that the Cold War (see pp.198–199) would turn nuclear led to the Campaign for Nuclear Disarmament (CND) calling for the US and the USSR to abandon their arsenals of nuclear weapons.

The CND symbol stands for peace.

People wore buttons to show support for the CND.

WOODSTOCK ▶

This four-day music festival, devoted to peace and love, was held on a farm in New York state at the peak of the Swinging Sixties in 1968. It was attended by 500,000 people who came to see artists such as Jimi Hendrix (right). The festival became a defining moment of the 1960s.

◀ SOUL MUSIC

A new kind of Black American music came to the fore in the 1960s. Soul, as it was known, combined elements of Black American gospel music, jazz, and rhythm and blues. It was made popular by stirring performances by artists such as James Brown and Aretha Franklin (left).

▼ PROTESTS IN FRANCE

In May 1968, French students, dissatisfied with the government, began a series of protests. French workers soon joined in by going on strike, and within a week, thousands of people were on the streets marching. The protests brought the country to a standstill for several weeks.

LGBTQIA+ rights

Throughout history, LGBTQIA+ (lesbian, gay, bisexual, transgender, queer, intersex, and asexual) people have suffered unfair treatment in society because of who they are and who they love. For example, until the 20th century homosexuality was illegal in most countries—and in some countries it still is. There has been a lot of progress in the fight for the LGBTQIA+ community to have the same rights as everyone else in recent decades, but there is still a long way to go.

THE FIGHT FOR EQUAL RIGHTS

1969
After police raid the Stonewall Inn, a gay bar in New York City, members of the gay community riot in protest. The event inspires the formation of a gay rights movement to campaign against discrimination (unfair treatment) toward LGBTQIA+ people.

1972
Sweden becomes the first country in the world to allow transgender people—those who feel that the gender they were assigned (given at birth) is not who they are—to change their gender by law.

2001
On April 1, the Netherlands becomes the first country in the world to legalize same-sex marriage. The first gay weddings (right) take place in Amsterdam shortly after midnight.

SAME-SEX COUPLES CUTTING CAKE

2015
The US legalizes same-sex marriage in all fifty of its states. By 2021, same-sex marriage is legal in 30 countries.

◄ **PRIDE PARADE**
On June 28, 1970, gay rights activists organized a march through New York City's streets to celebrate the first anniversary of the Stonewall riots. The Christopher Street Gay Liberation Day March, as it was called, was the first pride parade. Now pride events celebrating LGBTQIA+ culture take place in cities around the world and attract millions of people every year.

20th-century fashion

At the beginning of the 20th century, fashion choices were limited, with most people in a region wearing similar styles. But over the decades, fashion became more free. This was partly because improved travel gave designers access to styles from around the world. By the late 20th century, people were able to choose from a wide variety of fashion trends.

Wrapped around
Cheongsam

Where Shanghai, China
When 1920s

This high-necked, close-fitting dress (also known as qipao) is believed to have evolved from styles of the Qing era (see pp.140–141). It was made popular by upper-class women in Shanghai, and came to be associated with the rise of the modern Chinese woman.

Colonial style
Sapeurs

Where Congo
When 1930s

The arrival of French colonizers in Congo gave rise to the sapeur ("dressed up") culture. Local Congolese adapted French styles, such as three-piece suits and silk socks, to challenge the supposed superiority of the colonists by emulating their clothing in an extravagant way. Sapeur style has seen a revival in the modern day.

Postwar fashion
Dior's New Look

Where Paris, France
When 1940s

French designer Christian Dior's first clothing collection, the "New Look" was launched in 1947. It featured dresses with rounded shoulders, narrow waists, and full skirts. The style became fashionable in the years following World War II, as it was different from the functional clothing of the war period.

Snazzy formalwear
Zoot suit

Where US
When 1940s

This baggy suit style with shoulder pads and flared pants was inspired by the suits worn in dance halls in the 1930s. Zoot suits were popularized by Mexican- and Black American men from working class neighborhoods across the US, and went on to influence suit styles for decades.

Daring style
Miniskirt

Where London, UK
When 1960s

Breaking away from older fashions, young women of the 1960s began wearing dresses that were increasingly shorter. The miniskirt, popularized by designer Mary Quant, became the most popular trend by the end of the decade.

Rebels of fashion
Punk

Where London, UK
When 1970s

Punk fashion came from the music movement of the same name. People who followed this trend used torn fabrics and wore skinny jeans, studded belts and other metal accessories, and working boots. This style was designed to shock, and to showcase the wearer's individuality.

Street fashion
Hip hop style

Where New York
When 1980s

Hip hop music originated in the 1970s, and the fashion style that went with it became extremely popular in the 1980s. Hip hop fashion began with white sneakers, tapered jeans, tracksuits, jackets, and hooded sweatshirts. Over time, it has come to include trends such as gold chains, fur coats, large hats, and baggy clothing, inspired by Black American heritage.

Fusion fashion
Harajuku

Where Tokyo, Japan
When 1990s to present

Named after the Harajuku district of Tokyo, this fashion movement was popularized by the youth of the city who wanted to break away from mainstream styles. Followers of this street fashion wear unique, elaborate, and colorful outfits. There are many styles, which can be influenced by Gothic elements, animated characters, and other quirky trends.

Independent Africa

During the 1950s and 1960s, most African nations gained independence from their European colonial rulers. Freedom brought hope and opportunity, though many countries had to tackle the problems left behind by years of colonial rule. In the 21st century, however, many nations are experiencing economic growth and stability.

Colonization by European powers, who had looted the continent's wealth and natural resources, and imposed their own culture on the population, left some of the newly independent nations of Africa ill-equipped to face the challenges of independence.

In some countries, dictators took control and refused to give up their power. Many governments struggled with civil wars and conflicts between different cultures and ethnic groups. Natural disasters such as droughts ravaged some parts of the continent

and left millions of people hungry and poor. In South Africa, the government started a system known as apartheid (see pp.202–203), where Black people faced discrimination.

Despite this, many nations have achieved some stability in the 21st century. Countries such as Ghana and Nigeria have relied on their vast reserves of mineral resources, such as gold, diamonds, and oil, to boost their economies, while there are a growing number of countries with stable, democratic governments.

▲ PAN-AFRICANISM
In the early 20th century, a worldwide movement promoting solidarity between African people began. It aimed to strengthen the cultural bonds between people of African origin. Ghana's first prime minister, Kwame Nkrumah (above), was a firm supporter of the Pan-African movement and advocated for the unity of all Africans.

◄ ORGANIZATION OF AFRICAN UNITY
After gaining independence from European countries, 32 African nations established the Organization for African Unity (OAU) in 1963. The aim of the OAU was to encourage cooperation between all African countries. The OAU was replaced by the African Union in 2002.

POST-COLONIAL CONFLICTS

1975–2002	1994	1983–2005	2011
After gaining independence, Angola is caught up in a violent civil war that lasts 26 years—one of the longest civil wars in history.	In Rwanda, more than 800,000 Tutsi people are killed by the Hutu people in just 100 days. The Hutu government orders the slaughter.	Rebel groups and the Sudanese government fight against each other in a brutal civil war that ravages the country for 22 years.	The Libyan Civil War erupts between Muammar Gaddhafi's government and opposing rebel groups. Gaddhafi is eventually overthrown.

▼ NELSON MANDELA

South African activist and politician Nelson Mandela challenged the system of apartheid and was imprisoned for 27 years (see p.203). After his release in 1990, he helped create a system where every citizen could vote, regardless of their skin color. Mandela was elected as the country's first Black president in 1994.

◄ CHALLENGES OF URBANIZATION

Since gaining independence, countries in Africa have seen a rise in urbanization— the large-scale movement of people from villages to cities and towns. This has created multiple challenges such as a lack of proper housing facilities leading to an increase in slum areas, traffic on roads, and widespread pollution.

THE ENVIRONMENT ►

In 1977, Kenyan environmentalist and feminist Wangari Maathai started the Green Belt Movement, empowering women in the villages of Kenya to plant trees to counter deforestation as well as provide a source of food and fuel. By the early 21st century, more than 30 million trees had been planted. Maathai's efforts won her the Nobel Peace Prize in 2004.

◄ 2010 FIFA WORLD CUP

The FIFA World Cup is one of the most widely watched sporting events in the world. Nelson Mandela campaigned to have South Africa as the host country for 2010, which was eventually granted, making South Africa the first African nation to host the tournament. Thousands of people came out to support their national team.

CHILD IN TIME

Born in 1991, Thandiwe Chama is a young activist from Zambia. She has campaigned for better educational facilities in Zambia, as well as for the welfare of people suffering from diseases such as HIV/AIDS. Chama was awarded the International Children's Peace Prize in 2007.

Modern Latin America

Even though most countries in Latin America gained independence from Europe in the 19th century (see p.163), people with European roots have tended to hold on to power. The 20th century was a period of instability across much of the region, but in recent years most countries have been at peace.

The Great Depression of the 1930s (see p.187) and the outbreak of World War II had a disastrous effect on Latin America, which relied on selling raw materials to the rest of the world. Though many countries tried to improve their economies after the war, they had limited success, and poverty and the gap between rich and poor worsened.

This led to a series of military coups (in which power was seized from governments by armies) that put brutal dictators in control. Most of these were supported by the US, who used the excuse that they wanted to prevent these countries from falling into communist hands during the Cold War (see pp.198–199). By 1975, only Colombia, Venezuela, and Costa Rica had democratic governments. The situation improved from the end of the 1980s as newly elected governments took power, and the 21st century has brought peace to many nations that have long suffered from conflict. But many governments are fragile, and inequality and poverty are still serious problems.

▼ **MILITARY RULE**
Since 1945, most Latin American countries have, for at least part of the time, been ruled by military dictators who have banned democracy. One such dictator was Chilean general Augusto Pinochet (below), who overthrew the elected government of Chile and ruled until 1990.

▼ **UPRISINGS**
Revolutionary groups have risen up throughout Latin America to overthrow corrupt governments. In 1979, the Sandinista National Liberation Front (below) of Nicaragua ousted the dictatorship of the Somoza family.

◀ PINK TIDE

Since the end of the 20th century, some Latin American countries have chosen governments that support social reform— a wave called the "pink tide." Hugo Chávez, who took power in Venezuela in 1999, was the first elected leader under this wave. In 2006, Evo Morales (left) became the first Indigenous president of Bolivia. He held that post for 13 years, during which he started programs to reduce illiteracy, poverty, and racism.

FACT
The constitutions of both Costa Rica and Panama forbid them from having a standing army, although both have civilian forces.

▼ RECLAIMING ANCESTRAL LAND

The lifestyles of Indigenous peoples are under threat as their land is exploited by oil companies, loggers, miners, and farmers. But some Indigenous groups have successfully fought to reclaim their ancestral land. In 2019, the Waorani people of Ecuador (below) won a landmark victory when a court ruled that their land could not be sold to oil companies without their permission.

CONFLICTS AND COUPS

1964
Military rule is established in Brazil. The government improves the economy but bans all opposition. The dictatorship lasts till 1985.

1973
In Chile, the democratically elected government led by Salvador Allende is overthrown in a military coup by General Pinochet.

1980
The communist Sendero Luminoso (Shining Path) group begins a revolutionary war in Peru.

1982
The military government of Argentina invades the British-held Falkland Islands but is defeated. Argentines protest against the government, and Argentina returns to democratic rule in 1983.

1989–90
The US invades Panama, deposing dictator Manuel Noriega.

LATIN AMERICAN CULTURE ▼

Latin America is renowned for its music and dance. The Argentine tango (right) became known throughout the world in the early 20th century and has had a revival since the 1980s. The region's many notable writers include Colombian Gabriel García Márquez and Chilean novelist Isabel Allende.

The collapse of the USSR

In 1985, the new Soviet leader Mikhail Gorbachev came to power in the USSR and began to introduce political and economic reforms. He rejected the Brezhnev Doctrine, which allowed the USSR to send in its army to other communist countries if their governments were threatened. The USSR withdrew its troops and support from Eastern Europe. Without that support, communist-led governments such as in Poland and Hungary were forced to hold free elections. The USSR itself collapsed in December 1991 and communist rule in Eastern Europe came to an end.

THE FALL OF THE EASTERN BLOC

1985

Mikhail Gorbachev begins to reform the USSR with policies of glasnost (openness) and *perestroika* (reconstruction) to modernize the struggling country.

MIKHAIL GORBACHEV

1989

Hungary opens its closed border with Austria, creating a route to western Europe. Thousands of East Germans use it to flee into West Germany. Without Soviet support, communist governments begin to fall across Eastern Europe.

1990

After the fall of the Berlin Wall, East and West Germany are reunited into one country. In 1991, the German parliament votes to make Berlin the capital of a united Germany. Free elections are held in all former communist countries, and democratic governments come to power by 1991.

1991

Gorbachev survives a coup planned by hard-line communists and he bans the Communist Party. Ukraine and other republics leave the USSR, which collapses at the end of the year as Gorbachev resigns.

FALL OF THE BERLIN WALL ▶

In November 1989, a new communist leader in East Germany announced that the Berlin Wall would be opened to allow its citizens to visit West Berlin. Thousands of people poured through the openings, while demonstrators began to climb over the wall watched by nervous East German border guards. The symbol of a divided Europe was soon torn down and Germany was united.

KEY DEVELOPMENTS

1947
Japan begins to modernize its economy, expanding production and changing the way companies are run to make them more internationally competitive.

1959
Taiwan begins to attract foreign investment and moves its focus from agriculture to industry, starting the Taiwan Economic Miracle. Its economy grows swiftly.

1961
A period of rapid economic growth begins in South Korea as the country focuses on exporting goods.

1978
China's new leader, Deng Xiaoping, opens up the economy to foreign businesses and reduces government control of companies.

2013
China opens the world's longest high-speed rail route—nearly 1,430 miles (2,300 km) long—linking the capital city Beijing with the commercial center of Guangzhou.

Modern East Asia

At the end of World War II in 1945, large areas of East Asia were devastated and in need of rebuilding. Since then, the region has experienced an economic transformation, and in the 21st century countries such as Japan, China, and South Korea are among the most prosperous and productive in the world.

The post-war economic development of East Asia began in Japan, and then spread to Taiwan and South Korea. These countries lacked raw materials, but had low-cost, skilled labor available. As a result, they could manufacture goods and export them at low prices around the world. Consumer goods (such as household appliances), ships, cars, and computer technologies, were the main exports.

After the death of Chinese leader Mao Zedong in 1976, China also began to modernize. Today, it is one of the dominant economies of the world. In 2013, the Chinese government announced its new Belt and Road initiative. Seen as a successor to the ancient Silk Road (see p.51), this project aims to build a trade network across Asia, Europe, and Africa by constructing new railroad lines, ports, airports, and roads in 71 countries.

By the late 20th century, South Korea, Taiwan, Singapore, and Hong Kong had also achieved rapid economic growth and came to be known as the Four Asian Tigers. The next generation of resource-rich nations—Malaysia, Thailand, the Philippines, Indonesia, and Vietnam—continued to develop and are now called the Tiger Cub Economies.

▼ JAPAN

After its defeat in World War II, Japan quickly revived its economy. By the mid-1950s, production was back to prewar levels and its economy grew on average by 10 percent a year. Fast trains called Shinkansen *(below), ships, electronics, and other manufactured goods powered the economy forward.*

SMALL AND PROFITABLE ▲

Several of Asia's smaller countries also experienced economic success after the 1950s. While Taiwan benefited from its electronics and information technology (IT) industries, Singapore specialized in finance and shipping (above). These were all valuable areas in the interconnected postwar world.

An angled nose helps the Shinkansen move at high speeds.

6

R 67

22-7951 JR

MODERN INVENTIONS

East Asia has led the world in developing new electronic goods, such as digital cameras, video games, and personal stereos. In recent years, the region has also developed robotics, maglev trains (which run on magnets), and 3D-printed electric cars such as the LSEV.

A knee joint helps ASIMO run like a human.

DIGITAL CAMERA

ASIMO

LSEV

▼ SOUTH KOREA

In 1961, South Korea closed its borders to all imports except raw materials and began to promote its own conglomerates (big companies made up of lots of different businesses), such as Hyundai and Samsung. These produced cars, electronics, and other goods for export. As a result, the economy is now one of the largest in the world.

MODERNIZATION OF CHINA ▶

When Chinese leader Deng Xiaoping came to power in 1978, he introduced massive economic reforms. Farmers were allowed to work their land for profit and entrepreneurs were encouraged to start new businesses. In 1985, the government also stopped setting the prices for goods. Many old cities such as Shanghai (right) were transformed. In 2010, China overtook Japan as the world's second largest economy, and is on track to overtake the US, the world's biggest, by 2026.

The climate crisis

The negative impact of human activity on Earth's climate was first brought to wide public attention in the 1970s. Yet over the following decades, governments were slow to react to the issue. Today, young people around the world, angry at this inaction, are demanding environmental reforms.

▲ POLLUTION
When harmful materials, called pollutants, are added to the environment, they can damage the quality of our air, water, and land, which humans and animals depend on for survival. Burning fuel for electricity, and smoke from factories and cars, releases carbon dioxide and pollutes the air; sewage can make people ill and damage sea life; and chemicals used in farming can flow into the land.

Since the Industrial Revolution in the 18th century, human progress has been powered by the burning of fossil fuels such as coal, oil, and gas. As we switched to producing goods by machine in factories, we started to burn more fossil fuels for energy.

Burning these fuels releases carbon dioxide into the air, which traps the sun's heat, not letting it escape Earth's atmosphere. This is similar to how the glass of a greenhouse works, and is known as the "Greenhouse Effect." As carbon dioxide levels rise, temperatures rise, too, leading to warmer oceans, melting polar ice, and rising sea levels.

Young activists are impatient with slow government action to reduce carbon emissions. They are pressuring for more action, and are also doing what they can to reduce their own carbon footprint—the amount of carbon dioxide they release.

FACT
Sea ice reflects the sun's heat back up into space like a mirror. As Arctic ice melts, the ocean absorbs more sunlight and heats up, which scientists believe may result in ice-free summers by 2030.

▼ PLASTIC
The first plastics were only developed at the beginning of the 20th century, but in a relatively short time they have caused massive environmental problems. Plastic waste can take hundreds of years to break down, and chemicals in plastic can also pollute water. But many plastics can be reused and recycled into new materials.

▲ GLOBAL WARMING
The Greenhouse Effect causes temperatures around the world to rise in a phenomenon called global warming. This term was first used by US geoscientist Wallace Broecker, who brought worldwide attention to global warming in 1975. Higher temperatures make natural disasters such as forest fires more common.

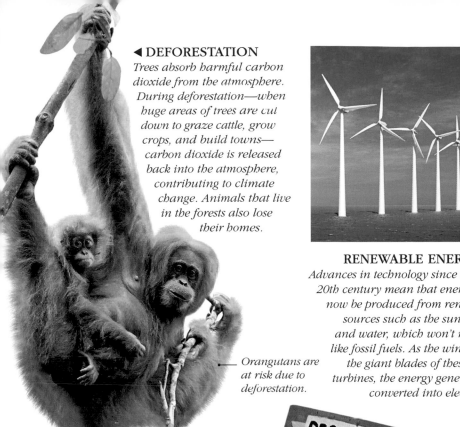

◄ DEFORESTATION

Trees absorb harmful carbon dioxide from the atmosphere. During deforestation—when huge areas of trees are cut down to graze cattle, grow crops, and build towns—carbon dioxide is released back into the atmosphere, contributing to climate change. Animals that live in the forests also lose their homes.

Orangutans are at risk due to deforestation.

RENEWABLE ENERGY ▲

Advances in technology since the late 20th century mean that energy can now be produced from renewable sources such as the sun, wind, and water, which won't run out like fossil fuels. As the wind spins the giant blades of these wind turbines, the energy generated is converted into electricity.

GRETA THUNBERG

In 2018, 15-year-old Greta Thunberg (born 2003) skipped school one Friday afternoon to sit alone outside the Swedish parliament with a banner that read "school strike for climate." Her strike inspired millions and launched a global climate movement.

◄ FRIDAYS FOR FUTURE

Created by the Swedish activist Greta Thunberg in 2018, Fridays for Future is an international campaign group led by young people. Students skip school on a Friday afternoon and gather to demand that global leaders take action to overcome the climate crisis.

The modern Middle East

With the discovery of vast oil fields in the early 20th century, the Middle East went through a period of rapid development and modernization. Small villages and settlements, home to nomadic Bedouin populations, grew into huge cities connected by fast highways. Today, 10 of the Middle East's countries—Iran, Iraq, Syria, Kuwait, Saudi Arabia, Bahrain, Qatar, United Arab Emirates (UAE), Oman, and Yemen—have 48 percent of the world's known oil reserves. The tremendous wealth brought by the oil industry has led to improved living conditions for many people. However, the region still faces huge problems—the long history of conflict (see p.201) is ongoing, and human rights abuses on issues such as freedom of speech and the treatment of women affect the region's standing on the world stage.

MODERN MEGACITIES
Over the years, the city of Dubai has transformed from a small trading center into a major international city with thousands of towering skyscrapers dotting the skyline. It is home to modern architectural marvels, such as the Burj Khalifa, the tallest building in the world, and the twisting Cayan Tower (right).

▲ **IRRIGATION CANALS**
Much of the Middle East is made up of desert, and the region does not get a lot of rainfall. Fresh water for farming is pumped up from underground water reserves and transported through stone or brick irrigation canals, such as this one in Saudi Arabia.

The Information Age

The development of the first programmable computers in the mid-20th century launched what is known as the Information Age. The first computers were huge and expensive but by the 1980s scientists had developed small, low-cost computers that people could use in their homes. By the 1990s, the invention of the World Wide Web had begun to transform the way we communicate, study, and work.

Electronic devices can turn information into electrical signals and back again. Two inventions in the mid-20th century powered electronics forward. All electronic devices are based on the transistor—a switch that controls the flow of an electrical signal, turning it on or off. The creation of the microchip, which can store millions of transistors on one tiny piece of material, made it possible to produce electronic gadgets that were much smaller, cheaper, and more reliable. By the 1980s, the electronic revolution was well underway as computers became cheaper to produce and more people were able to buy them for use at home, work, and in schools.

Today, technology makes it possible for us to communicate across long distances and gives us access to a world of information on the internet at the touch of a button. Yet some worry that we have become too reliant on our devices, and that cutting down on face-to-face communication has led to us feeling more isolated.

HISTORY OF COMPUTERS

1822 British inventor Charles Babbage designs a machine called the Difference Engine, which is able to perform difficult calculations.

1843 British mathematician Ada Lovelace works on Charles Babbage's new Analytical Engine, an ancestor of modern computers. She is the first computer programmer.

ADA LOVELACE

1946 US engineers develop the ENIAC (Electronic Numerical Integrator and Computer), the first programmable computer. It can perform 5,000 calculations per second.

1975 The Cray-1 is invented. This "supercomputer" can perform 240 million calculations per second. It is used to design nuclear weapons and for weather forecasting.

1982 The Commodore 64 is released, and becomes the biggest-selling home computer of all time. It opens up the world of video games, word processing, and spreadsheets to millions of people.

ALAN TURING

Alan Turing (1912–1954) was a British mathematician and a computing pioneer. In 1936, he came up with the idea of a machine that could solve any mathematical problem given the right instructions. He never built such a "Turing machine," but the idea led to the modern computer.

◀ PIONEERING WOMEN
Many of the early pioneers in the field of computer programming were women. Black American computer programmer Melba Roy Mouton led a group of NASA scientists, known as "computers," in their astronomical calculations. Another US computer scientist Grace Hopper (left) made a key contribution to the development of computer languages.

SMARTPHONES ▶

Smartphones such as the Apple iPhone, which was released in 2007, have changed the way we live our lives. We use them to access the internet, play games and music, take photos, and document our own lives on social media. On average, US adults now spend a quarter of their waking lives looking at their phones.

Industrial robots place car frames on an assembly line.

▲ ROBOTS

The first electronic programmable robotic arm was installed in a factory in the US in 1961. Robotic technology has since evolved, and robots are now able to recognize people and facial expressions, shop, cook, fly, play basketball, make music, perform medical procedures, and much more.

FACT

In 2017, the humanoid robot Sophia was granted citizenship of Saudi Arabia, making her the first robot to become a citizen of a country.

▲ THE WORLD WIDE WEB

In 1989, the World Wide Web was invented by British scientist Tim Berners-Lee. He wanted to create a space where scientists around the world could easily share information. In December 1990, the world's first World Wide Web server ran on this computer at CERN, a physics research laboratory in Geneva, Switzerland.

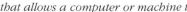

Sophia's humanlike hands can grasp objects.

ARTIFICIAL INTELLIGENCE ▶

The technology that allows a computer or machine to behave like a human is known as artificial intelligence or AI. Sophia is a realistic, human-shaped robot first activated in 2016. Her AI allows her to recognize faces and show emotion, and she will get smarter over time.

231

Glossary

abolition The act of doing away with something completely.

allies/allied forces People or countries working together. In World War I and World War II, the Allied forces were the countries fighting against Germany.

anti-Semitism Prejudice and hostility toward Jewish people.

Axis powers Nations on Germany's side in World War II, including Italy and Japan.

BCE Before Common Era. The years before 1 CE (Common Era). This abbreviation has replaced BC (Before Christ).

Bronze Age A period of ancient history when people mostly used bronze for making tools and weapons.

caliph The title of a political and religious leader of an Islamic empire, or caliphate.

capitalism An economic system based on private ownership of property and competitive conditions for business.

casualties People killed or injured as a result of war or an accident.

cavalry Military troops mounted on horseback.

CE Common Era. The years from 1 CE to the present day. This abbreviation has replaced AD (Anno Domini, which is Latin for "in the year of our Lord").

citizen A person who belongs to a city or a bigger community such as a state or country.

city-state A city, and its surrounding territory, that has its own independent government.

civil rights The rights of citizens to be socially and politically equal.

civil service All the government departments and employees of a country or state, not including the armed forces.

civil war A war between opposing groups of people in the same country.

civilization The culture and way of life of people living together in an organized and developed society.

colonization The act of sending settlers to establish a colony in another country, sometimes involving taking political control over the people already living there.

colony An area under the political control of another state; or the group of people who have settled there.

communism The political belief in a society in which ownership of property and wealth is shared.

constitution A set of laws that determines the political principles of a government.

culture The customs, beliefs, and behavior shared by a society.

dictator A leader who rules a country alone, with no restrictions on the extent of their power.

dynasty A royal family ruling a country for successive generations.

economy The system through which goods and services are produced, sold, and bought in a country or state.

empire A group of lands or peoples brought under the rule of one government or person.

epidemic A sudden spread of a disease within a specific region.

fascism A political movement stressing nationalism, which places the strength of the state above individual citizens' welfare.

feudal system A social system that developed in medieval Europe and Japan, in which lords granted land to people of lower rank in return for loyalty, military assistance, and services.

golden age A period of great success, development, or achievement.

guerrilla warfare A type of warfare in which small groups of fighters, who are not part of regular uniformed armies, make use of sabotage and surprise attacks against a larger force.

hominin A member of the biological group that includes humans and their extinct relatives.

Ice Age A period when global temperatures drop drastically and large areas become covered by vast sheets of ice. There have been at least five ice ages in Earth's history.

Indigenous When applied to people, the word indigenous describes the original settlers of a country or region.

Iron Age The historical period characterized by the use of iron for making weapons and tools.

medieval period Also known as the Middle Ages, the period in European history that lasted from about the 5th to the late 15th centuries CE.

Mesopotamia The region of modern-day Iraq lying between the Tigris and Euphrates rivers, where many of the earliest civilizations began.

metallurgy The study of metals and their uses.

metalworking The process of creating or shaping things out of metal.

missionary A religious person who seeks out and persuades others to adopt their religion.

monarchy A type of government in which a king or queen is recognized as the head of state, whether or not they hold real power.

nation An independent country, or a group of people who share historical or cultural ties.

nationalism Loyalty and devotion to a nation, and the political belief that its interests should be pursued as the primary goal of a political policy.

Neolithic Age The later Stone Age, during which improved stone tools and weapons were made and the first farming began.

nomadic Describing people who move from place to place without establishing a permanent settlement.

pandemic A sudden and widespread outbreak of disease.

peasant A worker on the land, usually an agricultural laborer.

persecute To oppress or harass a person or group because of their origins or beliefs.

philosophy A set of ideas or beliefs.

plantation A large area of fertile land within a landowner's estate where a certain type of crop is grown.

pre-Columbian The time period before the arrival of Christopher Columbus in the Americas.

republic A country without a monarch or emperor. Modern republics are usually led by presidents.

revolution A sudden and fundamental change in society brought about by an organized group of protesters. Can also be used to mean a major change in the way that people do things or think about things.

samurai A Japanese warrior who owes allegiance to a *daimyo* (a landowning noble) and follows a strict code of honor.

script The written characters that make up a writing system, such as an alphabet.

serf A peasant who is obligated to undertake agricultural work on their lord's land.

siege To surround a city or fortress with the intention of capturing it.

Silk Road An ancient trade route that extended from eastern China to the Mediterranean Sea.

socialism The belief that the government should have some control over the economy and be able to spread wealth more evenly among the people.

species A group of organisms that are similar to, and can breed with, each other.

state A country—or a region within a country—and its people. A state is ruled by a government.

suffrage The right to vote.

superpower A country with great political and military power, capable of influencing international politics.

terra-cotta A reddish-brown clay that is used for making pottery, sculptures, or ornaments.

treaty An official, written agreement between warring parties to bring hostilities to an end.

urbanization The large-scale movement of people from rural areas to urban areas such as towns and cities.

USSR The Union of Soviet Socialist Republics, the communist state that existed from 1922–1991 in the former Russian Empire, with its capital in Moscow.

West, the Europe and North America, or their ideals and culture when seen in contrast to other civilizations.

woodblock printing The process of using carved blocks of wood for printing on cloth or paper. This technique originated in China and was widely used across East Asia.

Index

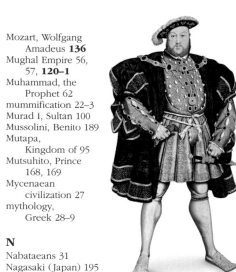

Acknowledgments

Dorling Kindersley would like to thank the following people for their help with making the book:
Pauline Savage for editorial assistance; Prof Nemata Blyden, Dr Vivian Delgado, Simon Griver, Seun Matiluko, Dr Gabriela Ramos, Corey Soper, and Yilin Wang for authenticity checks; Heena Sharma for design assistance; Anita Yadav for DTP assistance; Priyanka Sharma-Saddi and Saloni Singh for the jacket; Caroline Stamps for proofreading; and Helen Peters for the index.

Smithsonian reviewer:
Dr. F. Robert van der Linden, Curator of Air Transportation and Special Purpose Aircraft, National Air and Space Museum, Smithsonian

Smithsonian Enterprises:
Kealy Gordon, Product Development Manager
Jill Corcoran, Director, Licensed Publishing
Brigid Ferraro, Vice President, Business Development and Licensing
Carol LeBlanc, President

ACKNOWLEDGMENTS

Stock Photo: Suzuki Kaku (cr). **Bridgeman Images. Dorling Kindersley:** Durham University Oriental Museum (c). **Getty Images:** DEA / S. Vannini (cl). **107 Alamy Stock Photo:** Granger Historical Picture Archive (br); PBL Collection (tr). **108 Alamy Stock Photo:** Granger Historical Picture Archive (clb/astrolabe); Maria Adelaide Silva (br). **Dreamstime.com:** Heritage Pictures (tl). **109 Alamy Stock Photo:** Interfoto (cr); Niday Picture Library (tl). **Getty Images:** Photo 12 / Universal Images Group (cl). **110 Alamy Stock Photo:** Abu Castor (bl); IanDagnall Computing (cla, bc). **110–111 Alamy Stock Photo:** GL Archive (bc). **111 Alamy Stock Photo:** Pictorial Press Ltd (br); The History Emporium (tr). **Getty Images:** Hulton Archive / Print Collector / Ann Ronan Pictures (cr). **© The Metropolitan Museum of Art:** Harris Brisbane Dick Fund, 1936 (tc). **112 Alamy Stock Photo:** The Picture Art Collection (clb). **Bridgeman Images. 113 Alamy Stock Photo. Mary Evans Picture Library:** IBL Collections (bl). **114 Bridgeman Images:** Tarker (bl). **114–115 Alamy Stock Photo:** lukas bischoff (bc). **115 Alamy Stock Photo:** J Marshall - Tribaleye Images (bc). **Bridgeman Images. 116 Alamy Stock Photo:** Granger Historical Picture Archive / Granger, NYC (bc); Cavan Images (tr); David Pimborough (br). **117 Alamy Stock Photo:** Prisma Archivo (tr). **Dreamstime.com:** Enchanted _fairy (cr). **Shutterstock.com:** JR Moreira (br). **118 Alamy Stock Photo:** Florilegius (bc); Prisma Archivo (bl); North Wind Picture Archives (cr). **118–119 Alamy Stock Photo:** Prisma Archivo (br). **Getty Images:** Imagno (tc). **119 Alamy Stock Photo:** Heritage Image Partnership Ltd (tr); North Wind Picture Archives (cr). **120 akg-images:** Roland and Sabrina Michaud (bl). **Dreamstime.com:** Rafał Cichawa (bc). **120–121 Alamy Stock Photo:** Classic Collection (tr). **121 Alamy Stock Photo:** The History Collection (br). **Dorling Kindersley:** Durham University Oriental Museum (cb). **122 Alamy Stock Photo:** AF Fotografie (bl); The Granger Collection (tr). **Science & Society Picture Library:** (br). **123 Alamy Stock Photo:** Granger Historical Picture Archive (bl, bc). **Bridgeman Images:** Look and Learn (br). **Getty Images:** Science & Society Picture Library (tc); UniversalImagesGroup (cr). **124 Alamy Stock Photo:** Archive Collection (tr); Prisma Archivo (bl). **125 Alamy Stock Photo:** Heritage Image Partnership Ltd (tc); Sputnik (c). **Bridgeman Images. Shutterstock.com:** Everett Collection (cr). **126 Alamy Stock Photo:** Ian Dagnell (bl); Peter Horree (tc). **127 123RF.com:** Serhii Kamshylin (tr). **Alamy Stock Photo:** Peter Horree (br); De Luan (c). **Dorling Kindersley:** Science Museum, London (tl). **128–129 The New York Public Library:** The Miriam and Ira D. Wallach Division of Art, Prints and Photographs: Print Collection, The New York Public Library. "On the Grounds of the Shinmei Shrine in Shiba: the Shatetsurô Restaurant" The New York Public Library Digital Collections. 1838 - 1840. https://digitalcollections.nypl.org/items/6c765830-2d1f-0135-0a58-05c4c0524ce0 (t). **128 Alamy Stock Photo:** Doug Steley (clb). **129 Alamy Stock Photo:** agefotostock / Historical Views (bc); Album (cl). **Getty Images:** UniversalImagesGroup (br). **© The Metropolitan Museum of Art:** Gift of Mrs. Russell Sage, 1910 (bl); The Hans Syz Collection, Gift of Stephan B. Syz and John D. Syz, 1995 (bl/Imari). **130–131 Bridgeman Images:** Peter Newark Military Pictures (bc). **130 Alamy Stock Photo:** Album (tr). **Dreamstime.com:** Chris Kelleher (bc). **Getty Images:** The New York Historical Society (bl). **131 Alamy Stock Photo:** Niday Picture Library (br); North Wind Picture Archives (tl). **Getty Images:** Richard T. Nowitz (tr). **132 Alamy Stock Photo:** Nicolas De Corte (tl). **Dreamstime.com:** Heritage Pictures (bc). **132–133 Alamy Stock Photo:** Pictorial Press Ltd (tc). **133 Alamy Stock Photo:** Album (cr); World History Archive (bl). **Bridgeman Images:** Wilberforce House Museum (tr). **Getty Images:** Photo Researchers (br). **134–35 Getty Images:** Heritage Images (cl). **136 Alamy Stock Photo:** The Natural History Museum, London (cra); Science History Images / Photo Researchers (bl); Pictorial Press Ltd (br). **137 Alamy Stock Photo:** Collection / Active Museum / Le Pictorium (tl); North Wind Picture Archives (tr); Pictorial Press Ltd (clb); The Granger Collection (br). **138 Alamy Stock Photo:** Artexplorer (c); Photo 12 (bl); Christine Osborne Pictures (br). **139 Alamy Stock Photo:** Chronicle (tr). **Getty Images:** David Attie / David Ochs Archives (bl); Steve Pyke / Premium Archive (br); Francois Lochon (c). **140 Bridgeman Images:** Bonhams, London, UK (cl). **Getty Images:** Print Collector (bl). **© The Metropolitan Museum of Art. 141 Alamy Stock Photo:** Pump Park Vintage Photography (br). **Shutterstock.com:** Stefan Auth / imageBROKER (cl). **142 Alamy Stock Photo:** Artokoloro (bl). **Bridgeman Images:** Leonard de Selva (tc). **143 Alamy Stock Photo. Bridgeman Images:** Rava (tc). **144 Alamy Stock Photo:** Granger Historical Picture Archive (bc); World History Archive (tl); Tatu (clb). **144–145 Bridgeman Images:** Archives Charmet (bc). **145 Alamy Stock Photo:** Falkensteinfoto (tl); North Wind Picture Archives (cla); Interfoto (br). **146–147 Alamy Stock Photo:** Niday Picture Library (tc). **146 Alamy Stock Photo:** Lanmas (cb); Pictorial Press Ltd (br). **147 Alamy Stock Photo:** Heritage Image Partnership Ltd (tr). **Getty Images:** Frederic Lewis (tc); De Agostini / DEA / G. Nimatallah (br); Otto Herschan Collection (clb). **148 Alamy Stock Photo:** North Wind Picture Archives (cl); Print Collector (bl). **Getty Images:** Science Museum / SSPL (cr). **149 Alamy Stock Photo:** Historic Collection (c); Interfoto (bl). **Dorling Kindersley:** Science Museum, London (cl). **Dreamstime.com:** Magnus Binnerstam (tr); Hupeng (br). **150–151 Alamy Stock Photo:** Martin Shields (cr). **150 Alamy Stock Photo:** Everett Collection Inc (bl). **152 Alamy Stock Photo:** Heritage Image Partnership Ltd (bl). **Getty Images:** John van Hasselt / Corbis (br). **153 Bridgeman Images. Dorling Kindersley:** Colin Keates (c). **Mary Evans Picture Library:** Sueddeutsche Zeitung Photo (bc). **154 Alamy Stock Photo:** Masterpics (bc); The Picture Art Collection (cr). **155 akg-images:** (tl). **Alamy Stock Photo:** Masterpics (clb); Scenics & Science (br). **Dreamstime.com:** Christianm (bc). **Getty Images:** Fototeca Storica Nazionale (cr). **156 Alamy Stock Photo:** Granger Historical Picture Archive / Granger, NYC (cr); Nativestock.com / Marilyn Angel Wynn (clb). **156–157 Getty Images:** Dea Picture Library (bc). **157 Alamy Stock Photo:** Historic Images (cl); Pictorial Press Ltd (br). **Shutterstock.com:** Granger (t). **158 Dorling Kindersley:** Powell-Cotton Museum, Kent (tr). **159 Alamy Stock Photo:** PvE (bl). **Bridgeman Images:** Look and Learn (tl). **Getty Images:** Chris Hellier (cl); Hulton Deutsch (r). **160 Alamy Stock Photo:** Heritage Image Partnership Ltd (tr). **Mary Evans Picture Library:** Winchester College / Mary Seacole Trust (bl). **160–161 Alamy Stock Photo:** Science History Images (br). **161 Alamy Stock Photo:** Science History Images (cla). **Dreamstime.com:** Geargodz (cra). **Getty Images:** Bettmann (tc). **162 Alamy Stock Photo:** agephotostock (cr); Painting (bl); Bart Pro (br). **Bridgeman Images:** Archives Charmet (tr). **163 Alamy Stock Photo:** EDU Vision / © Estate of Juan O'Gorman / ARS, NY and DACS, London (tl); Granger Historical Picture Archive (tr); www.BibleLandPictures.com (cr); Niday Picture Library (br). **164–165 Alamy Stock Photo:** Science History Images (cl). **165 Alamy Stock Photo:** Chronicle (br). **166–167 Alamy Stock Photo:** Interfoto (bc). **166 Alamy Stock Photo:** FL Historical 1A (tr); The Granger Collection (bl). **167 Alamy Stock Photo:** Pictorial Press Ltd (tr). **Bridgeman Images:** CCI (tl). **Getty Images:** Print Collector (br). **168–169 © The Metropolitan Museum of Art. 168 Alamy Stock Photo:** CPA Media Pte Ltd (bl). **Getty Images:** Hulton Archive / Stringer (tr). **© The Metropolitan Museum of Art. 169 Alamy Stock Photo:** Interfoto (cr); MeijiShowa (tl, br). **170 Alamy Stock Photo:** Granger Historical Picture Archive / Granger, NYC (cra); Niday Picture Library (br). **170–171 Alamy Stock Photo:** Science History Images / Photo Researchers (cb). **171 Alamy Stock Photo:** American Photo Archive (cla); Maurice Savage (tc); Science History Images / Photo Researchers (crb). **Getty Images:** Bettmann (cb). **Library of Congress, Washington, D.C.:** LC-DIG-ppmsca-19211 (digital file from original recto) LC-DIG-ppmsca-19212 (digital file from original verso) (cra). **172 Bridgeman Images:** Look and Learn (tr). **Getty Images:** ullstein bild Dtl. (bl). **172–173 Alamy Stock Photo. 173 Alamy Stock Photo:** Dinodia Photos (tl). **Dreamstime.com:** Shahid Mehmood (cr). **Getty Images:** NurPhoto (br). **© The Metropolitan Museum of Art. 174–175 Getty Images:** Bettmann (cl). **176–177 Alamy Stock Photo:** World History Archive (bl). **177 Alamy Stock Photo:** CPA Media Pte Ltd (tr). **Getty Images:** Keystone (cr); Mondadori Portfolio (cla); SovFoto (br). **178 Alamy Stock Photo:** (bl). **Getty Images:** The Print Collector (tc). **179 Alamy Stock Photo:** Everett Collection Historical (tr). **Getty Images:** Buyenlarge (bl); F. Lukasseck (br); Hulton Archive / Stringer (tl). **180–181 Alamy Stock Photo:** Science History Images (cr). **180 Getty Images:** Majority World (bc). **182 Alamy Stock Photo:** World History Archive (c). **183 Alamy Stock Photo:** Sputnik (tr). **Getty Images:** Heritage Images (clb); Hulton Deutsch (c, cr); Photo 12 (br). **184 Alamy Stock Photo:** Heritage Image Partnership Ltd (bc). **Getty Images:** AFP (bl). **184–185 Getty Images:** Joe Sohm / Visions of America (br). **185 Alamy Stock Photo:** PA Images (cra). **Getty Images:** Image Press (tl); Juan Mabromata (cl). **186 Alamy Stock Photo:** Interfoto (cr); Pictorial Press Ltd (bl). **Getty Images:** Michael Ochs Archives / Stringer (tr). **Shutterstock.com:** Granger (cl). **187 Alamy Stock Photo:** Everett Collection Historical (cl). **Dreamstime.com:** Tupungato (bc). **Getty Images:** MCT / Tribune News Service (tc). **188–189 Getty Images:** Keystone / Stringer (cl). **189 Alamy Stock Photo:** Shawshots (br). **190 Getty Images:** (cr); Henry Guttmann Collection (bl); Central Press (br). **191 Getty Images:** SovFoto (br); Wall (tc); The Print Collector (bl). **192 Alamy Stock Photo:** Granger Historical Picture Archive (cra); US National Archives (bc). **193 Alamy Stock Photo:** Niday Picture Library (br). **Getty Images:** Insights (tr); Keystone (cl); Stephenson (tl). **194 Getty Images:** Mondadori Portfolio (bl). **194–195 Alamy Stock Photo:** Art Directors & TRIP (cb). **Getty Images:** Hulton Archive / Stringer (tc). **195 Alamy Stock Photo:** Granger Historical Picture Archive (cra); XM Collection (cr). **Getty Images:** Library of Congress (br). **Shutterstock.com:** Underwood Archives / UIG (ca). **196 Alamy Stock Photo:** Dinodia Photos (c, tr). **Getty Images:** Bettmann (br). **197 Alamy Stock Photo:** Reuters (bl). **Getty Images:** Bettmann (crb); Central Press (tl). **198 Getty Images:** ullstein bild / Lehnartz (t). **Shutterstock.com:** Sipa (bl). **199 Alamy Stock Photo:** Everett Collection Inc (ca). **Getty Images:** Bettmann (cb); Universal Images Group / Sovfoto (r); Stringer / MPI (tl). **200 Alamy Stock Photo:** Interfoto (bc). **Bridgeman Images:** National Army Museum (tr). **Getty Images:** Joyce Naltchayan (cr). **201 Getty Images:** John Cantlie (br); Chip HIRES (cr); Keystone (tr); Marco Di Lauro (bl). **202 africamediaonline.com:** Museum Africa (cr). **Alamy Stock Photo:** TT News Agency (tl). **Getty Images:** Gallo Images (br); Terence Spencer / Popperfoto (bl). **203 Getty Images:** AFP (r); Pool Bouvet / De Keerle (clb). **204 Getty Images:** Keystone-France (cl); There Lions (tr); Wally McNamee (cr). **205 Alamy Stock Photo:** Michael Honegger (br); Sueddeutsche Zeitung Photo (tr); Pictorial Press Ltd (cr). **206 Getty Images:** Bettmann (bl). **Shutterstock.com:** AP (br). **206–207 Getty Images:** AFP (tr). **207 Alamy Stock Photo:** Everett Collection Historical (cb). **Dreamstime.com:** Julian Leshay (br). **Getty Images:** Bettmann (bl). **208 NASA:** (bl). **209 Alamy Stock Photo:** Sputnik (clb); Xinhua (crb). **Getty Images:** Stocktrek Images (bl). **NASA. 210 Dorling Kindersley:** National Railway Museum, York / Science Museum Group (bl). **Getty Images:** Photo Josse / Leemage (c). **210–211 Dorling Kindersley:** Shuttleworth Collection, Bedfordshire (bc). **211 Alamy Stock Photo:** Granger Historical Picture Archive (cla). **Dorling Kindersley:** R. Florio (cra); RAF Museum, Cosford (clb). **NASA. 212 Alamy Stock Photo:** ClassicStock (cr); Chuck Franklin (bl). **Getty Images:** Fox Photos / Stringer (cb). **213 Getty Images:** Archive Photos / Jack Robinson (cl); AFP (bl); Barry Z Levine (cr); Keystone / Stringer (tc). **214–215 The New York Public Library:** Diana Davies (cl). **215 Alamy Stock Photo:** Reuters (cr). **216 Alamy Stock Photo:** Abaca Press (bl); Everett Collection Historical (br). **Bridgeman Images:** Pictures from History (tr). **Getty Images:** Lipnitzki (c). **217 Getty Images:** H. Armstrong Roberts / ClassicStock (tl); Michael Ochs Archives / Stringer (cr); UniversalImagesGroup (tr). **Getty Images / iStock:** Korkusung (bl). **218 Alamy Stock Photo:** Ninja Flags (cb); Sura Nualpradid (tl). **219 Alamy Stock Photo:** Reuters (br). **Getty Images:** Phil Cole (bl); Walter Dhladhla / AFP (cl); Micheline Pelletier (cr). **Getty Images / iStock:** Peter (tc). **220 Getty Images:** Toni Anne Barson (tl); Robert Nickelsberg (cl); Andrew Holbrooke (bl). **220–221 Shutterstock.com:** Dolores Ochoa / AP (bc). **221 Alamy Stock Photo:** PA Images (cr). **Getty Images:** Gaston Brito (tl). **Getty Images / iStock:** Tempura (br). **222–223 Getty Images:** Tom Stoddard Archive (cr). **222 Alamy Stock Photo:** ITAR-TASS News Agency (cl). **224 Dreamstime.com:** Efired (br). **Getty Images:** ullstein bild (bl). **225 Alamy Stock Photo:** Andrew Benton (cla); Newscom (tl/camera); Horizon International Images Limited (clb). **Dreamstime.com:** Ekaterina Khliustina (fcla). **Getty Images:** Xiaodong Qiu (r). **226 Alamy Stock Photo:** Corine van Kapel (tl); roberthardìng (bc). **Getty Images / iStock:** Byronsdad (crb). **227 123RF.com:** tebnad (tc). **Alamy Stock Photo:** michael melia (bc). **Dreamstime.com:** Donyanedomam (tl); Per Grunditz (tr). **228–229 Getty Images:** Pawinee Sangsawang / EyeEm (cr). **228 Alamy Stock Photo:** Tom Hanley (bl). **230 Alamy Stock Photo:** Alpha Historic (bl); Science History Images (bc); Balfore Archive Images (cra). **231 Alamy Stock Photo:** imageBROKER (tl); Reuters (bc). **Dreamstime.com:** Yalcinsonat (tr). **Science Photo Library:** CERN (cl). **234 Getty Images:** Science & Society Picture Library (tr). **235 Dreamstime.com:** Ylstock (br). **236 Alamy Stock Photo:** Prisma Archivo (br). **237 Alamy Stock Photo:** IanDagnall Computing (tl). **238 Alamy Stock Photo:** Chuck Franklin (bl).

All other images © Dorling Kindersley
For further information see:
www.dkimages.com